IMAGES of America
WISCONSIN VETERANS HOME
AT KING

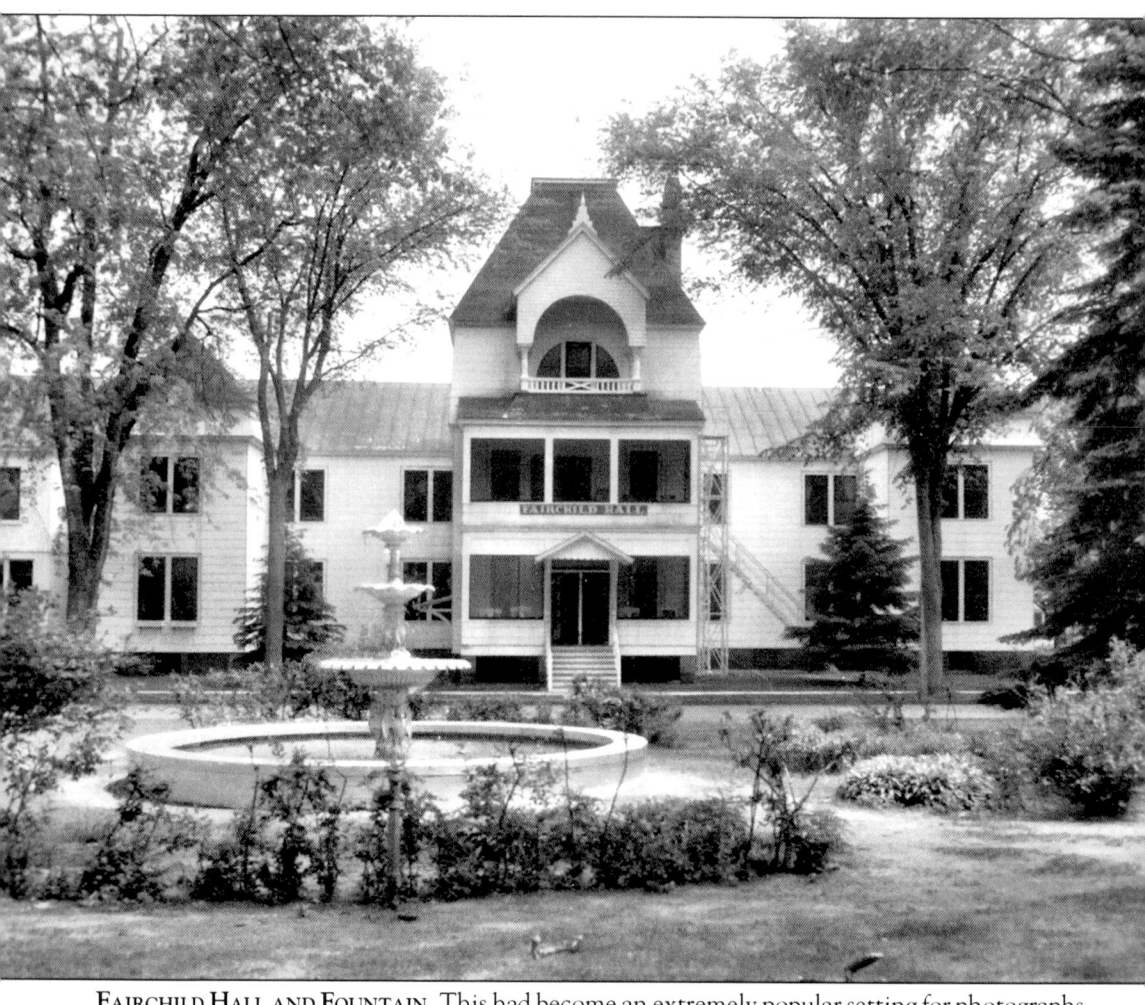

FAIRCHILD HALL AND FOUNTAIN. This had become an extremely popular setting for photographs at the home. Postcards and photographs alike were taken from the same angle. The fountain with Fairchild Hall as a backdrop was hard to resist.

IMAGES of America

WISCONSIN VETERANS HOME AT KING

Kim J. Heltemes

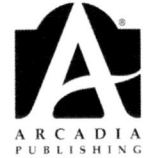

ARCADIA
PUBLISHING

Copyright © 2004 by Kim J. Heltemes
ISBN 978-0-7385-3285-1

Published by Arcadia Publishing
Charleston, South Carolina

Printed in the United States of America

Library of Congress Catalog Card Number: 2004105031

For all general information contact Arcadia Publishing at:
Telephone 843-853-2070
Fax 843-853-0044
E-Mail sales@arcadiapublishing.com
For customer service and orders:
Toll-Free 1-888-313-2665

Visit us on the Internet at www.arcadiapublishing.com

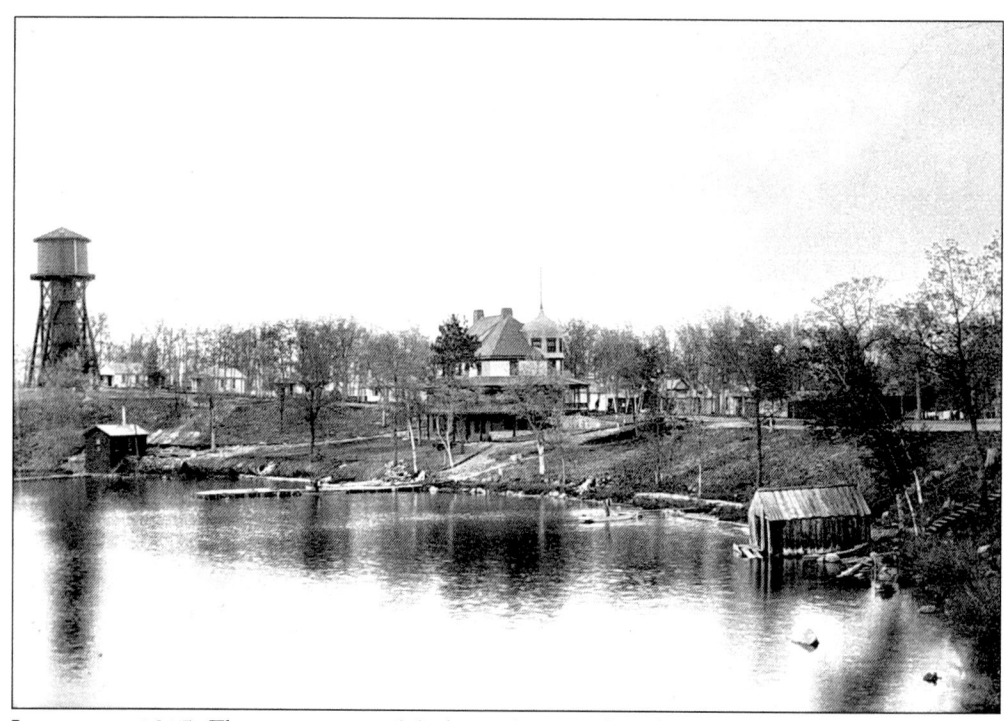

LAKEFRONT 1915. There were many lakefront photographs taken of the Home, but this is one of the nicest ones found. Taken from a 1915 album, this scene clearly shows the Home in its earliest days. The stairway on the right goes to Marden Hall. The streets have not yet been filled with cottages. The Commandant's House is in the middle.

Contents

Acknowledgments 6

Introduction 7

1. The Home Takes Shape 9
2. A Walk in the Park 57
3. Street Scenes 67
4. Across the Road 77
5. The Waterfront 83
6. National Historic District and Cottages 87
7. People, Places, and Things 119

ACKNOWLEDGMENTS

This work is dedicated to Kathy and our sons, Chris and Eric, who support my endeavors in every way.

This work could not have been done without the help of many people. The Home's Public Information Officer, Rich Calcut, was the primary reason for this book. He was instrumental in obtaining most of the old photographs to be used in the book. The librarian, Linda Hagen, helped whenever she could without reserve. Gary Hartleben and Ron Johnston, security officers, were a tremendous help. Gary is the Home's "historian" and was more than willing to share his knowledge. The Wisconsin Veterans Museum director, Richard Zietlin, was an inspiration for me. Mark Ebner, of the Waupaca Historical Society, was always willing to look for more photographs of the Home. It was his suggestion to try Arcadia Publishing for the book's publication. Friends Jim and Sue Waid were always there to help. Elizabeth Jobe, an editor at Arcadia, has been a nice addition to all that have lent a hand. They have all been great to work with and I hope they are proud of their contributions to this book.

It's hard to do a book on a veterans topic without thinking of my dad, Eugene Heltemes, a World War II Army veteran, and my Uncle Roy Wyman, a World War II Navy veteran and past member of the Home.

Introduction

My memories of the Wisconsin Veterans Home at King go back to the mid-1960s while working on Onaway Island, straight out from the Home on Rainbow Lake. As an employee of the Boy's Brigade, Neenah, Wisconsin, my spare time was spent at the Home. Nothing was more fascinating than listening to World War I veterans and their experiences. The museum had my interest—my hair was even cut at the home's barbershop. Walking down the roads, among the cottages, the Home held its own appeal. It's because of my teenage years there that I started collecting photos of the Home.

Hosea W. Rood last wrote the history of the Grand Army Home of King, Wisconsin in 1926. Rood was the Wisconsin Department Grand Army of the Republic patriotic instructor. This edition has been written by the Wisconsin Department Sons of Union Veterans of the Civil War junior vice commander of 2003–2004.

Although the 1926 version included some photographs, it only gave a brief idea of how the early Home looked. Trying to update that work, the author has done so without making the edition complicated or confusing. While the descriptions are brief, it is well known a person could write a book about each photograph if given enough time.

The Home has changed many times. Looking at the building blueprints of various years, it would be hard to determine a method for the reader to see all the changes. One would have to study each year's blueprints. Many buildings were moved to make room for modern structures. Some of the cottages just simply fell apart when they tried to move them. Other cottages were sold off and moved from the grounds. Several of these locations are known. Some of the cottages are not accounted for in the photographs because there was not a photograph of those buildings to be found.

In 1985, the Home was nominated for the National Registry of Historic Places through the work of Carol Lohry Cartwright of the Wisconsin State Historical Society. This area in the National Registry is considered the Historic Veteran's Cottage District, comprised of 31 cottages and staff buildings, including the Chapel, Ove Medical Center, and the commandant's residence.

It all started in 1887, at the Milwaukee Grand Army of the Republic Encampment. Department Commander Henry P. Fisher suggested that the state make provisions for a veteran's home. The National Home in Milwaukee, which didn't include widows or spouses as members, didn't have the capability to handle the amount of applicants it was getting. After Fisher's suggestion, which included talk of supporting the veterans in their own homes, the motion was eventually made by Dr. Frederick A. Marden to set up a committee of five to consider the advisability of a home, even if temporary, in which the veteran and spouse or widow could live. The motion passed and the committee of five was appointed. They were Dr. Marden, A.O. Wright (secretary of the State Board of Charities and Reform), B.F. Bryant, James Cumberledge, and J.H. Marston. Marden was named as head of the committee. These five men were the incorporators of the Home. Deciding they could manage the Home better than a state or national institution could, the Home came under the management of the Grand Army of the Republic (GAR). This was the start of the first veteran's home to allow the veteran and spouse or widow in a retirement setting.

After looking over six sites for the Home (Waupaca, Sheboygan, Watertown, Evansville, Berlin, and New Lisbon), the incorporators, after a two day meeting, decided on the Waupaca site on the Chain O' Lakes. Incorporation was officially March 10, 1887. On March 15, 1889, the city of Waupaca held an election for the proposal of the city borrowing $7,500 for the purchase of the land, buildings, and 78 acres for the Grand Army Home. Approved with a vote of 249 to 52, the proposition passed. The money was borrowed from the State of Wisconsin. According to Rood, "the city of Waupaca in its corporate capacity gave $7,500 toward the purchase of the Greenwood Park Property for the Wisconsin Veteran's Home, including the deeds which were given by the Greenwood Park Association directly to the Corporation of the Wisconsin Veteran's Home. One condition in the deed as first drawn was that in case the property ever cease(d) to be used for the purpose of a Soldier's Home for the veterans of the Civil War, it would revert to the city of Waupaca. The Home at the time was a feeble institution with a doubtful future, and the people of Waupaca thought this a wise business precaution. To this the Corporation objected on the ground that in the course of time and nature it must eventually cease to be used as a home for veterans of the Civil War. Because of this objection the deed was redrawn as to give the city of Waupaca a residuary interest to the extant of $7,500 in the property in case it should cease to be used for some charitable or benevolent purpose."

In 1889, the Home was in need of money for improvements. The Wisconsin Legislation approved $50,000, but only on the condition that the Home was deeded to the state. The Board agreed to this as long as GAR could control the Home. On May 23, 1890, the Home was conveyed to the state. The GAR control lasted until 1917, when the federal government objected to the Home being run by a non-federal agency while it used federal funds. The State of Wisconsin then took over control of the Home but left G.A.R to run the Home. Commandant Jerome A. Watrous, of the famous Iron Brigade, was the last of the GAR to run the Home. He resigned on September 6, 1920, his 80th birthday. GAR management of the Home officially ended in 1929, but remained active until 1947.

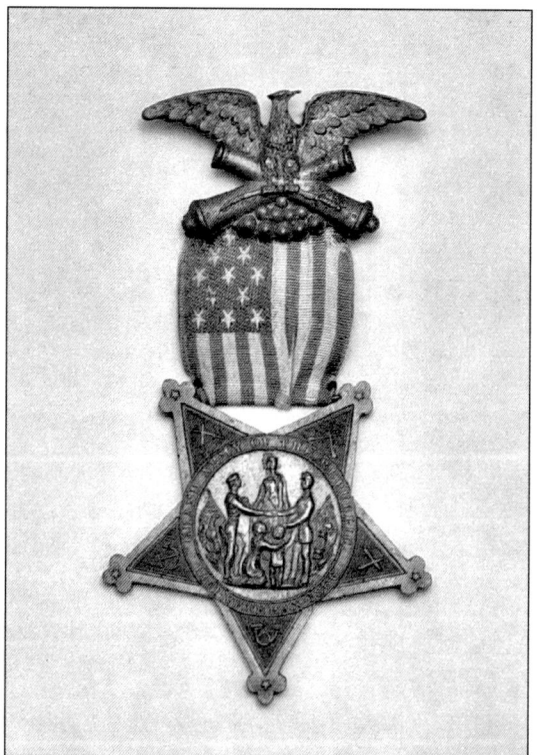

GAR 1866 MEMBERSHIP BADGE.

One

THE HOME TAKES SHAPE

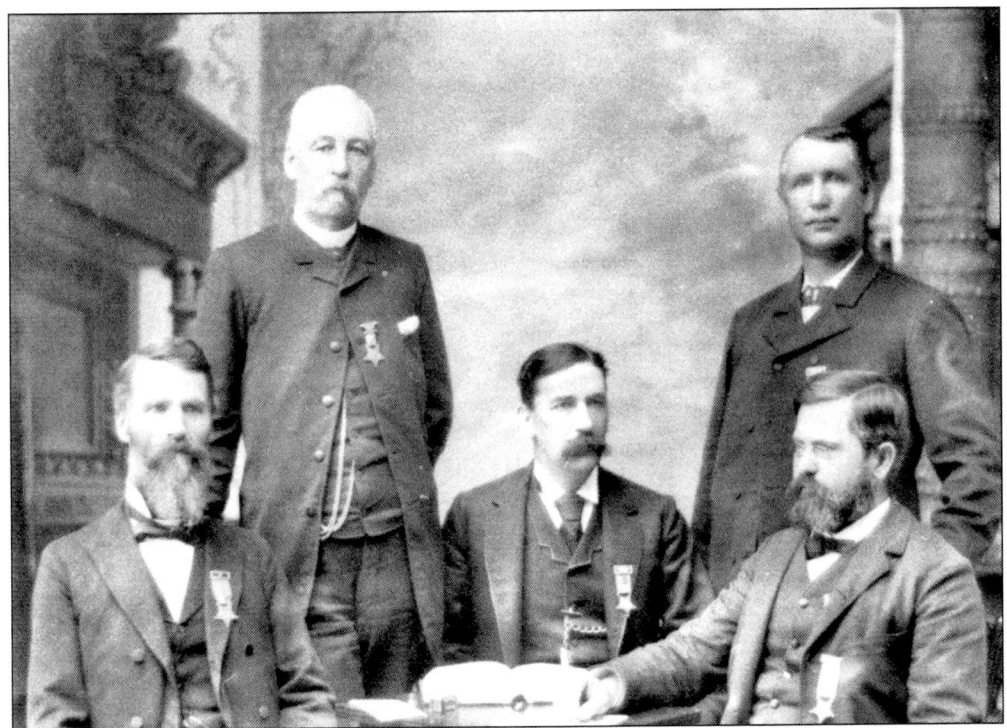

INCORPORATORS. The five incorporators of the Home pose, wearing their G.A.R badges, for a photo in 1897. Seated left to right are Benjamin F. Bryant, Dr. Frederick A. Marden, and Albert O. Wright. Standing from left to right are Joseph H. Marston and James Cumberledge.

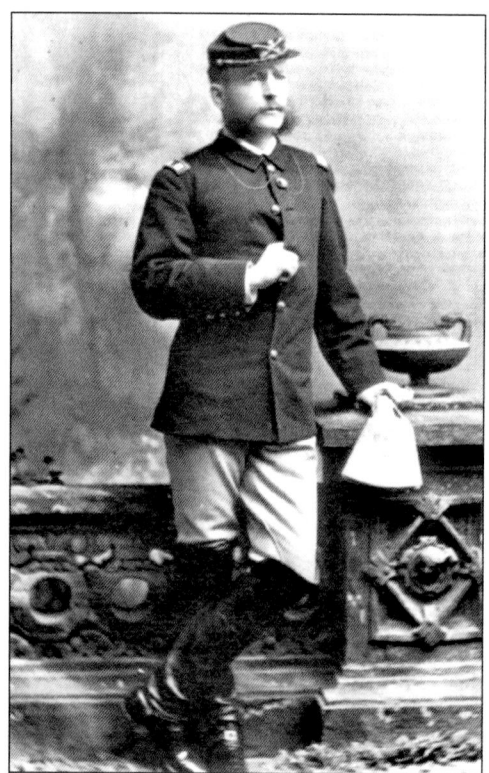 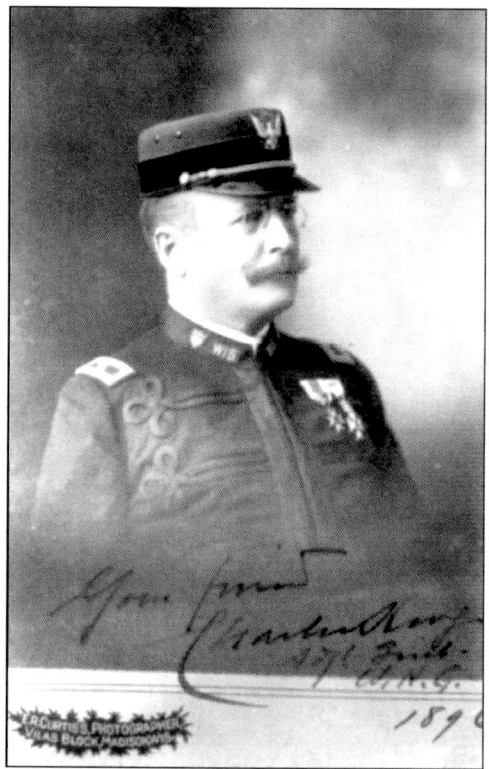

GENERAL CHARLES KING (1844–1937). As taken from a marker on the grounds, "Charles King, one of America's most illustrious soldiers, was born in New York and came to Milwaukee in 1845." His father was Rufus King, editor and publisher of the *Milwaukee Sentinel* and first commander of the famed Civil War Iron Brigade. Charles King graduated from West Point, took part in the Civil War, and served on active duty in until 1879, when a serious battle wound during an Indian Campaign forced his retirement. Returning to Wisconsin, King began a writing career popularizing the exploits of the U.S. Cavalry in the west. He also transformed the states militia system into the modern National Guard and commanded the Guard during the labor riots in Bay View. King taught for many years at St. John's Military Academy in Delafield. Reentering the federal service during the Spanish American War, King attained the rank of Brigadier General and later participated in World War I. Spending more than seventy years in uniform—longer than any soldier in American history—King also wrote and published extensively on military life. The Village of King in Waupaca County bears his name.

To the right is an 1896 photograph of General King.

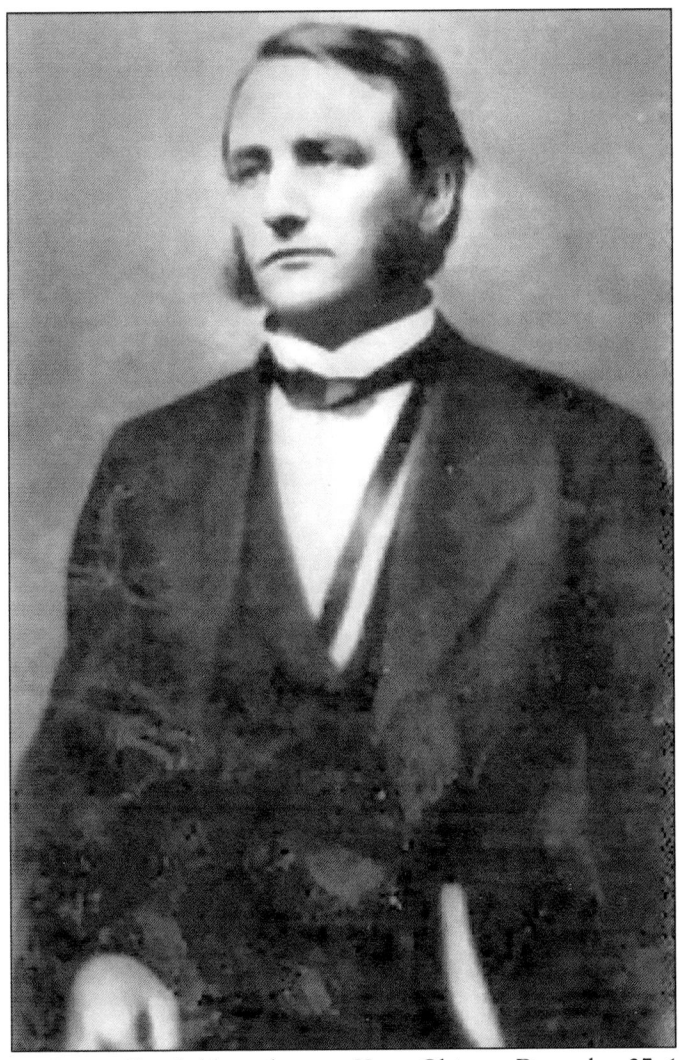

LUCIUS FAIRCHILD. Lucius Fairchild was born in Kent, Ohio on December 27, 1831. He moved to Madison in 1846. After attending Prairieville College (Carroll College), he worked as a court clerk. Fairchild enlisted into the First Wisconsin Infantry at the start of the Civil War in April 1861 as a private. He was made a lieutenant colonel in 1862 of the Second Wisconsin Infantry of the famed Iron Brigade. In 1862, he was made a full colonel. During the 1863 battle of Gettysburg, he lost his left arm. In October 1863, he was made a brigadier general and returned to Wisconsin in November 1863. In 1864 he became the secretary of state under Governor James Lewis. As a thirty-four-year-old, he was elected governor of Wisconsin in 1866. Also in 1866, he helped organize the Wisconsin Chapter of Soldiers and Sailors National Union League. Fairchild helped organize the Wisconsin Grand Army of the Republic in an effort to get support for and from the Civil War veterans. Getting the veterans to vote as a unit gave him more political clout. He was elected for two more terms as governor, making him the first three-term governor of Wisconsin. After ten years as consul general of England and France, and U.S. minister to Spain, Fairchild returned to become a driving force in the Iron Brigade Association and the Wisconsin GAR. He became the Wisconsin state commander of the GAR, as well as the national commander of the GAR. Always an advocate for the veterans, Fairchild died on May 23, 1896 in Madison, Wisconsin. He is buried at the Forest Hill Cemetery in Madison.

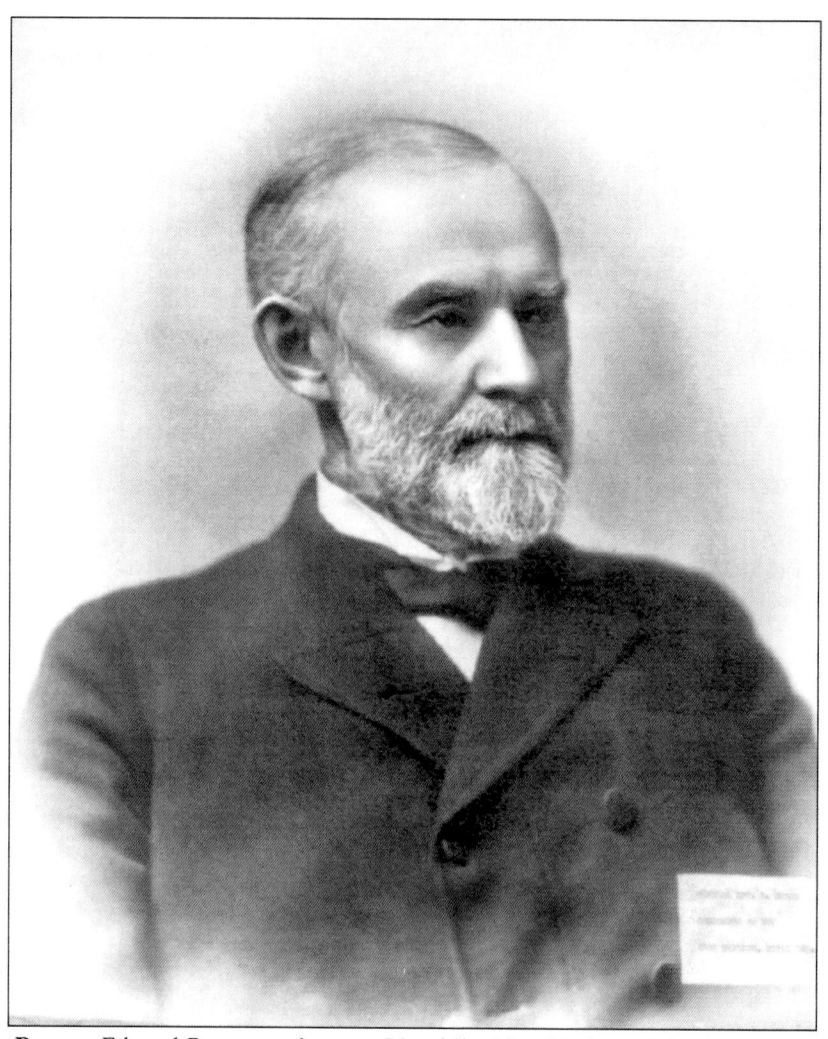

EDWARD BRAGG. Edward Bragg was born in Unadilla, New York on February 20, 1827. After graduating from Geneva College in Geneva, New York, he was admitted to the bar in 1848. He practiced law in his hometown until 1850, when he moved to Fond du Lac, Wisconsin to resume his law practice. He served as the district attorney for some time. In 1860, he became a delegate to the Democratic National Convention. On July 16, 1861, he joined the Union Army as a captain of the Sixth Wisconsin Infantry. He was made a major on September 17, 1861; a lieutenant colonel on June 21, 1862; colonel on March 24, 1863; and brigadier general on June 25, 1864. Bragg was mustered out of the service on October 9, 1865.

After the Civil War he was appointed postmaster of Fond du Lac in 1866. He served two terms in the State Senate in 1868 and 1869. He was the delegate to the Democratic Convention again in 1872, 1880, and 1896. He was elected to the United States Senate as a democrat from 1877 to 1883. He served on the Committee of War Claims from 1879 to 1881. Re-elected to the Senate from 1885 to 1887, he served on the Committee of Military Affairs. It was during this time period that Bragg was in a feud with Lucius Fairchild over the control of the Wisconsin Grand Army of the Republic. Bragg was an ardent democrat and Fairchild was a staunch republican. Bragg retired from public service in 1906 after stints as envoy of Mexico, consul general at Cuba, and consul general of China. He died in Fond du Lac on June 20, 1912, and is buried in the Rienzi Cemetery.

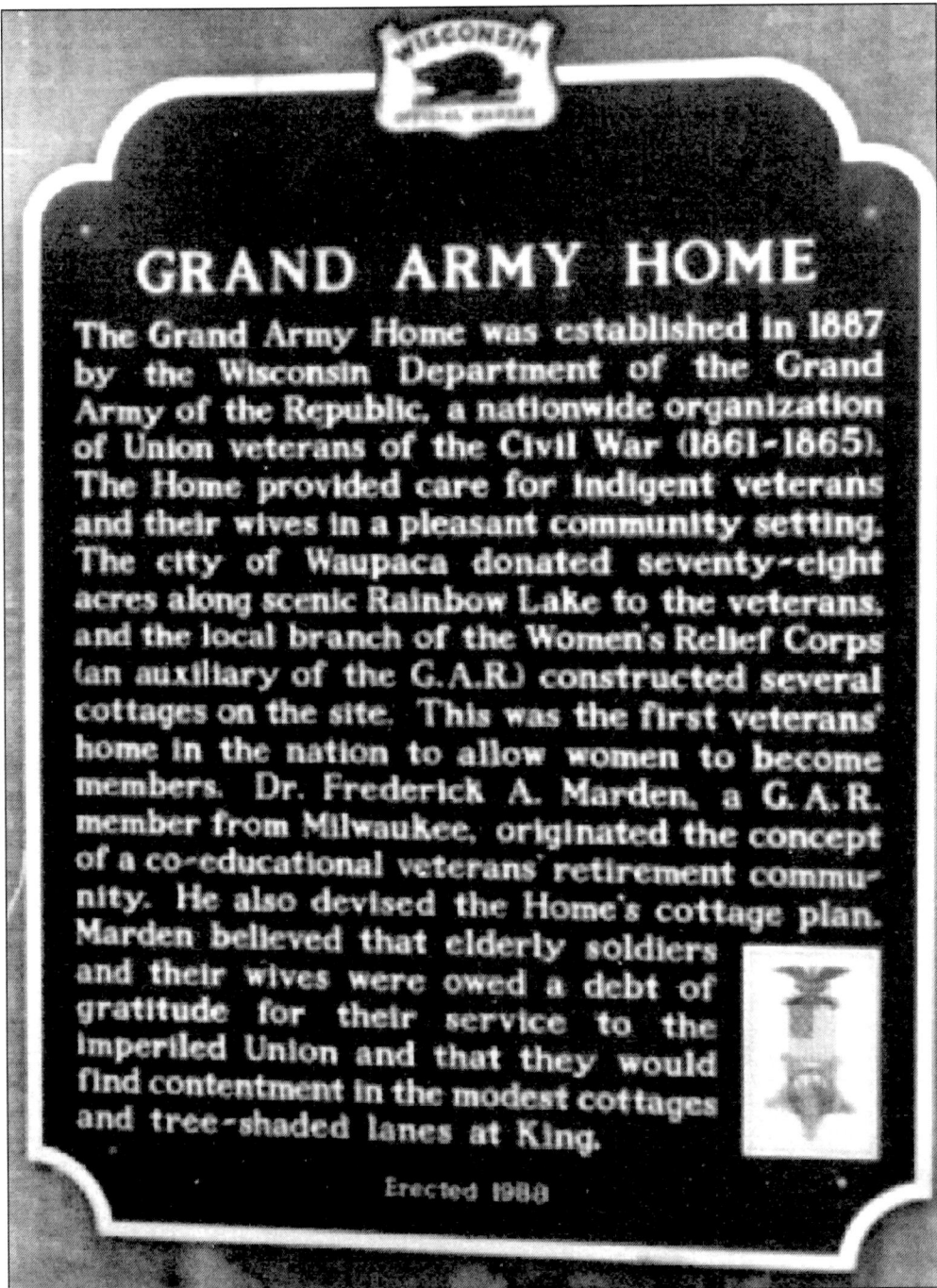

HOME MARKER. This marker is outside of the Marden Hall. It gives the visitor a brief introduction of the start of the Home.

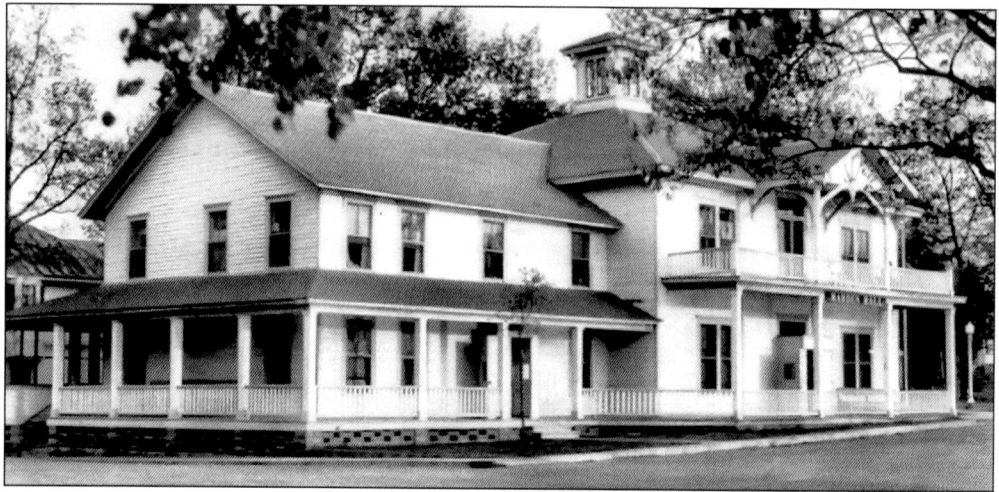

MARDEN HALL. Marden Hall, originally the Greenwood Park Hotel, was situated on the raised shoreline overlooking Rainbow Lake of the Chain O' Lakes. Built in 1881, it started out as a resort, but as such it only lasted a few years. On August 20, 1887, the Wisconsin department commander of the Grand Army of the Republic, Michael Griffin, announced the selection for the Home by the incorporators as Greenwood Park Hotel.

The wooden structure, with first and second story porches, was the initial building for care of the veterans. Eventually, the building was used for the widows.

Shortly after the mysterious death of Dr. Frederick Marden in Milwaukee, on September 24, 1887, the building was named in honor of him. Dr. Marden, one of the five incorporators of the Home, served in the Navy during the Civil War. Marden is credited with the insight of having a veteran and spouse living together in a caring environment in small cottages, so they wouldn't have to be split up. He served as the president of the first Board of Trustees.

Marden Hall was torn down in 1971 and a new Marden Hall now takes its place.

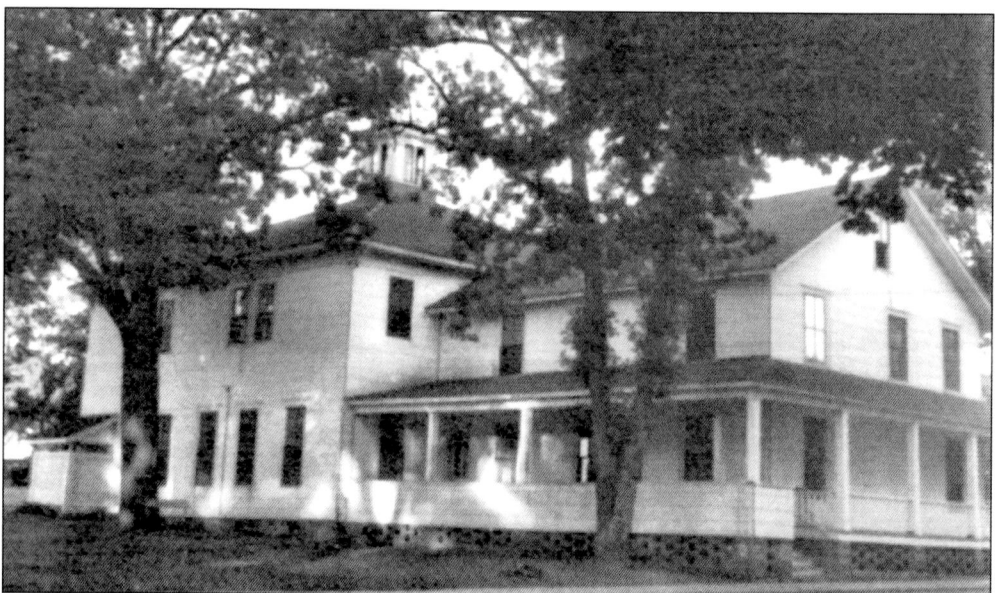

MARDEN HALL. Marden Hall is shown from the side—not as glamorous as the front. Most photos taken of Marden Hall are from the front.

MARDEN HALL. The Marden Hall (Greenwood Hotel) was torn down in 1971 to make room for a modern structure. Shown in the middle of destruction, this was the oldest building on the Home property and a landmark on the Chain O' Lakes.

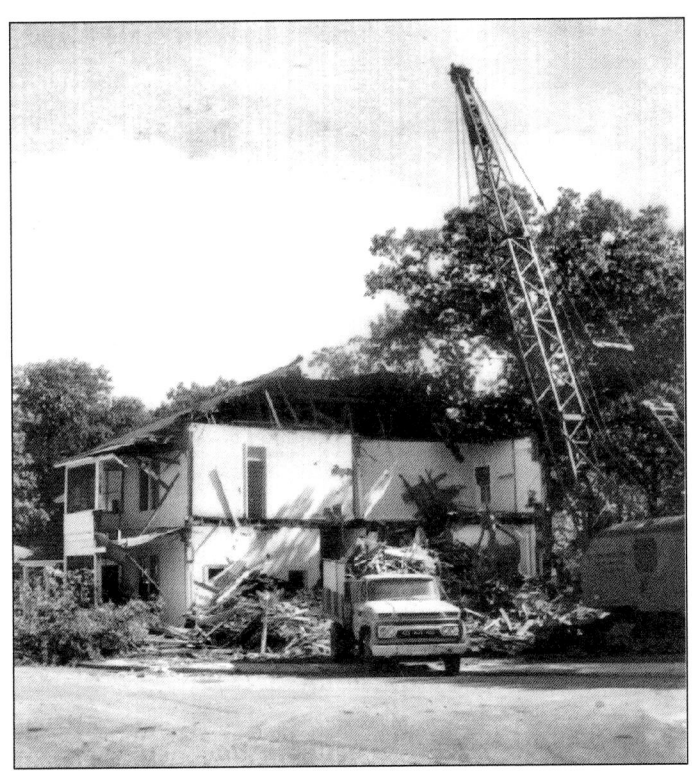

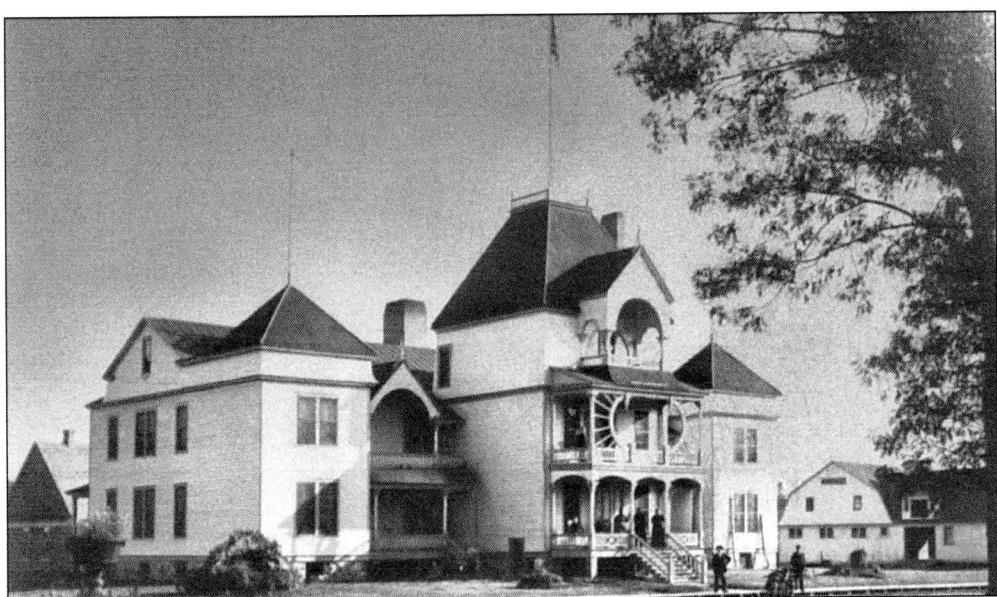

FAIRCHILD HALL AND BARD. This is a view of Fairchild Hall, with a surprising view of a barn on the right. The barn is not listed as a building number on any of the blueprints of the grounds. This might be the only photo of this barn.

BLDG NO.	NAME	BLDG NO.	NAME	BLDG NO.	NAME
101	Commandant's	216	Cottage	403	Houston Hall
102	Headquarters	217	Cottage	404	Harnden Hall
103	Boat House	218	Cottage	405	Nurse's Res.
104	Q.M. Residence	219	Cottage	406	Power House
105	Cottage	220	Cottage	407	Cottage
106	Cottage	221	Cottage	408	Adjutant's
107	Cottage	222	Cottage	409	Cottage
108	Cottage	223	Cottage	410	Cottage
109	Cottage	224	Cottage	411	Cottage
110	Cottage	225	Cottage	412	Cottage
111	Cottage	226	Cottage	413	Cottage
112	Cottage	227	Cottage	414	Cottage
113	Cottage	228	Cottage	415	Cottage
114	Cottage	229	Cottage	416	Cottage
115	Cottage	230	Cottage	417	Pump House
116	Cottage	231	Cottage	501	Ove Center
117	Cottage	232	Cottage	502	Hospital Annex
118	Cottage	233	Cottage	505	Asst. Q.M. Res.
119	Cottage	235	Ice House	507	Cottage
120	Cottage	301	Fairchild Hall		
121	Cottage	302	Amusement		
122	Cottage	304	Marston Hall		
123	Cottage	305	Robert Law Bld		
124	Cottage	306	Griffin Hall		
125	Cottage	307	Roberts Hall		
200	Bandstand	312	Cottage		
205	Library	320	Barn		
206	Post Office	321	Farm Cottage		
207	Furniture Shop	324	Barber Shop		
208	Carpenter Shop	327	Chapel		
209	Paint Shop	401	Marden Hall		
210	Lumber Shed	402	Bryant Hall		

BUILDING NUMBERS. This is a combined listing of various buildings that existed throughout the history of the Home. Not all are listed.

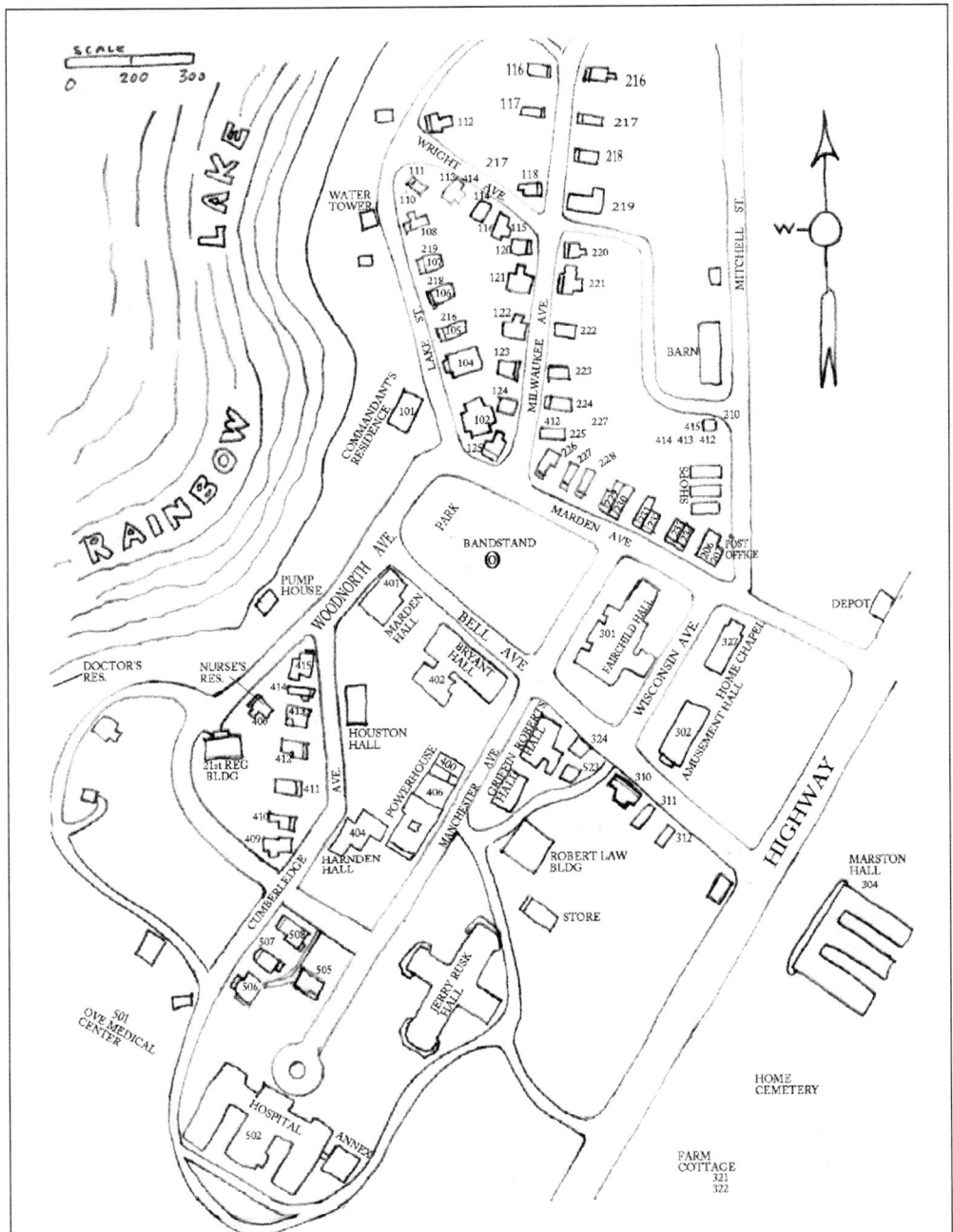

MAP. This map, when coordinated with the building list (*opposite page*), will give the reader an idea where a building of interest was and may still be located. Several street names have been changed as the Home changed. This map is also a combined example of builing location. It does not show building locations for any particular year.

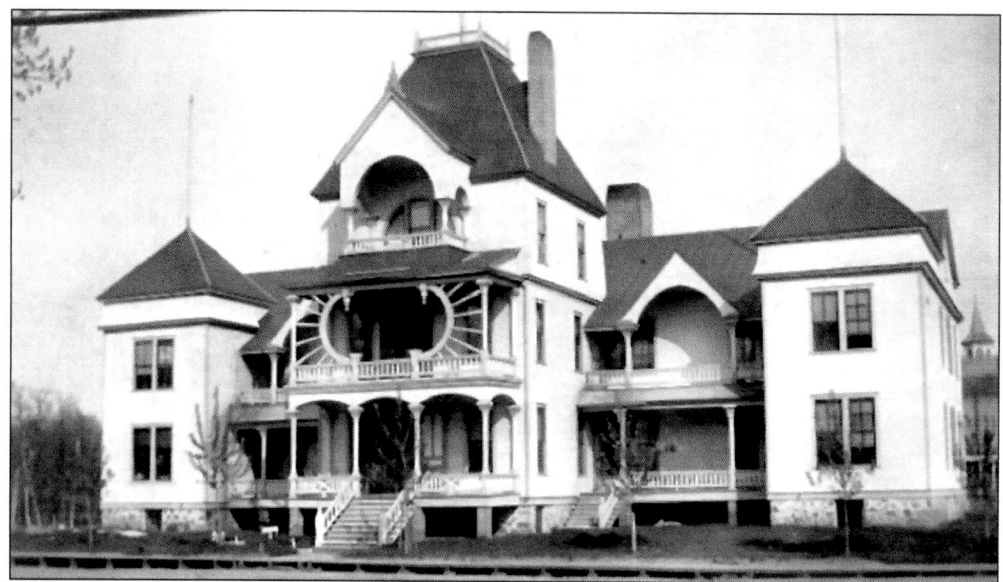

FAIRCHILD HALL. Fairchild Hall, built in 1891 at a cost of $12,000, was originally called the Old People's Home. An addition to the hall was done in October of 1906. The new addition had a capacity of 80 for the dining room, as well as a kitchen, pantry, and storeroom on the first floor. The second floor had quarters for 15 more members. The third floor was a dormitory style room with a tower above it. Fairchild Hall was considered the nicest looking building on the grounds. It was also modernized for conveniences. Later, the wooden structure had the museum in the basement and for some time held the library.

Fairchild Hall was named in honor of Lucius Fairchild in 1896 after his death. Fairchild, a driving force in Wisconsin veteran's rights, was a dedicated republican and Grand Army of the Republic supporter.

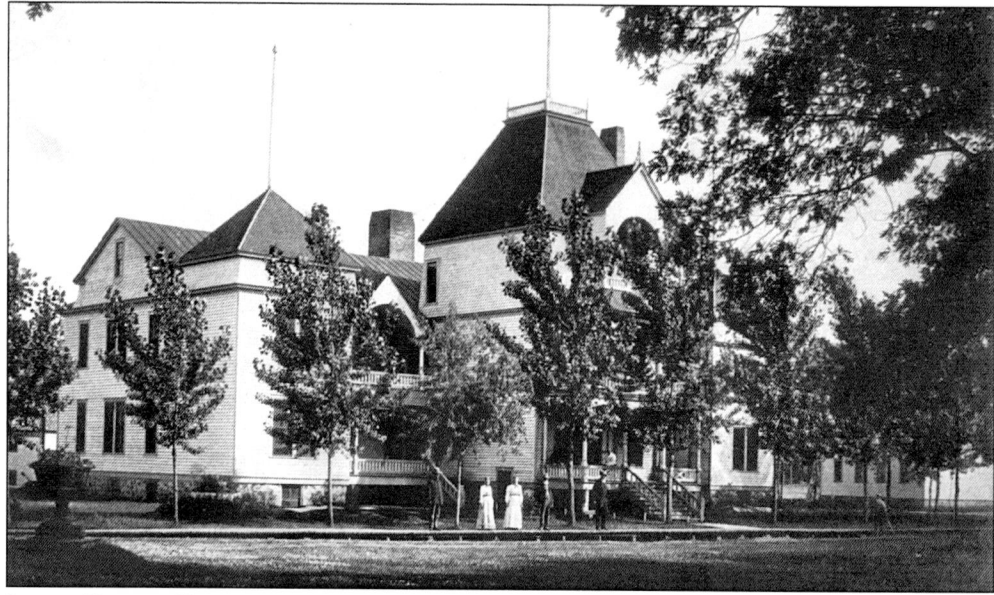

LATER VIEW OF FAIRCHILD HALL. This view was taken later, when the trees had grown along Manchester Avenue.

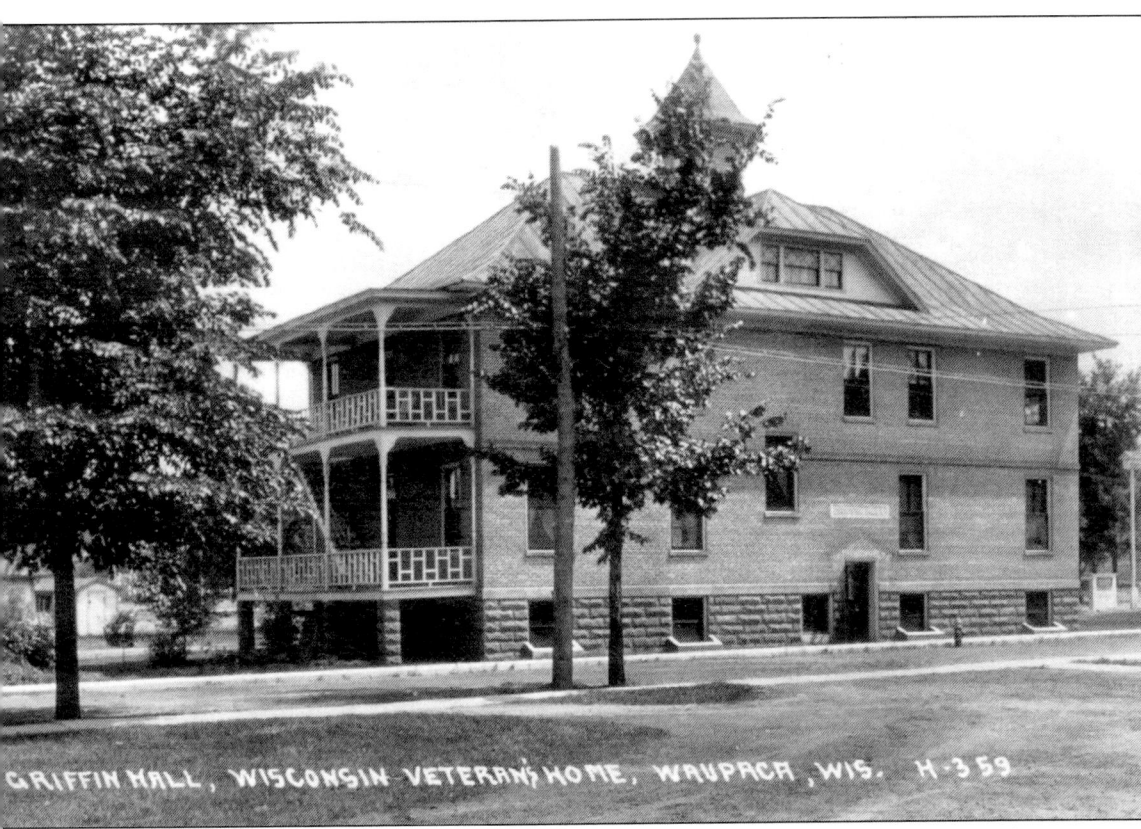

GRIFFIN HALL. Griffin Hall was located on Manchester Avenue, just south of Roberts Hall. It was a two-story brick and stone building with a two-tiered porch on the north end. Seven living quarters and a sitting room were on both floors. The basement was a recreational room with billiard and card tables. The building was also where voting took place.

Griffin Hall was named after Michael Griffin. Griffin was born in Ireland on September 9, 1842. His parents moved from Canada, Ohio, and then to Wisconsin, making Newport, Wisconsin their home. During the Civil War, Griffin enlisted into Company E, 12th Wisconsin Infantry. Mustered out as a lieutenant, he returned to Kilbourn, Wisconsin, now known as Wisconsin Dells. He practiced law, was a cashier at the Kilbourn City Bank, and got into politics. After a stint as State Assemblyman of Sauk County, he moved to Eau Claire, Wisconsin to practice law. He served as a State Senator from 1880 to 1881. It was during his role as Wisconsin department commander of the Grand Army of the Republic that he oversaw the birth of the Veterans Home in King. In 1894, he was elected to Congress to fill a vacancy and was elected for the following two terms. Griffin died on December 29, 1899.

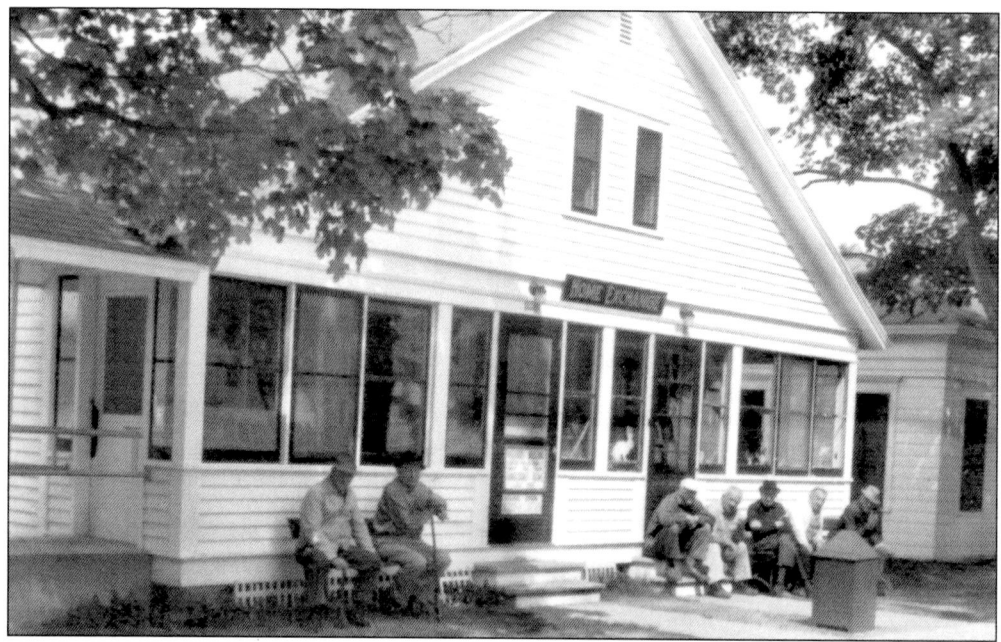

HOME EXCHANGE. The Home Exchange was a wooden structure. Split down the middle, the house was the coffee shop, a place to display handmade crafts, and a place for Home members to purchase clothing. It was located next to the post office near the corner of Marden and Mitchell Avenues. This building was torn down to make way for Stordock Hall.

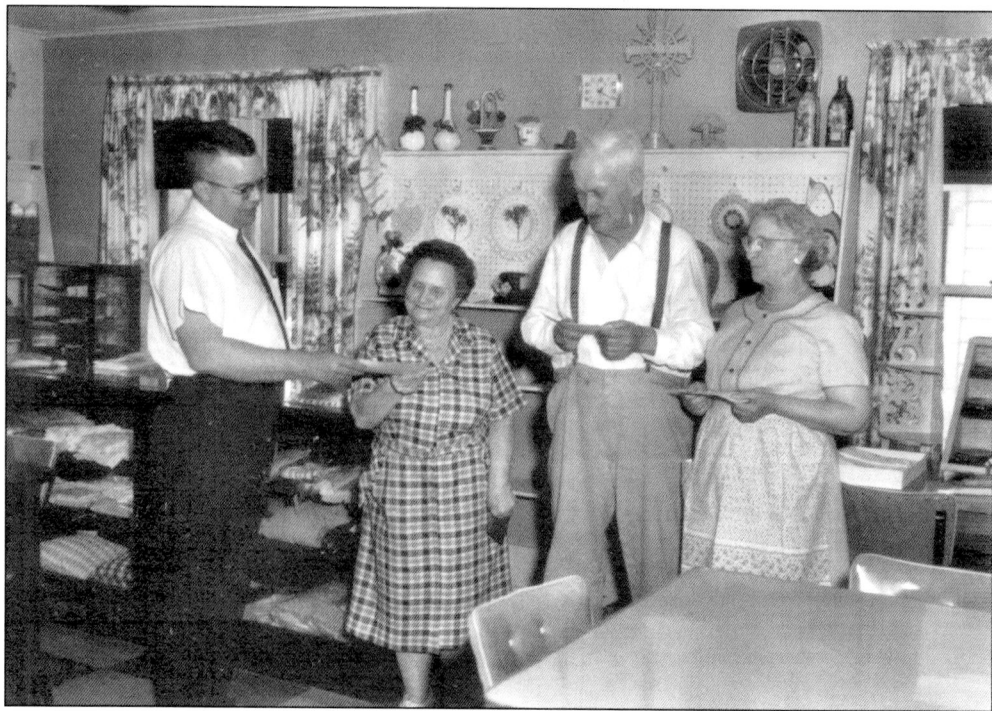

HOME EXCHANGE INTERIOR. The inside of the Home Exchange is shown with clothing articles for Home members.

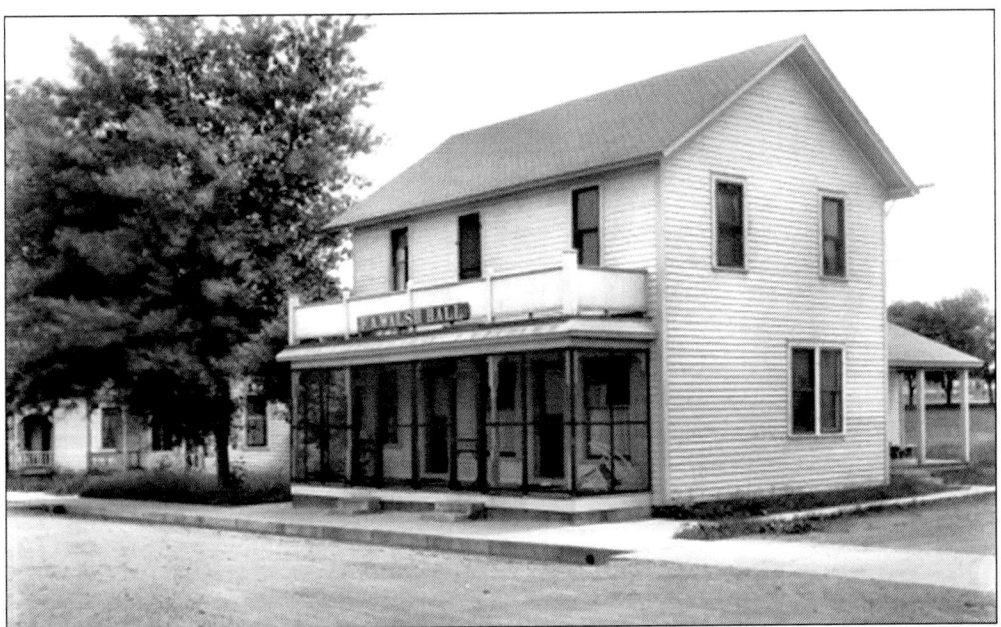

WALSH HALL. This is the only view of Walsh Hall, located after an exhausting search. Walsh Hall was named after Francis A. Walsh. Walsh had donated money for the building's repair as he had with other buildings on the grounds. Walsh Hall was located on Bell Avenue.

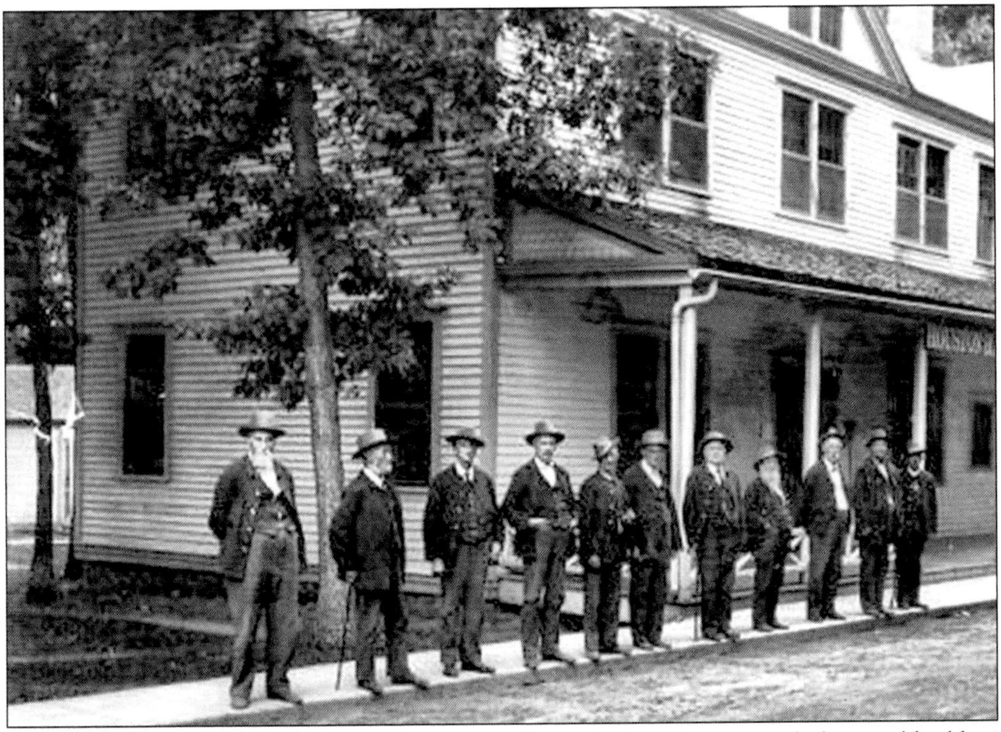

HOUSTON HALL. Formally known as Assembly Hall, this hall was later named after an old soldier, who realized how well the members of the Home were treated. With the death of Walter L. Houston, the Home was willed over $4,900. This hall was located on Cumberledge Avenue.

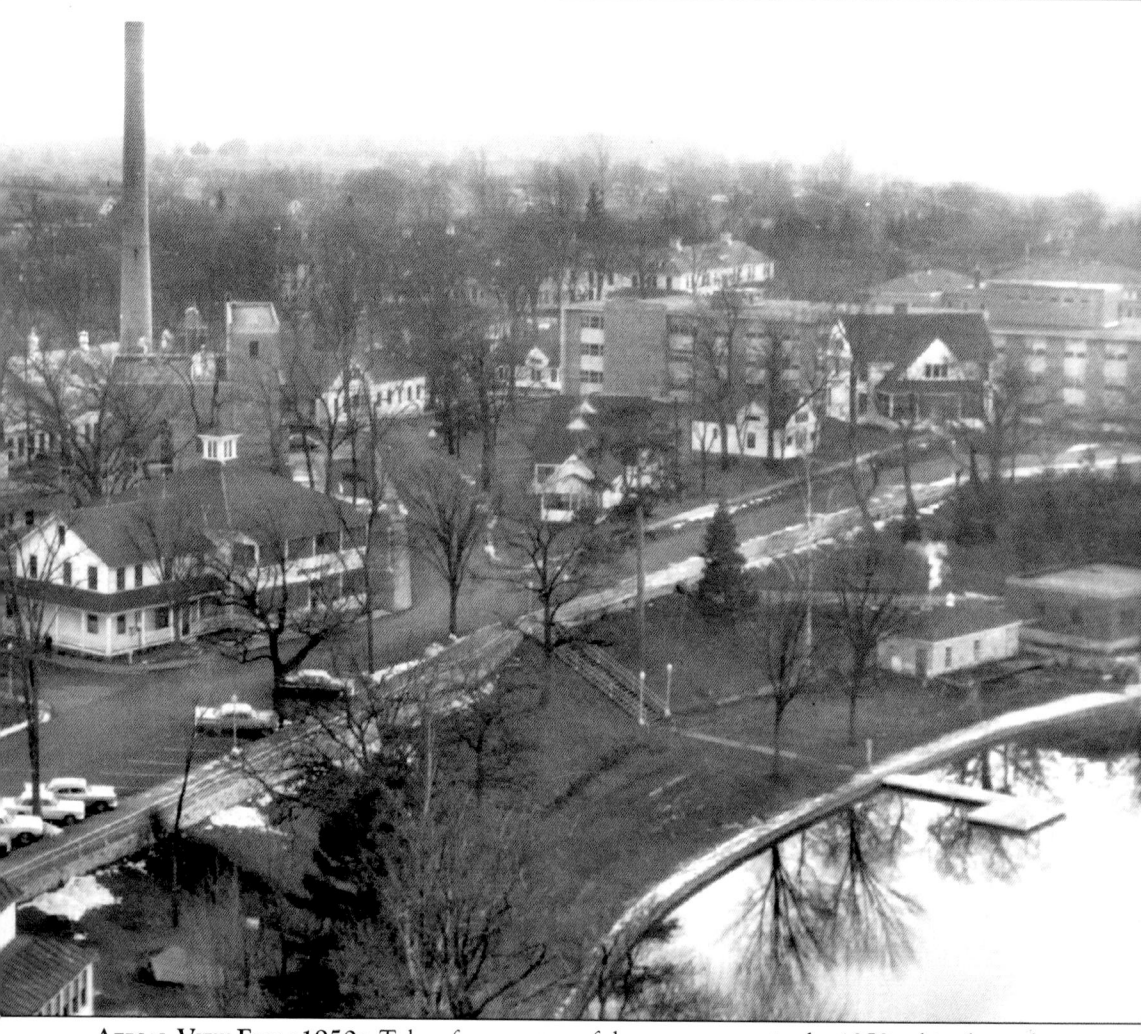

Aerial View From 1950s. Taken from on top of the water tower in the 1950s, this photo shows Marden Hall on the left, Building Number 415 in the middle, the nurses' residence to its right, and the 21st Regimental Building facing the lake. The water facilities are on the lakeshore. This is one of several docks going out to Rainbow Lake that the Home had throughout the years.

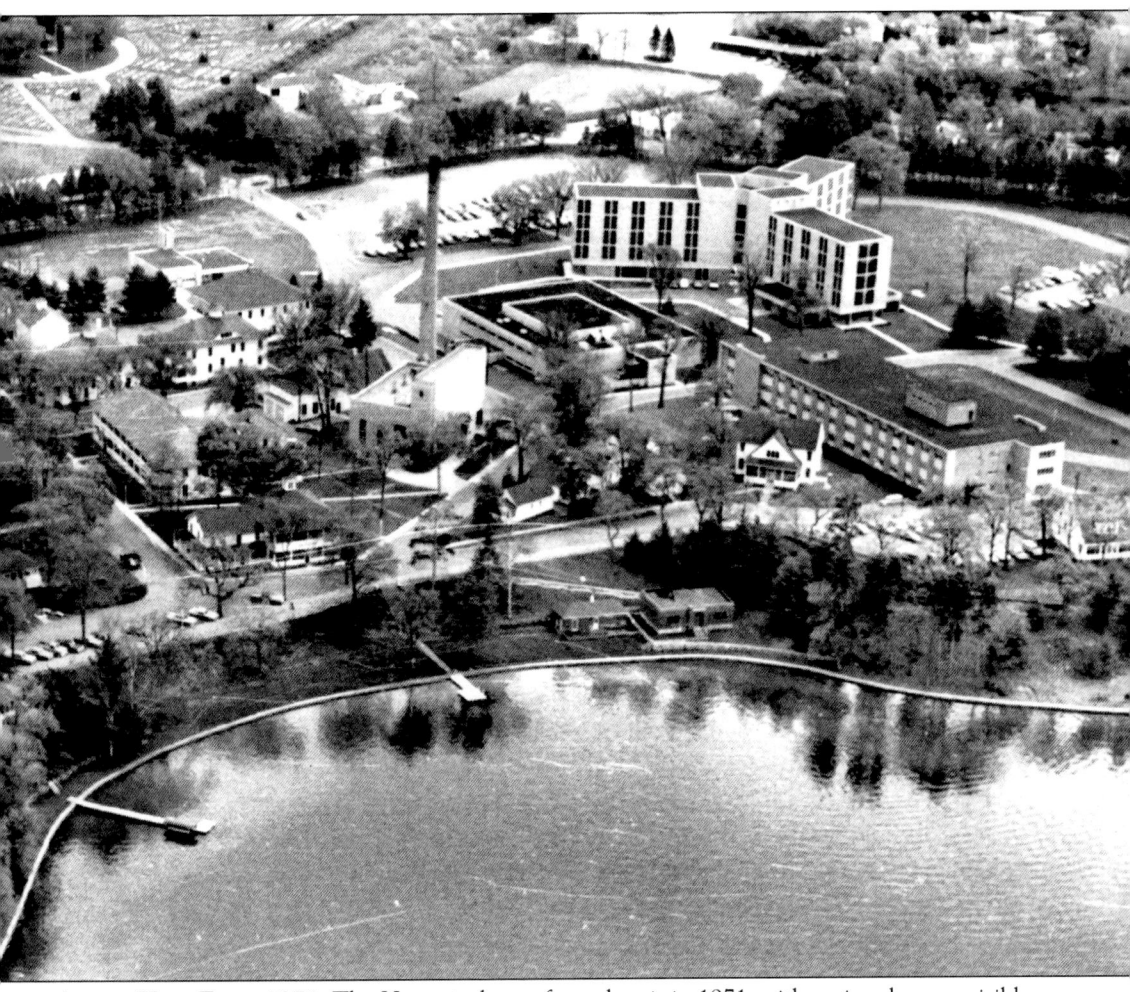

AERIAL VIEW FROM 1971. The Home is shown from the air in 1971, with major changes visible. This photo shows the location of the doctors' residence in relation to the rest of the Home. It is on the far right, just right of the 21st Regimental Building. There were only two views found of the home that included the doctors' residence. Still standing on the left side of the photo is Marden Hall, with Bryant Hall behind it. The white buildings on the center left are Roberts Hall, Griffin Hall, and the Law Building. Just to the left of the Power House is the Fire Department Building. The small white building on the far left would be Building Number 310.

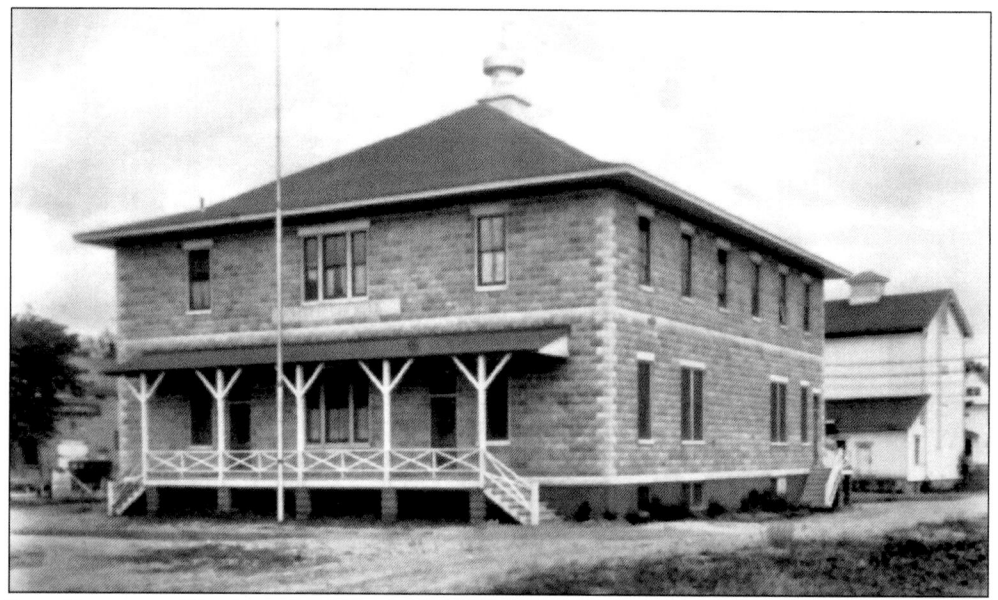

LAW BUILDING. The Law Building, as it was known, was built in 1923 of concrete block, one of the first fire-safe buildings on the grounds. Built by the Home workers and carpenters, the building was two stories with an eight-and-one-half ft. high basement. The Quartermaster Department and Commissary equally shared the first floor. The second floor had eleven rooms for employees. Home workers made the concrete blocks from molds on the grounds. They also made the window sills.

This building was named for Robert Law, who served as an officer of the Home, including the president of the Board of Trustees in 1917.

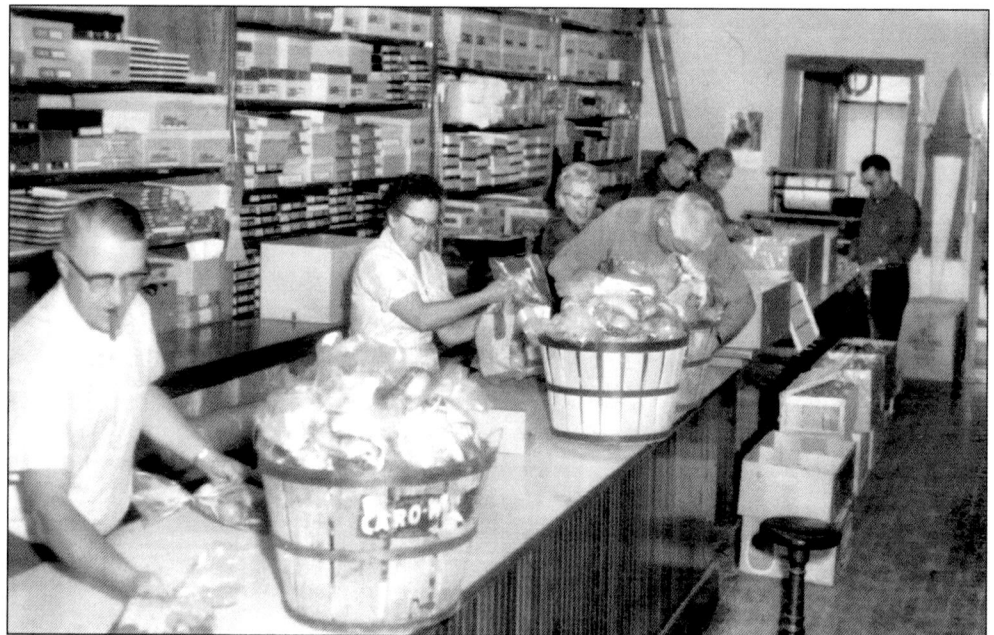

LAW BUILDING INTERIOR. In the only view found of the interior of the Commissary, it shows employees handling dry goods for the Home.

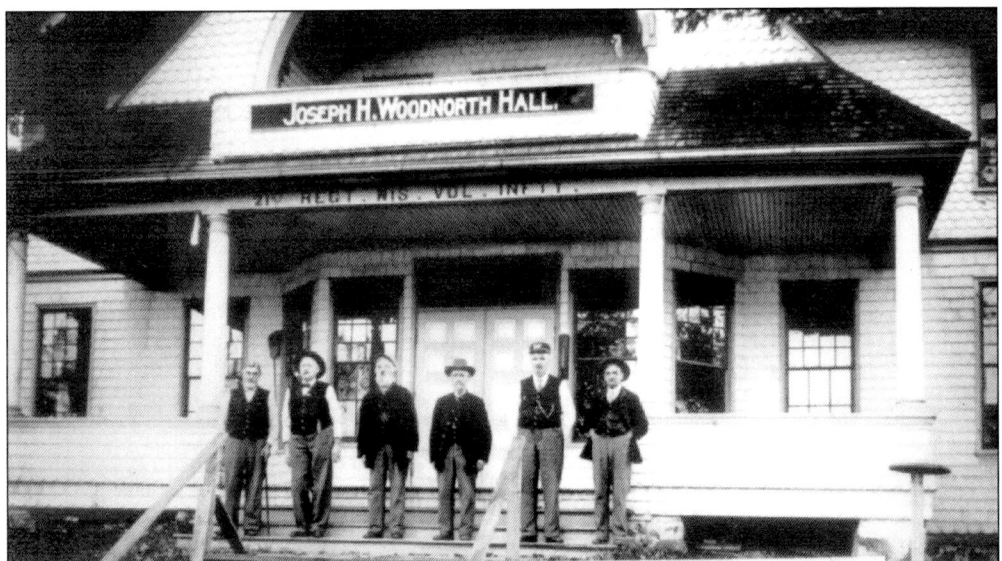

TWENTY-FIRST REGIMENTAL BUILDING. The surviving members of the 21st Regiment paid for this building, used to house members of the 21st Wisconsin Infantry. Built in 1894, it was located on one of the most commanding sites on the Chain O' Lakes, overlooking Rainbow Lake. Part of the building was also used as the Home library from 1894 to 1921. The building was on Woodnorth Avenue, where it meets Clark Avenue.

The building was named for Joseph H. Woodnorth, a member of the 21st Wisconsin Infantry and commandant of the Home from 1903 to 1910. Woodnorth's service to the Home started in 1888 as secretary of the Board of Trustees.

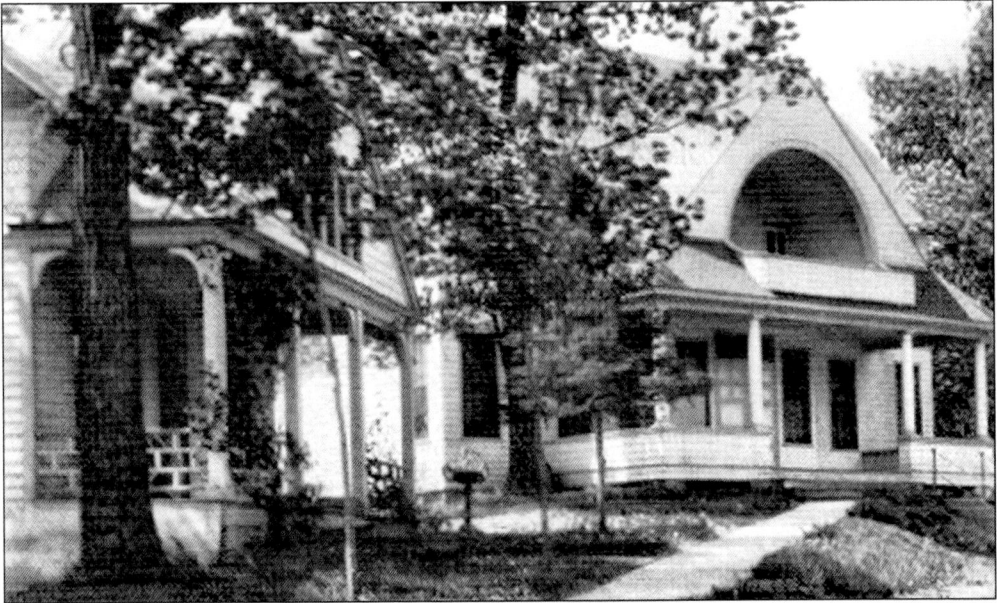

NURSES' RESIDENCE AND 21ST REGIMENTAL BUILDING. The nurses' residence is on the left side of the photograph, while the 21st Regimental Building is on the right. Both were located on Woodnorth Avenue, with the 21st Regimental building holding a commanding view over Rainbow Lake.

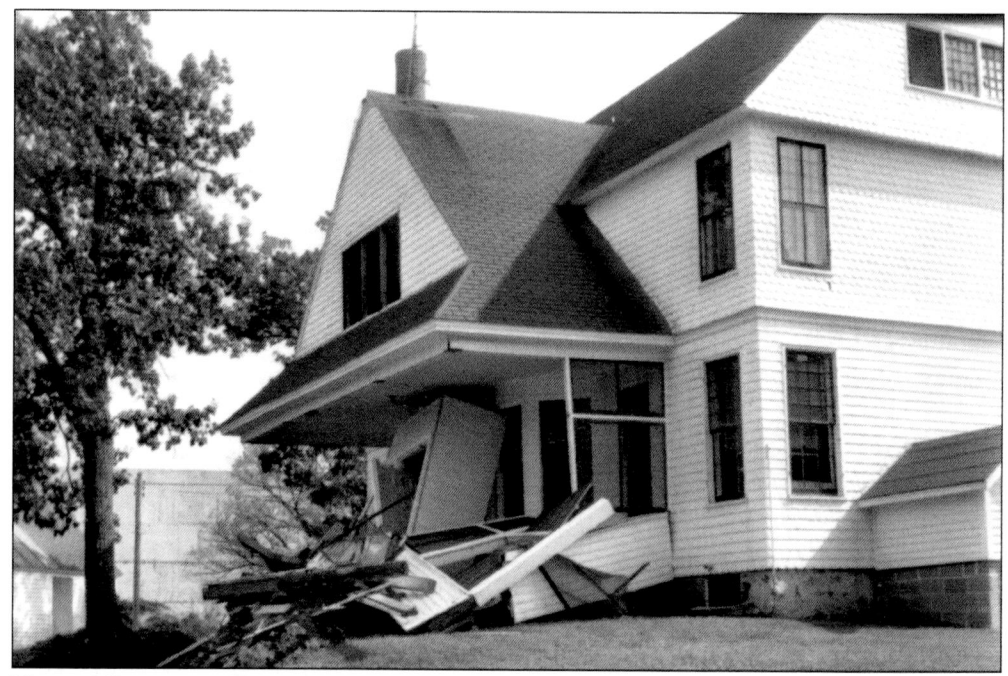

NURSES' RESIDENCE TORN DOWN. This photo was taken as the Nurses' quarters were being removed. An aerial view of the Home was taken in 1971, after the building was razed.

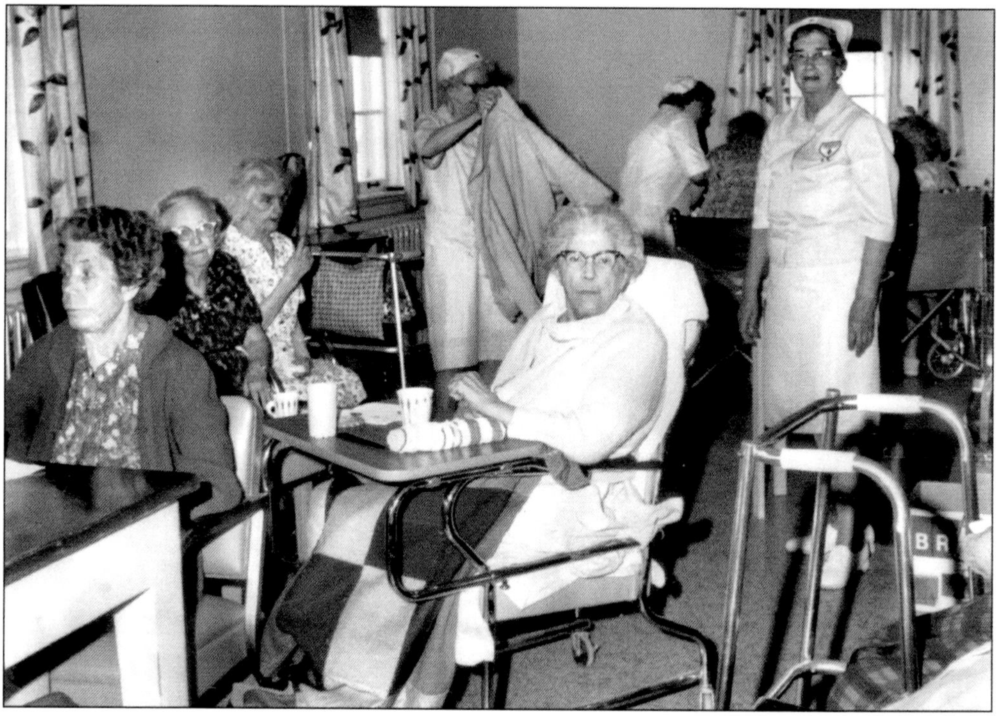

NURSES AT WORK. The work of the nurses must be commended. They are the center of activity at the Home. Since World War I, the Home has become a nursing facility. The days of the retirement home with minimal health care have long since been gone.

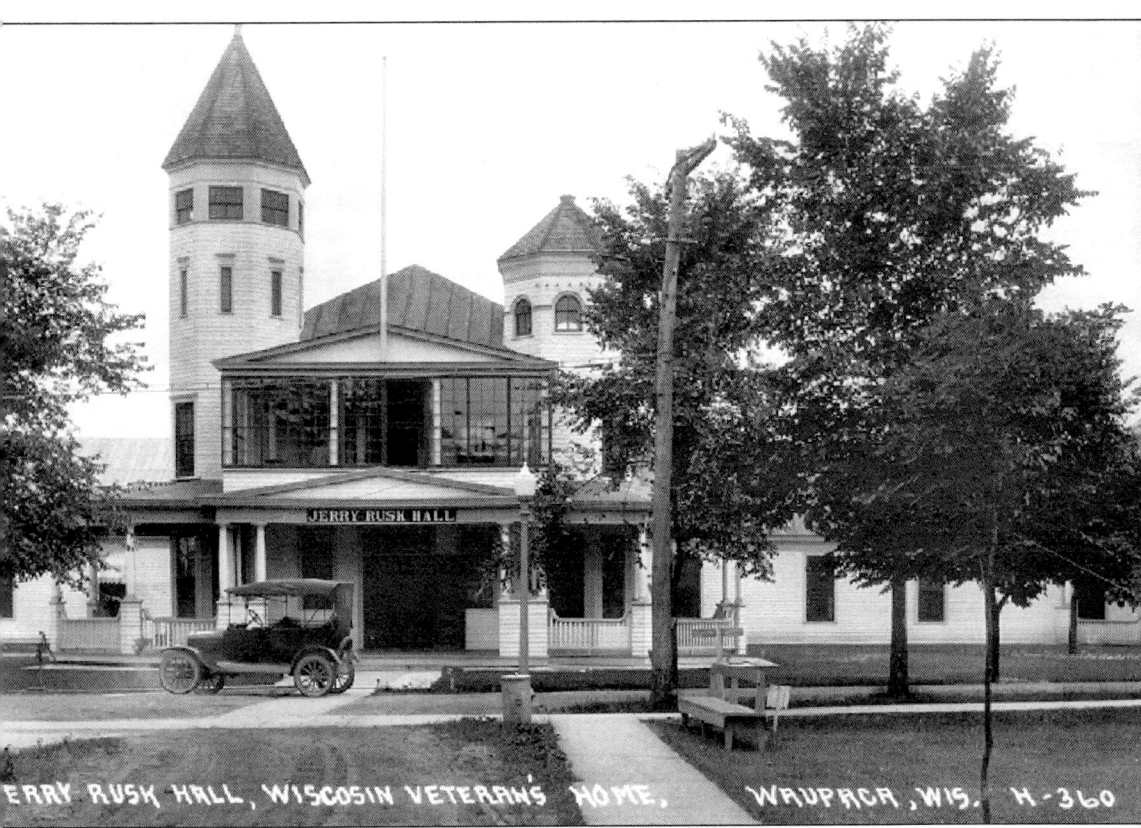

RUSK HALL. Rusk Hall was used to house old couples. Built in 1896, it had modern improvements and could house 60 people. In 1898, at a cost of $875, more rooms were finished on the second floor. This improvement then gave Rusk Hall a capacity of 74. The building was made in the shape of a cross, with porches on three of the wings. It had two towers in the center section that could be seen throughout the grounds. On Friday June 7, 1929, Rusk Hall was ablaze. The fire destroyed the south wing and caused fire and water damage to the remaining structure. The surviving structure was later razed.

Rusk Hall was named for Jeremiah M. Rusk, governor of Wisconsin when the Home was established. Rusk, achieving the rank of brigadier general in 1865, served in the 25th Wisconsin Infantry during the Civil War. Returning to Viroqua, Wisconsin after the war, Rusk became involved in the Republican Party. After six years in Congress he was elected to governor in 1882. A three-term governor, Rusk held this position until 1889 when he became the secretary of agriculture for President Benjamin Harrison.

Rusk died on November 21, 1893, and is buried in Viroqua, Wisconsin.

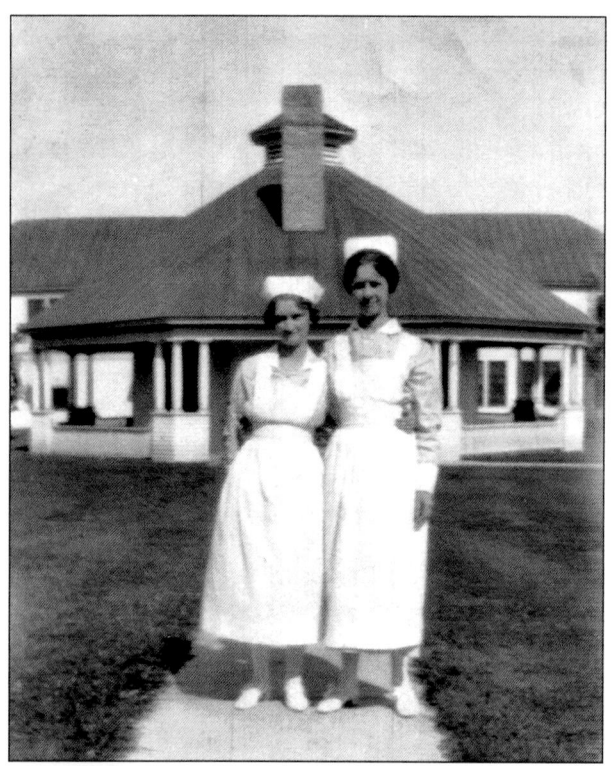

RUSK HALL IN 1922. Two nurses stand in front of one of the wings of Rusk Hall to have their photograph taken. This photograph shows more of the detail in the octagon shaped porches of Rusk Hall. Most photographs of this building were taken from the front. This is the only view found from a side of the building.

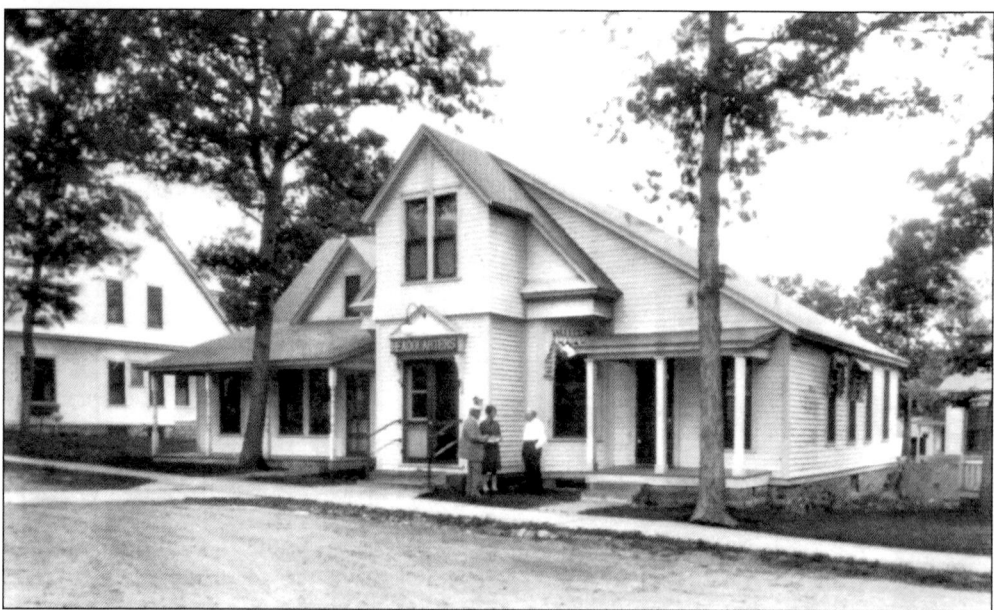

HEADQUARTERS. Referred to as the Office, this building was located on Lake Street, across the street from the commandant's residence. Inside were the offices of the commandant, adjutant, and bookkeeper. It also had a safe, in which the deeds for the properties were kept, as well as other important papers. Besides the Vault Room were the Consultation Room, a telephone booth, and several sleeping rooms on the second floor. It was built at a cost of $5,445.90 in 1889 or 1890. The members admitted to the Home stopped here first to fill out paperwork.

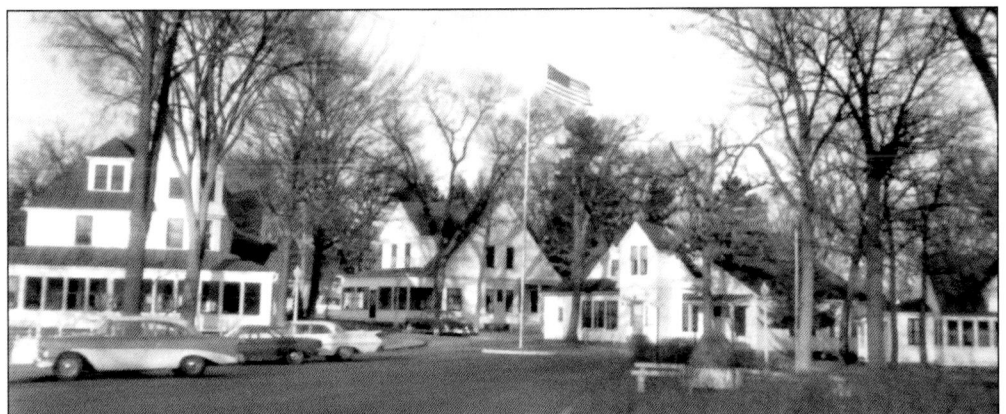

ADMINISTRATOR'S COURTYARD. This photo, looking north, was taken from the southwest side of the park. It shows, from left to right, the commandant's residence, adjutant's residence, Headquarters, and Cottage Number 125. In the foreground is the edge of the park. The buildings are on the corner of Marden Avenue and Lake Street.

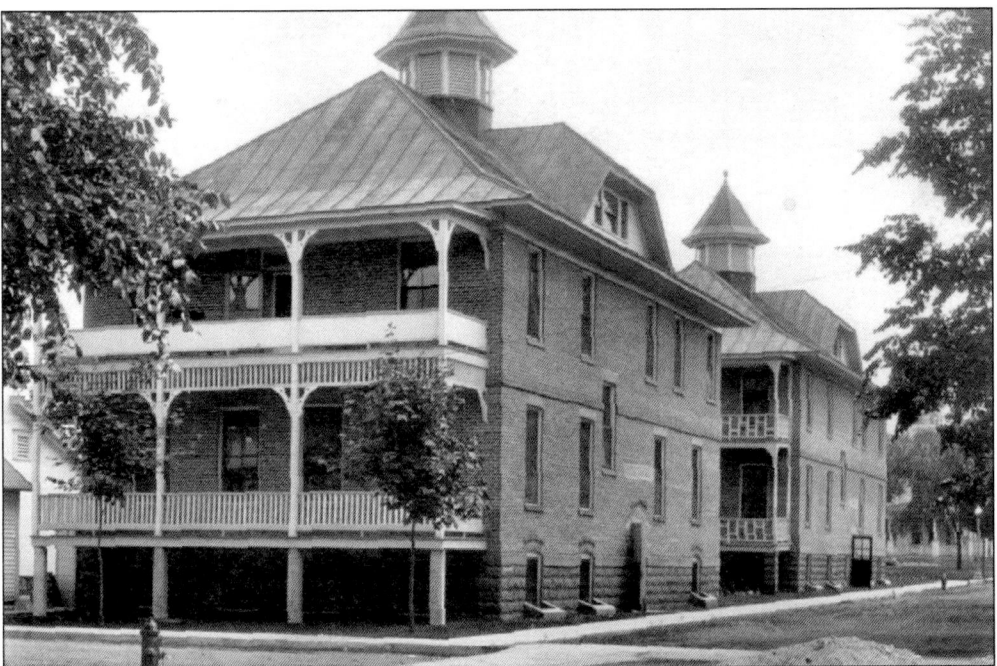

ROBERTS HALL. Roberts Hall was built north of where Griffin Hall stood on Manchester Avenue. Like Roberts Hall, Griffin Hall was also a brick building and they appear very much alike in this photo. Roberts Hall had laundry on the first floor and living quarters for 14 unmarried employees on the second floor. The building stood across from the park. This building also had a two-tiered porch on the north end.

The hall was named for Robert N. Roberts. Roberts was born in Newton, Ireland on Oct 3, 1842. His parents moved to Waupaca, Wisconsin in 1856. Having served in the Civil War in Company B of the 38th Wisconsin Infantry, he rose to the rank of major. He returned to Waupaca to work as a clerk in his father's store. After his father's death, he organized the City Bank of Waupaca, later known as the National Bank of Waupaca. He was president until his death on January 11, 1903.

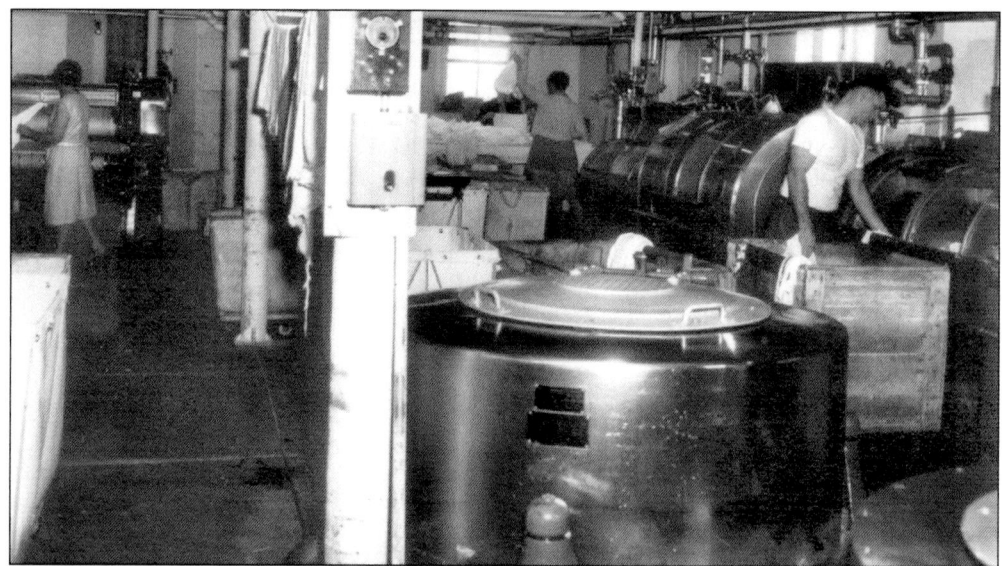

ROBERTS HALL INTERIOR. The laundry was done inside Roberts Hall, shown here is a 1966 view of the laundry room. In 1950, the laundry had 12 employees.

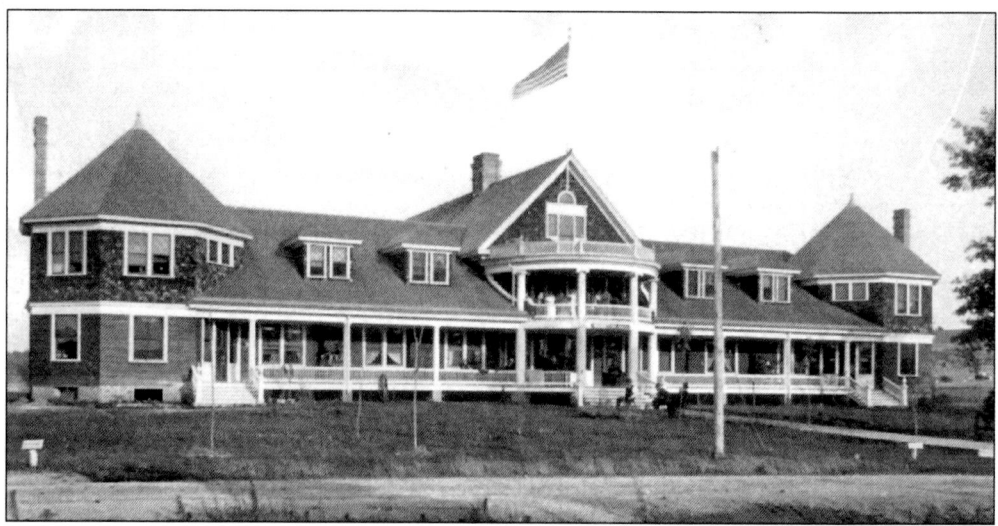

MARSTON HALL. Marston Hall, a wooden structure built in the 1880s, was located east of the electric car (trolley) tracks—present day Highway QQ. Located far away from the rest of the home, next to the Home's cemetery, the building was called "Canada" by the residents. It could hold 116, but meals were not served there. They were served at Bryant Hall, which meant that a resident had to walk quite a distance for meals. It was especially difficult to do this in the winter, considering the health of some of the members. Based upon an evaluation by the Women's Relief Corp. in 1887, Marston Hall was upgraded in 1888 with a kitchen, dining room, and 16 rooms overhead, allowing a total of 160 residents. Members did enjoy sitting on the long front porch as the trolley and traffic went past.

Marston Hall was named in honor of Joseph H. Marston, one of the original five incorporators. Marston was a long time member of the Board of Trustees, and for a time, president of the board.

Razed in mid-July 1985, Marston Hall lasted longer than any of the other wooden-framed structures from the late 1880s.

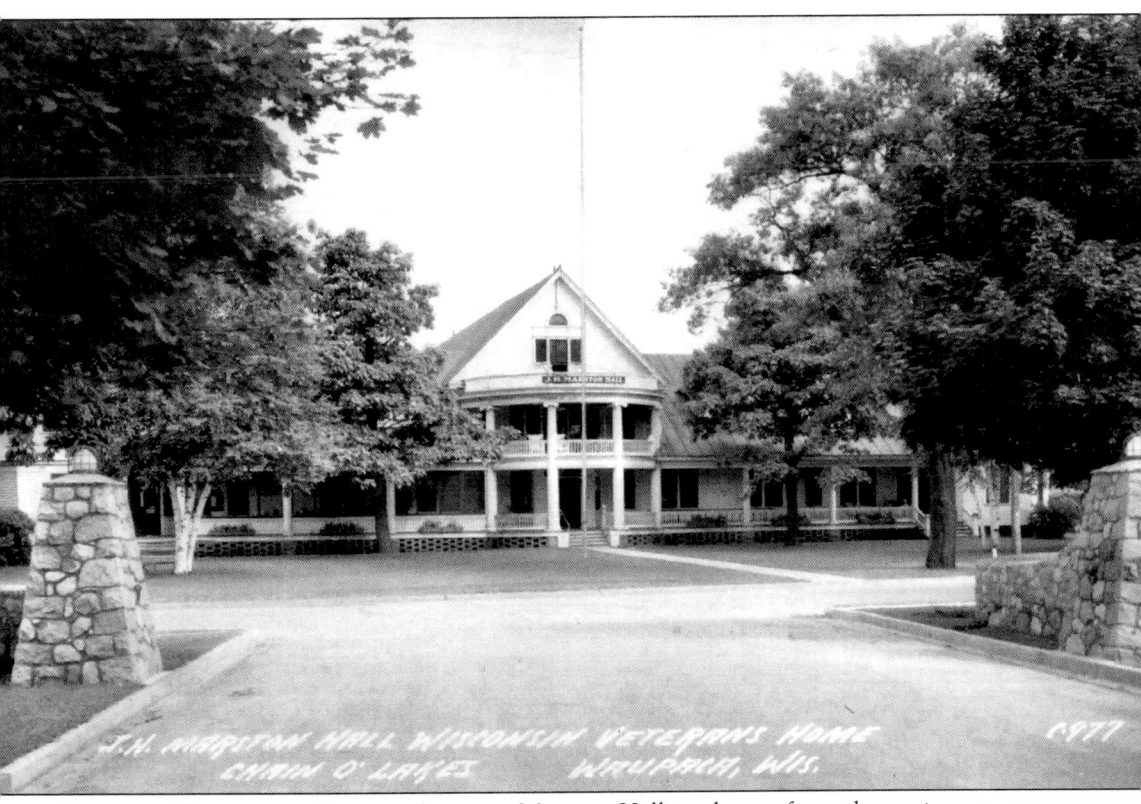

MARSTON HALL FROM MARDEN AVENUE. Marston Hall is shown from the main entrance looking east. Situated across the road from the main part of the Home, Marston Hall is in its prime condition—nicely painted, mature trees for shade, and a well-groomed lawn.

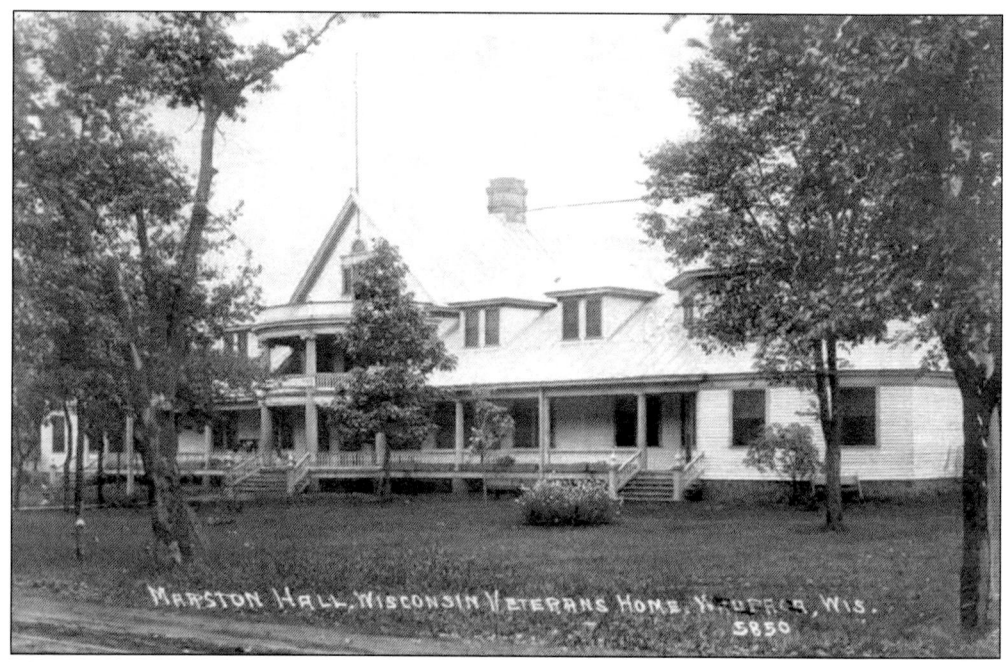

MARSTON HALL POST CARD. This is a 1926 post card view of Marston Hall. This view shows some of the south side of Marston Hall, as well as a better view of the porches on its west side.

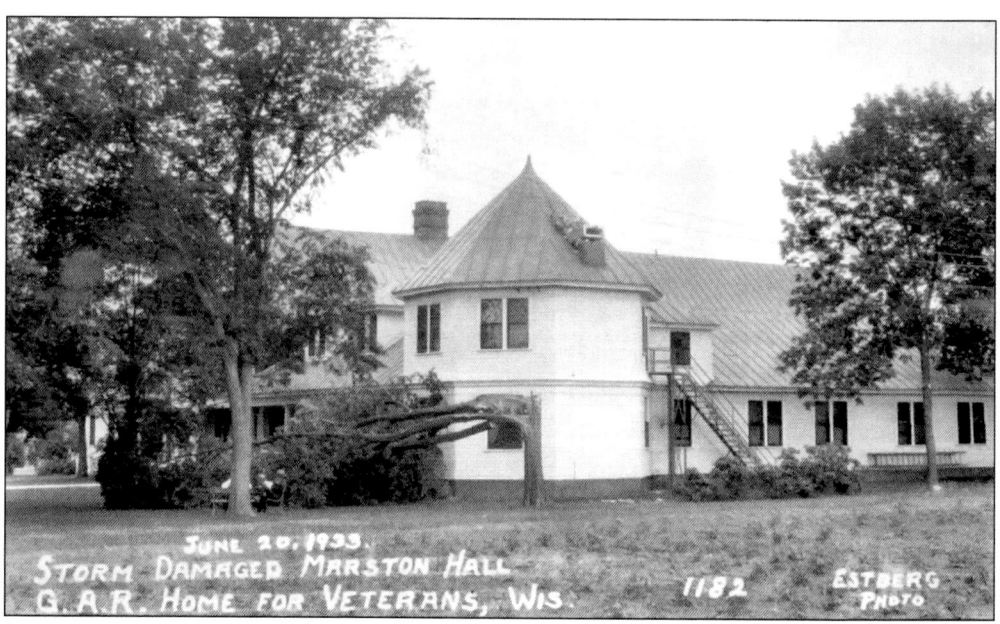

STORM AT MARSTON. There was a storm in 1933 that did damage to Marston Hall and the trees surrounding the hall. The Power House was also damaged.

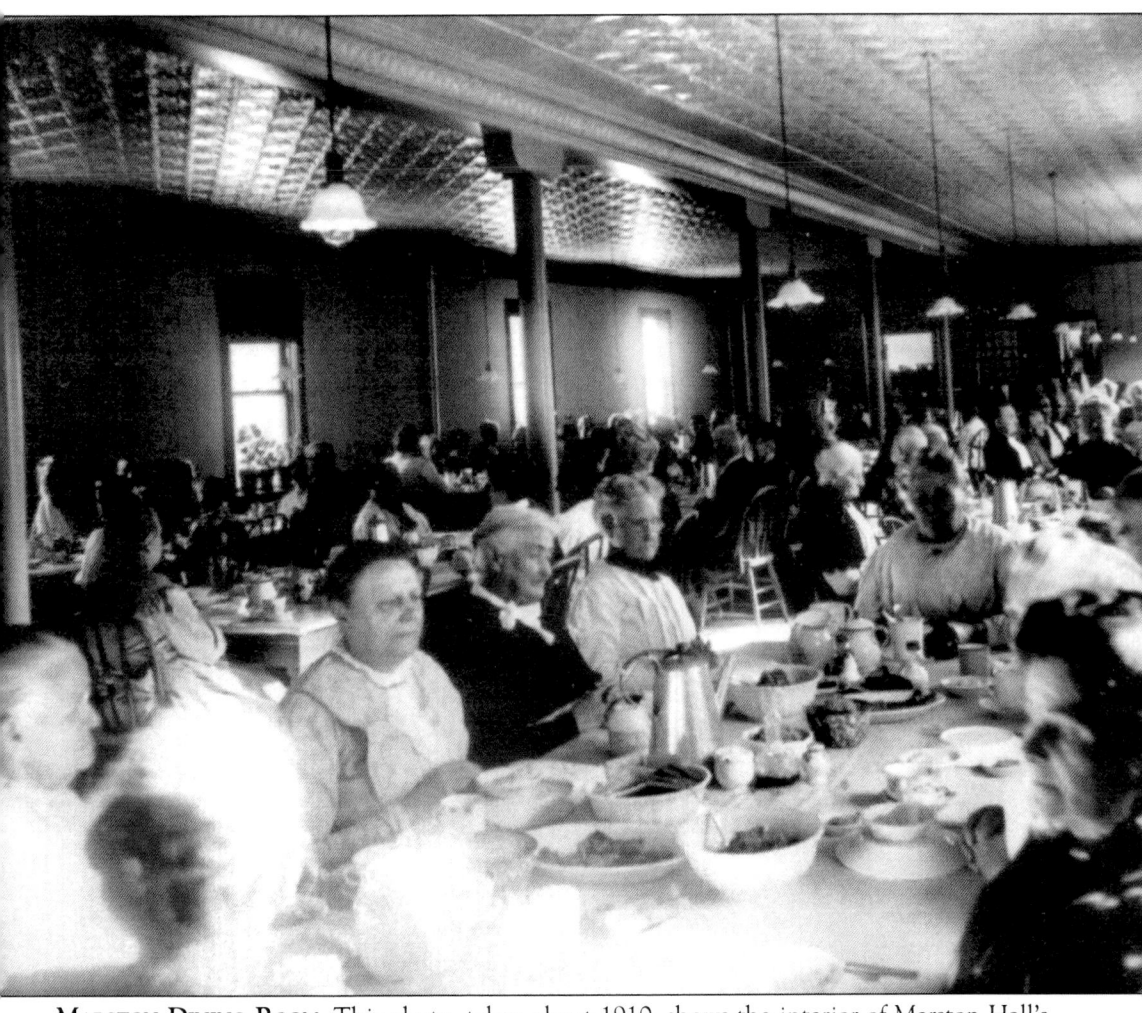

MARSTON DINING ROOM. This photo, taken about 1910, shows the interior of Marston Hall's Dining Room. This view is similar to photos of the other dining rooms on the grounds.

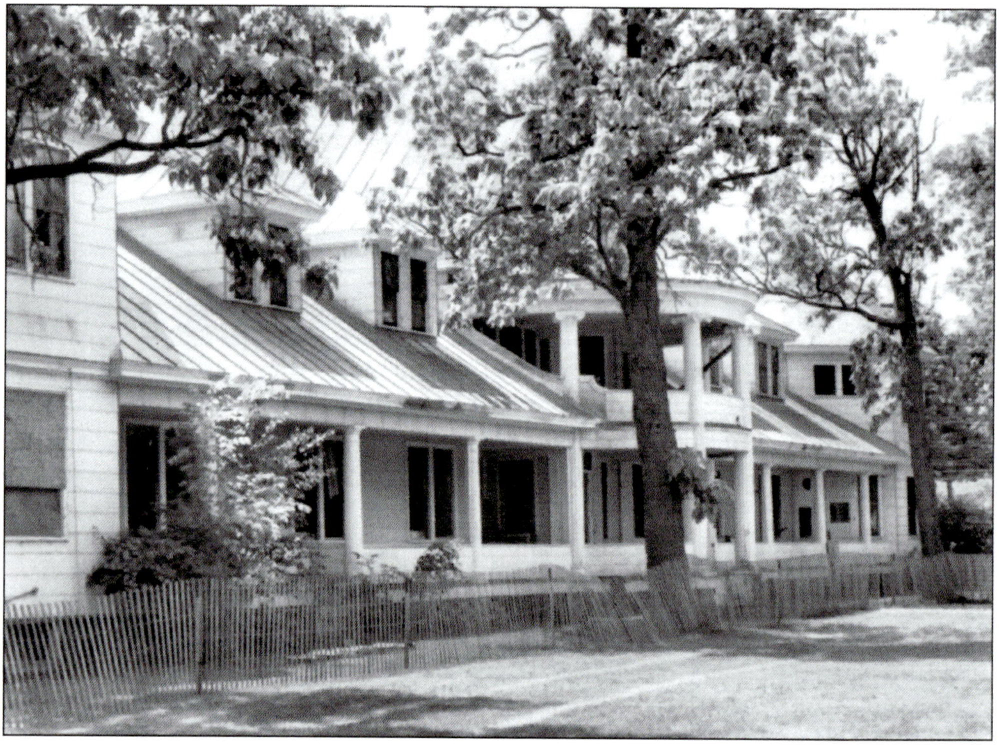

MARSTON BOARDED UP. Destined to be torn down in mid-July of 1985, after a fight for preservation, Marston Hall is pictured here in its final days. It was boarded up and used for storage before demolition.

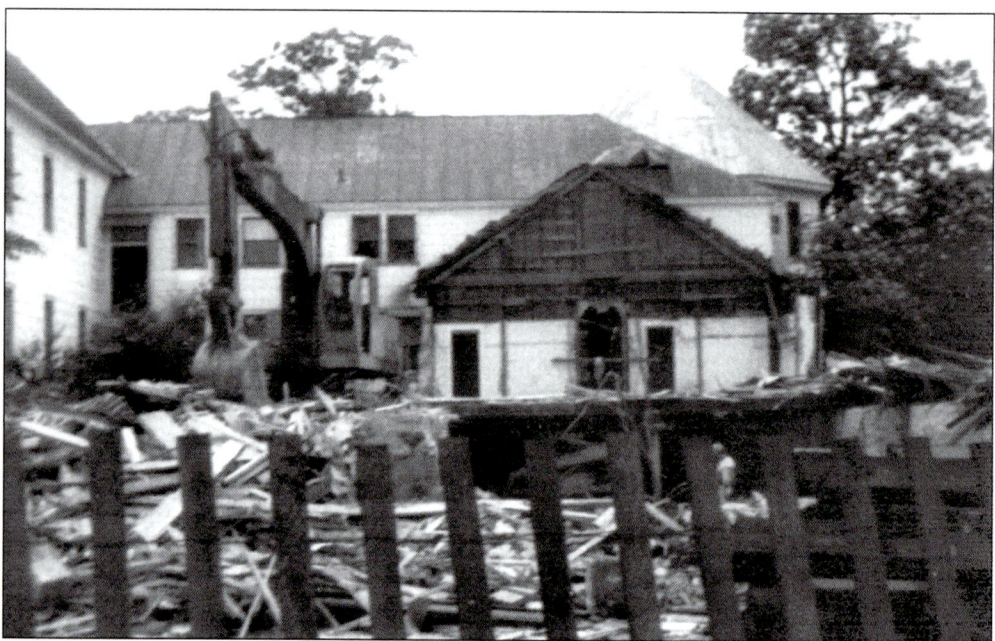

MARSTON TORN DOWN. After some controversy regarding tearing down a historical building, this image shows Marston Hall as it was razed.

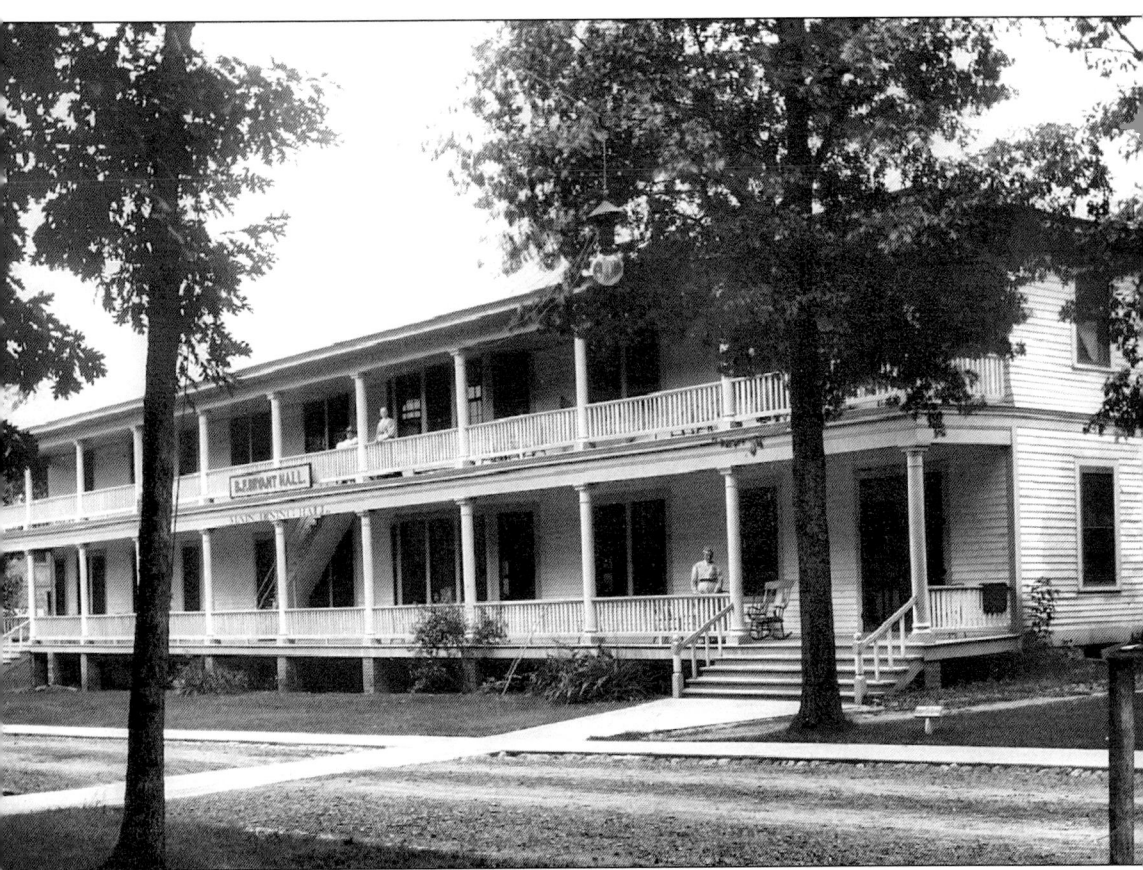

BRYANT HALL. Bryant Hall, along with 20 other cottages, was built in 1889. The hall was located behind Marden Hall on Bell Avenue. Originally the two-story wooden structure, called the Main Dining Hall, housed women on the second floor. Because of this, the hall was also known as the "Hen House." The large dining room was for members from the cottages, Marden Hall, Griffin Hall, and the Walsh Building. There was a smaller dining room attached to Bryant Hall, called the "Nickelplate," it served employees from the Power House, the laundry, and the farm. The basement held the more important bakery, where one-and-one-half barrels of flour were used daily.

Bryant Hall was named for Colonel Benjamin F. Bryant. Bryant, one of the five incorporators and later commandant of the Home from 1910 to 1914, was the treasurer of the board in the early years of the Home. Ill health forced his retirement from the board in 1914. Taking up residence in one of the small cottages, he still acted as a legal counsel. His ailments finally took his life on April 9, 1919, at the age of 81.

The photo shows a sign, "Bryant Hall," from the top walk rail. Notice that beneath this sign it says "Men's Dining Hall."

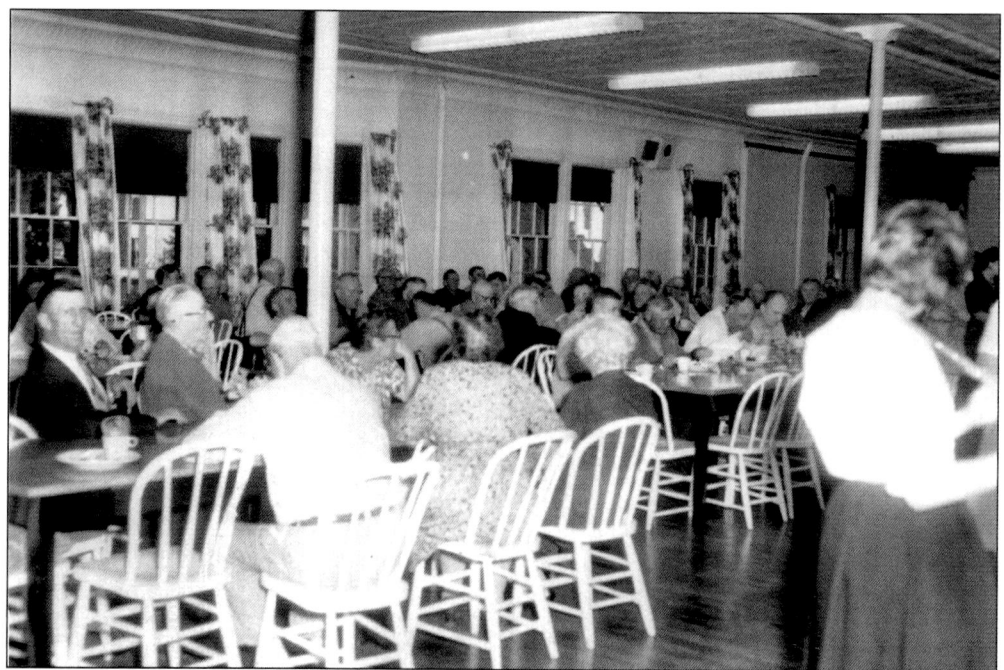

BRYANT HALL DINING ROOM. This is the inside view of the Bryant dining room from the mid-1960s.

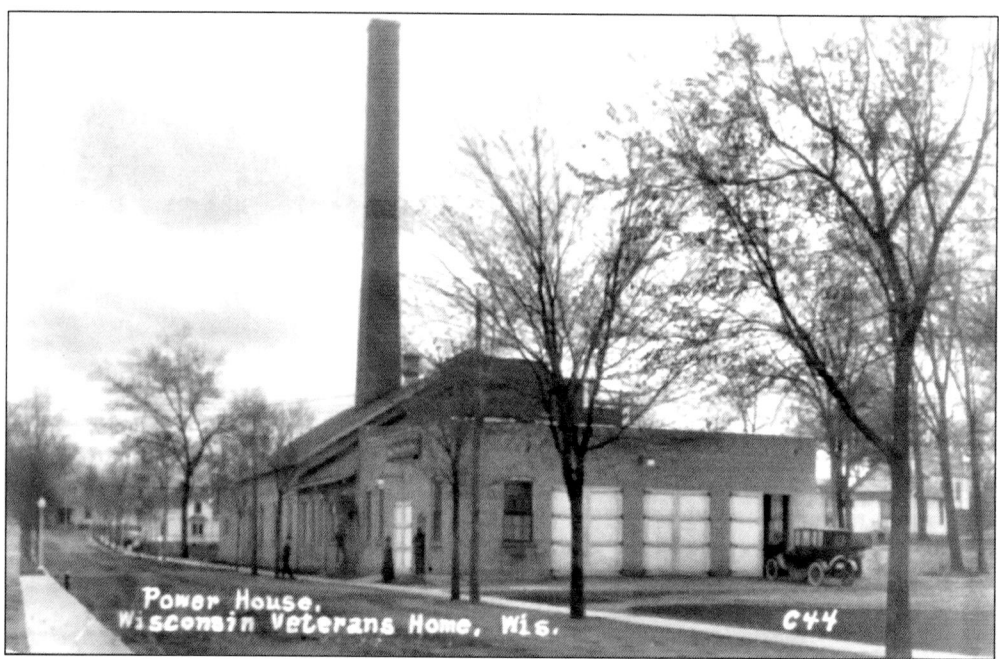

POWER HOUSE. The original Power House was a coal-burning, steam-generating facility. The north end, seen in the photograph, had garage doors. The engine room was in the center of the building. The fire engine and fire department were located there. The boiler room was under the smokestack area. Coal was stored on the south end. The Power House was located on Manchester Avenue, it was replaced in 1951.

POWER HOUSE ROOF. This photograph shows some of the roof damage from a storm in 1933. The smokestack tumbled into the mid-section of the building.

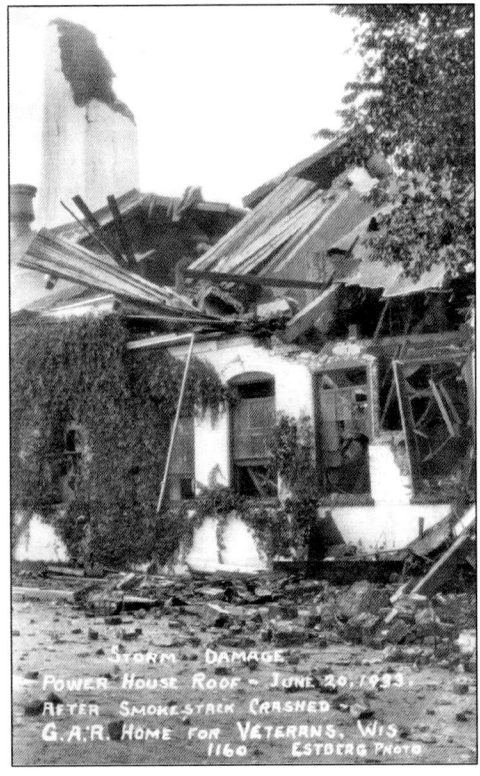

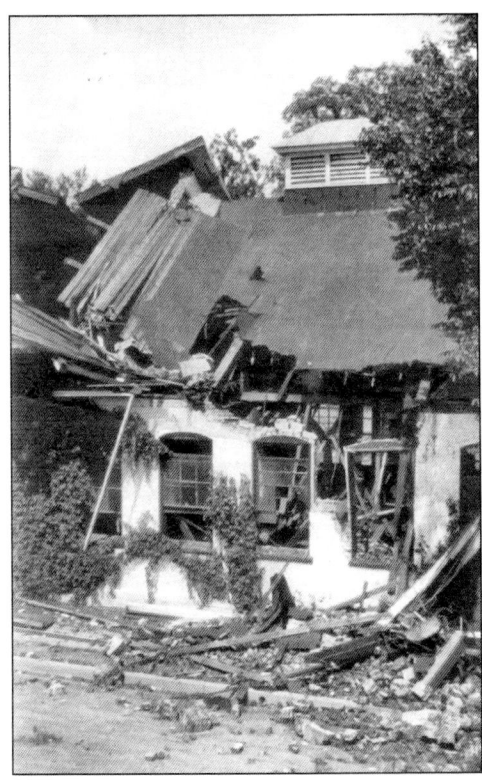

POWER HOUSE ROOF. There were several photographs taken of the storm damage to the Power House.

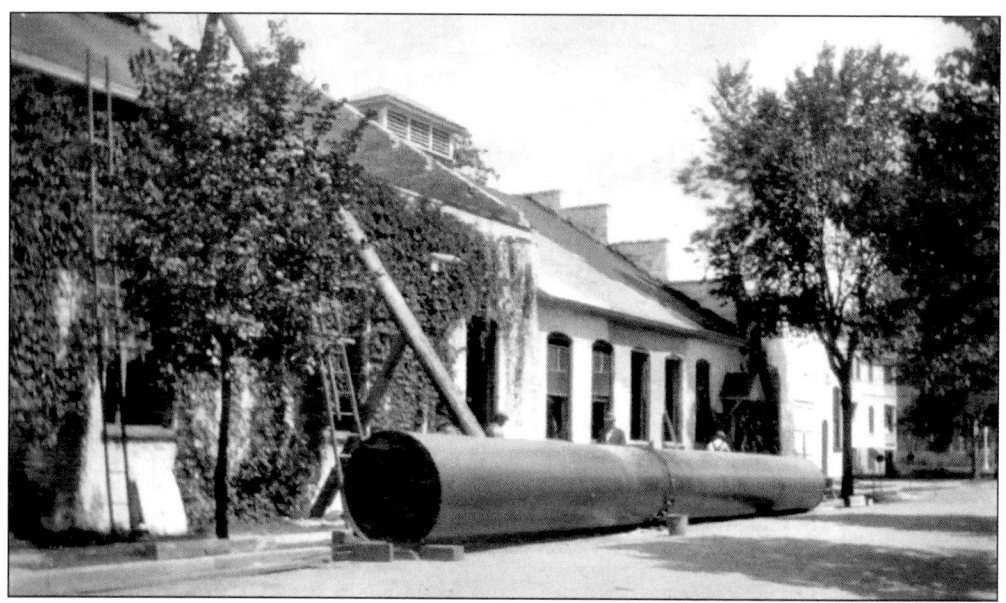

A NEW POWER HOUSE STACK. A new smokestack was erected to replace the damaged stack from the June 1933 storm.

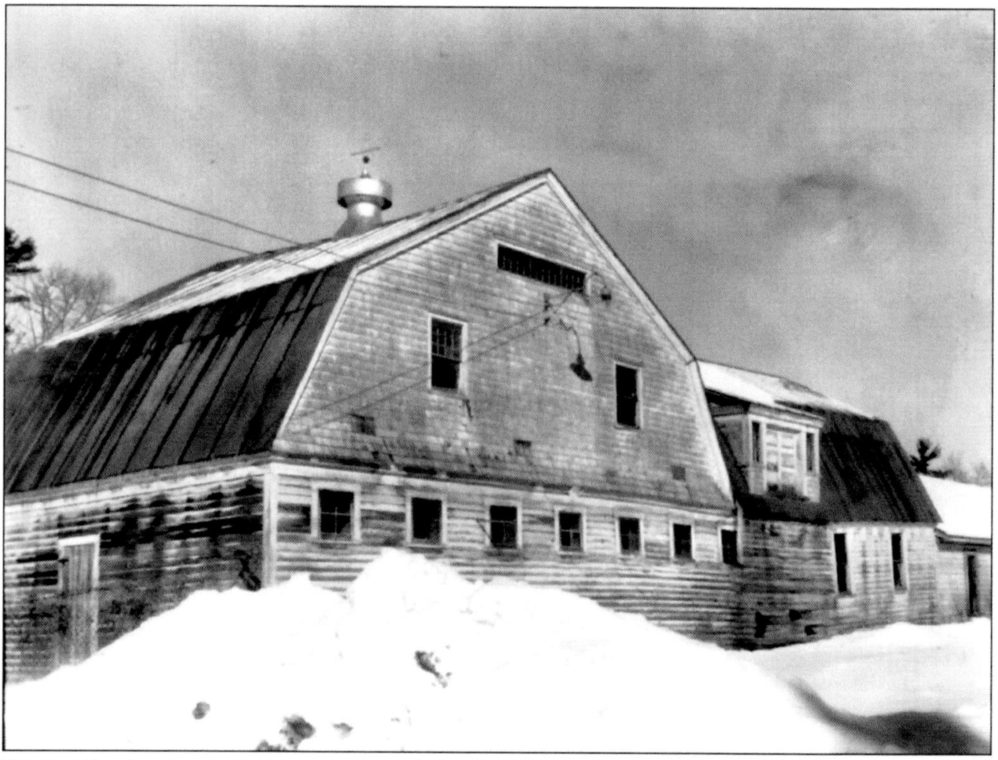

BARN. The barn was on the property when the 78 acres were purchased. It was located north of the shops on Mitchell Avenue. Used as a barn and storage until the end, the barn was torn down to make way for Ainsworth Hall. This is the only known photo of the barn, it shows the most ragged condition of any of the buildings on the grounds.

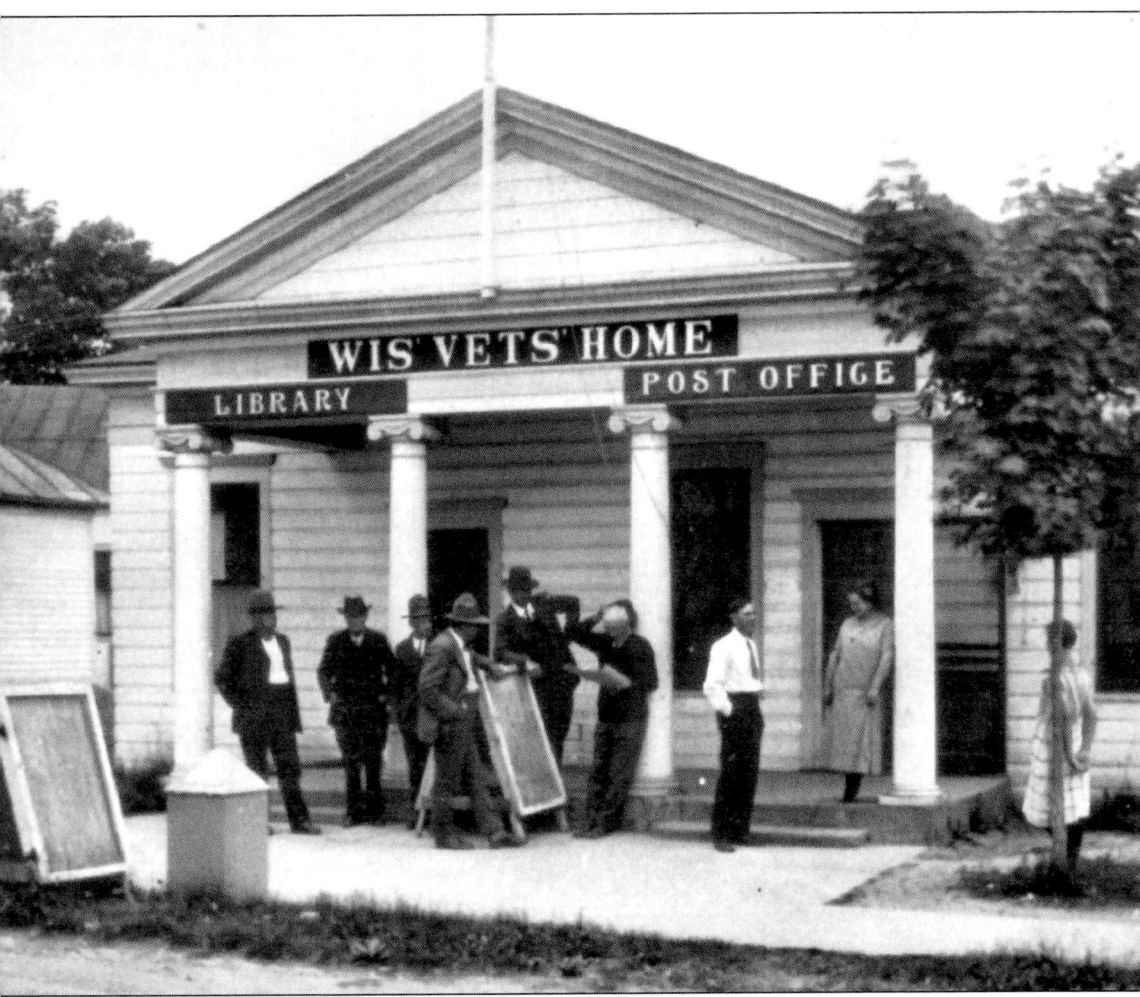

Post Office and Library. Before 1921, the library was in the 21st Regimental Building (Woodnorth Building). It was probably moved to the post office building in 1921. In 1923, it had about a thousand books. Some of the books were donations from the Women's Relief Corp. They supplied the Home's library with magazines, books, and papers.

The records of the Home state that the postmaster first began work at the Home in 1896. The first post office was in one of the small cottages across from Houston Hall on Cumberledge Avenue. That location was probably Building Number 414 or one of the adjoining buildings. Later, it was moved to the location pictured. This building was located on the corner of Marden Avenue and Mitchell Avenue. It was the first building on the right as a person traveled onto the grounds from the Marden entrance. The first year the post office handled $2,000 in money orders and in 1923 they handled almost $40,000 in money orders.

This building was removed to make room for the present day Stordock Hall.

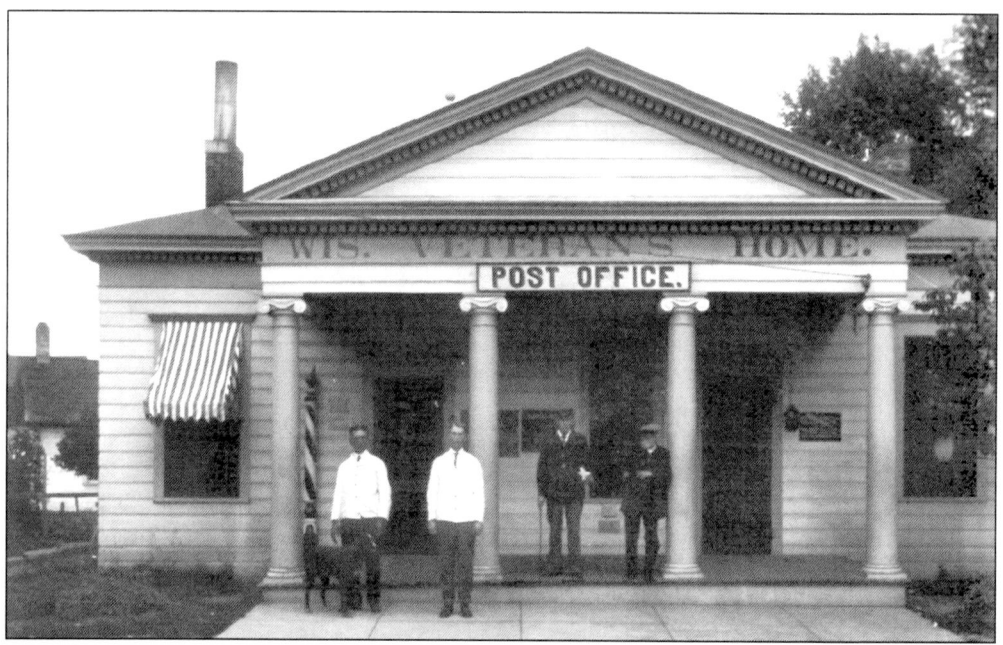

POST OFFICE AND BARBERSHOP. The barbershop was located next to the post office in this view. Later, in 1921, the library was located on the side of the post office, replacing the barbershop. The barbershop was, at one time, located just east of Roberts Hall on Bell Avenue. This view is at the corner of Marden Avenue and Mitchell Avenue.

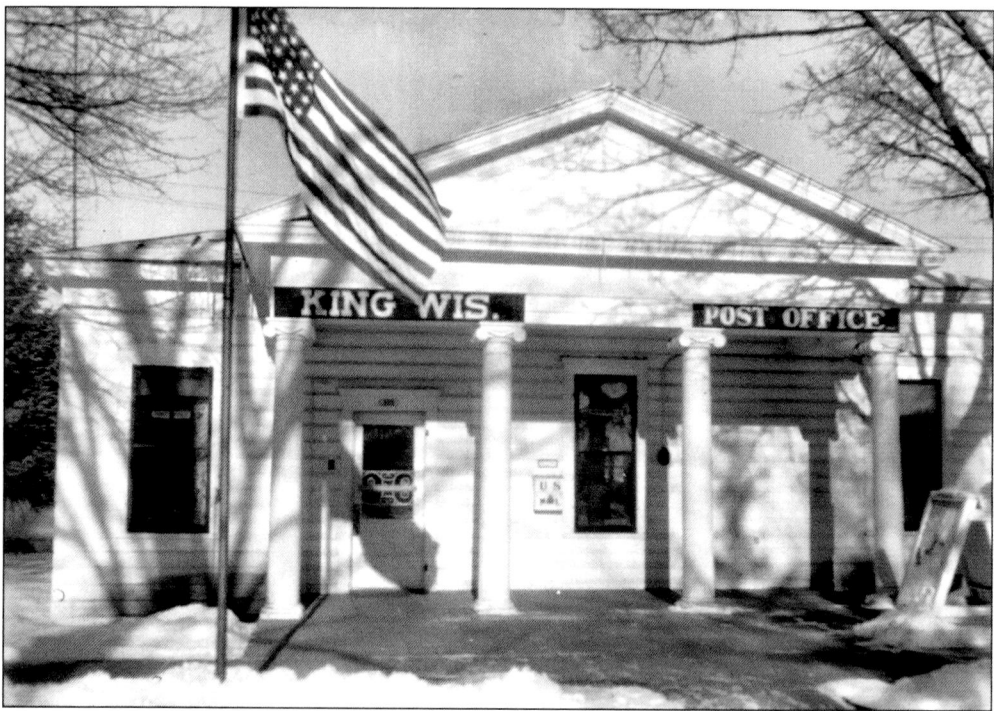

POST OFFICE 1966. By 1966, the volume of mail from the post office warranted the use of the whole building. The building was no longer split for dual usage.

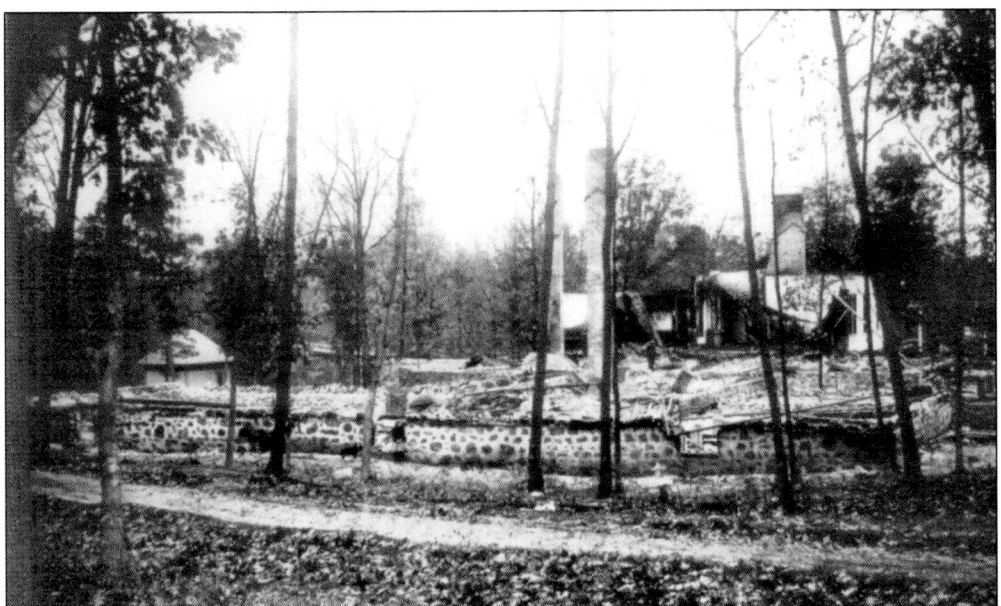

REMAINS OF FIRST HOSPITAL. On November 9, 1889, fire swept the hospital building, burning it to the ground. Patients were temporarily moved to the Amusement Hall. Cots were set up as beds. Without a way to treat patients, the Home denied incoming applicants. A photograph of the first hospital could not be found.

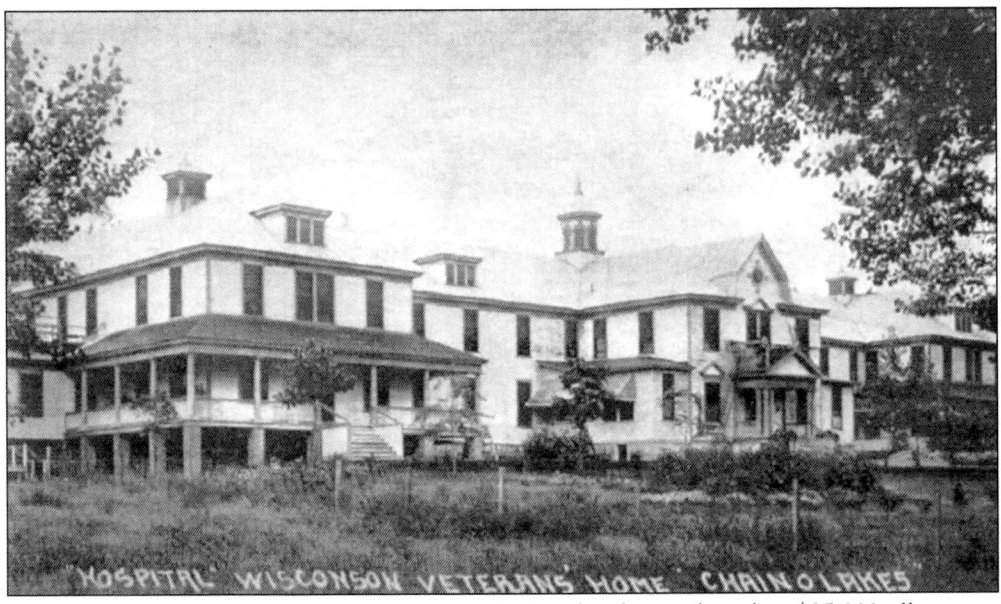

THE NEW HOSPITAL. A new hospital was built shortly afterward, with a $35,000 allowance. The new building, built with an "E" shape, was a two-story, wooden structure. A dining room, kitchen, pantry, and storeroom occupied the center of the first floor. The head surgeon had his office in this middle section. There were no patient rooms above the dining room. The outer wings had room for 150 in 120 rooms that were each 12 ft. x 14 ft.

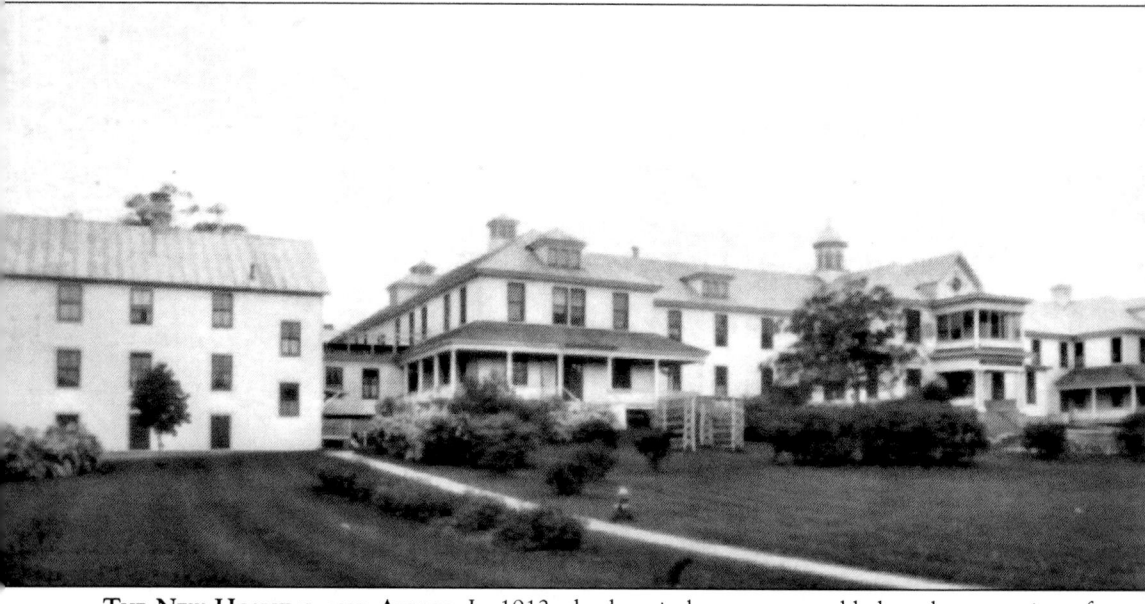

THE NEW HOSPITAL AND ANNEX. In 1912, the hospital annex was added to the east wing of the hospital, connected by a 20 foot corridor. Later, the morgue was located below the corridor. The annex could handle 30 more patients. The cost of the annex was $6,500, of which the Women's Relief Corp. donated $528 and Comrade Frank A. Walsh of Milwaukee gave $500.

The hospital also had a central air transfer system for fresh air and a central heating system from concrete ducts that ran from building to building.

The building was used until 1929, when the Ove Medical Center was built. Since then, the old hospital was named the Hospital Annex. The old hospital was razed in 1965.

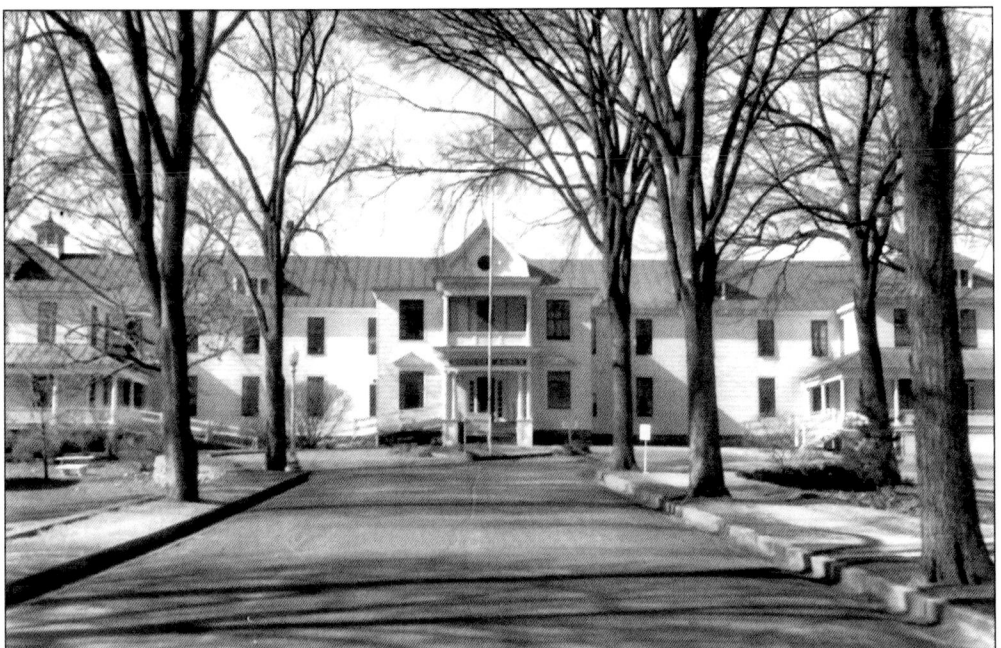

CENTER VIEW OF HOSPITAL. This view shows the front of the center section of the hospital. Located at the end of Manchester Avenue, the hospital had a flagpole in the center of a circle drive in front of its main doors.

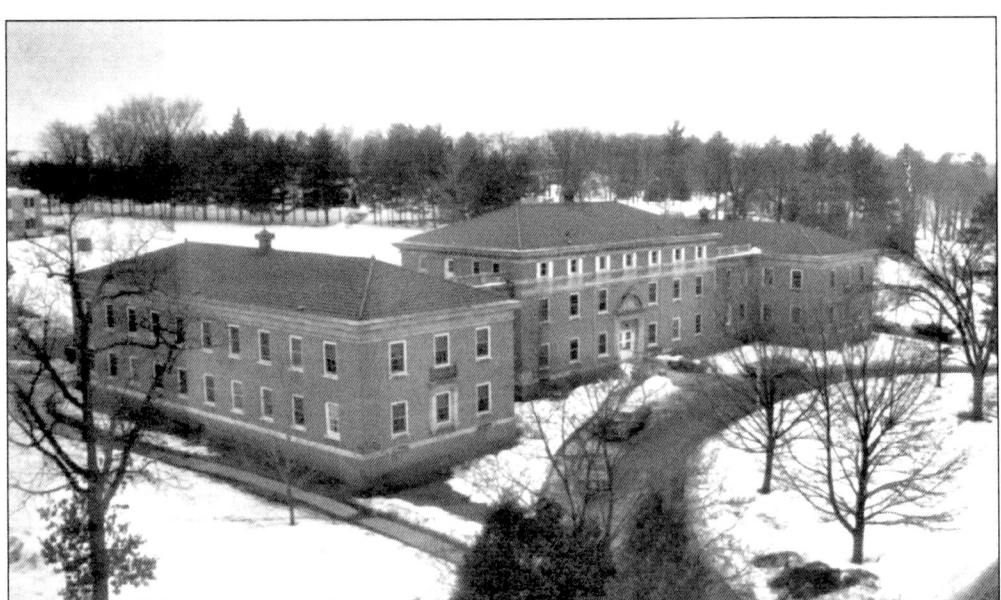

OVE MEDICAL CENTER. The Ove Medical Center was built in 1929. This building is significant in that it started the modernization of brick structures to be built in the future. No longer were the wooden firetraps to be built. Brick and concrete were safer and lasted longer. The Ove had inpatient and outpatient services, as well as routine surgery capacities. The Ove still stands today and is used for the Veterans Assistance Program. This building is in the National Historic Registry.

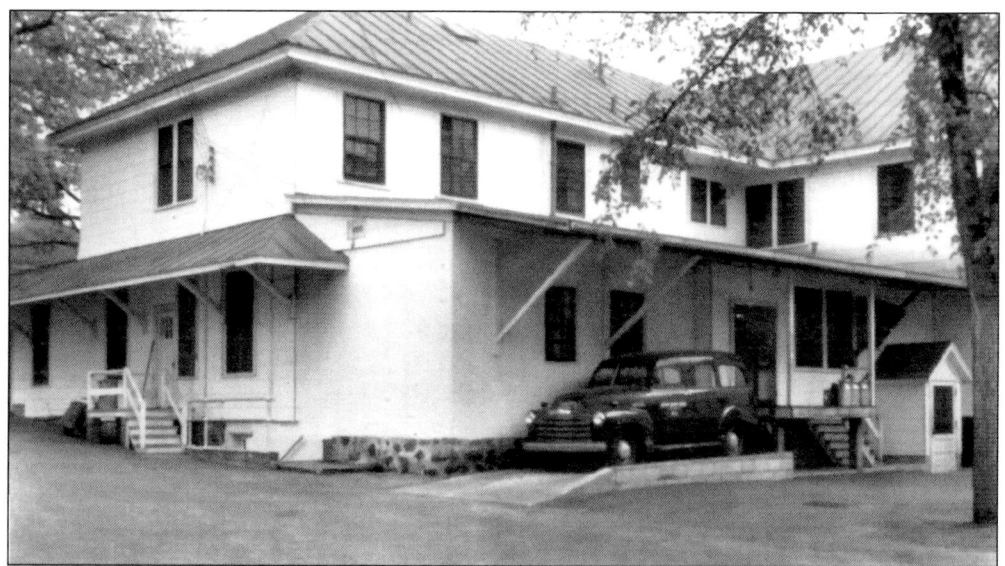

SERVICE AREA. In an unknown photo with a service vehicle, this is probably a view of the back of one of the dining areas at the Home—note the milk cans on the back porch.

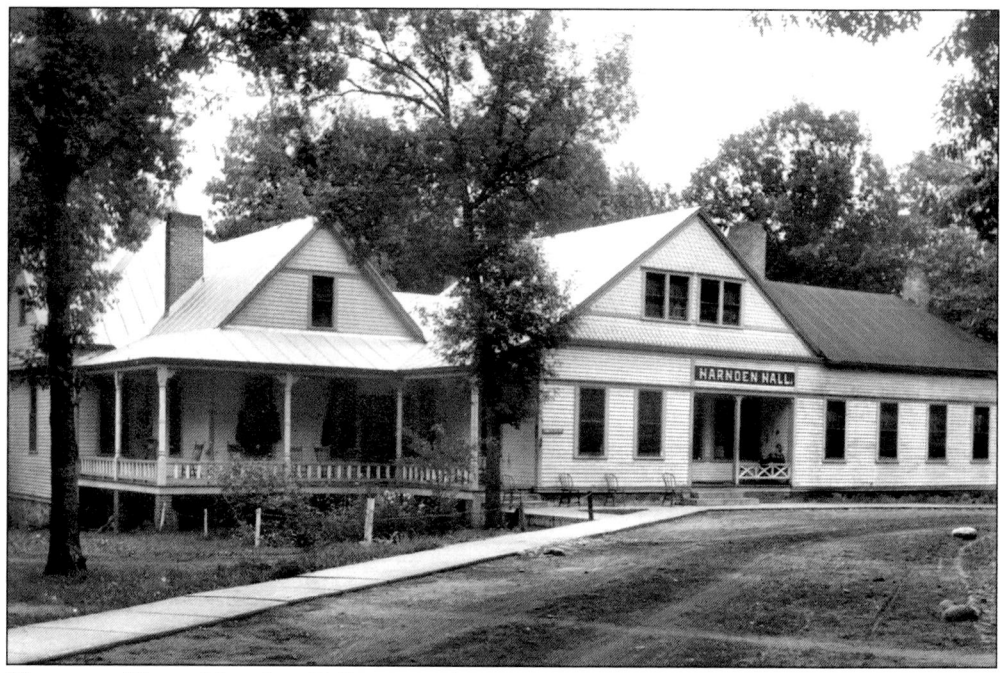

HARDNEN HALL. Harnden Hall, a wooden structure with a metal roof, was located on Cumberledge Avenue, about 400 feet south of Marden Hall. Known as "Ram Pasture," Harnden Hall housed men.

Harnden Hall was named in honor of Lt. Col. Henry Harnden of the First Wisconsin Cavalry. Harnden was most noted as commander of the forces that chased and captured Confederate President Jefferson Davis in Georgia. Harnden was the Wisconsin department commander of the Grand Army of the Republic in 1889. Harnden died on March 17, 1899. His grave marker is in Forest Hill Cemetery in Madison, Wisconsin.

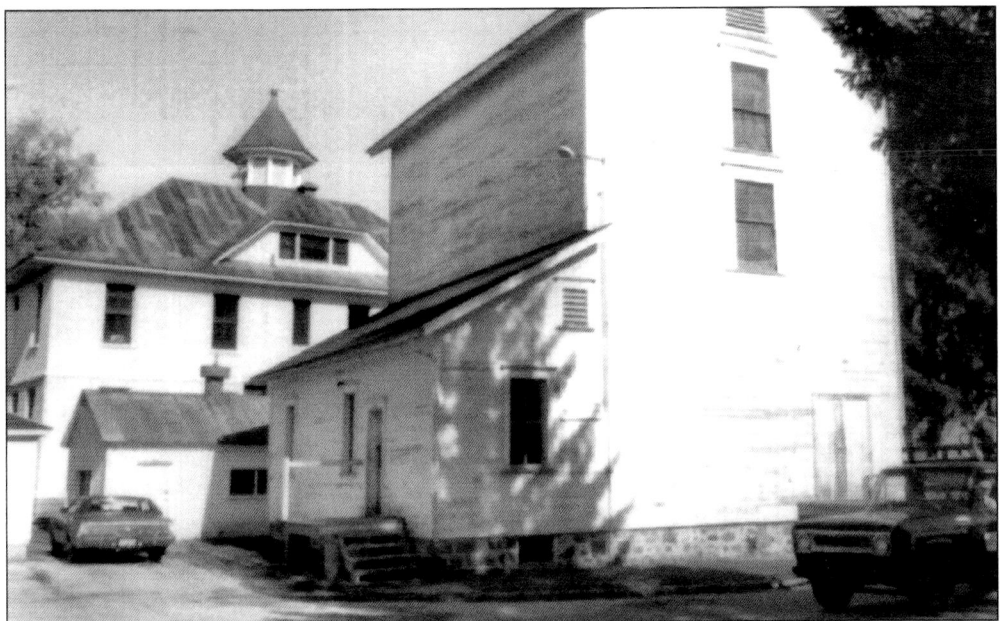

COLD STORAGE. The cold storage building was located east of Roberts Hall and Griffin Hall. Needed to help store food, this building was put up for sale at a cost of $2520.30 in 1887 or 1889. According to Quartermaster M.C. Russell in an 1889 report, "the new cold storage building will prove to be an excellent investment for the Home."

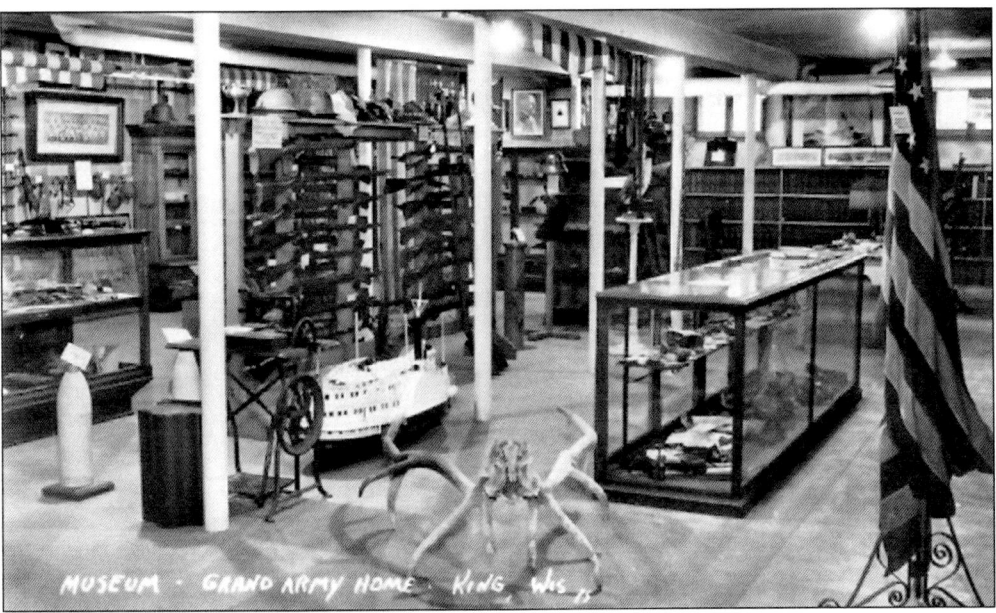

MUSEUM. At the urging of Col. C.L. Brosius, the museum was assembled in the basement of Fairchild Hall. Brosius was the commandant of the Home for six-and-one-half years. He took time off from his duties at the Home to serve in World War II. The museum had Civil War, Spanish-American War, World War I, and World War II items. There were also many Wisconsin Civil War battle flags in the museum at one time. Some of these items are now stored in the Wisconsin Veterans Museum in Madison, Wisconsin.

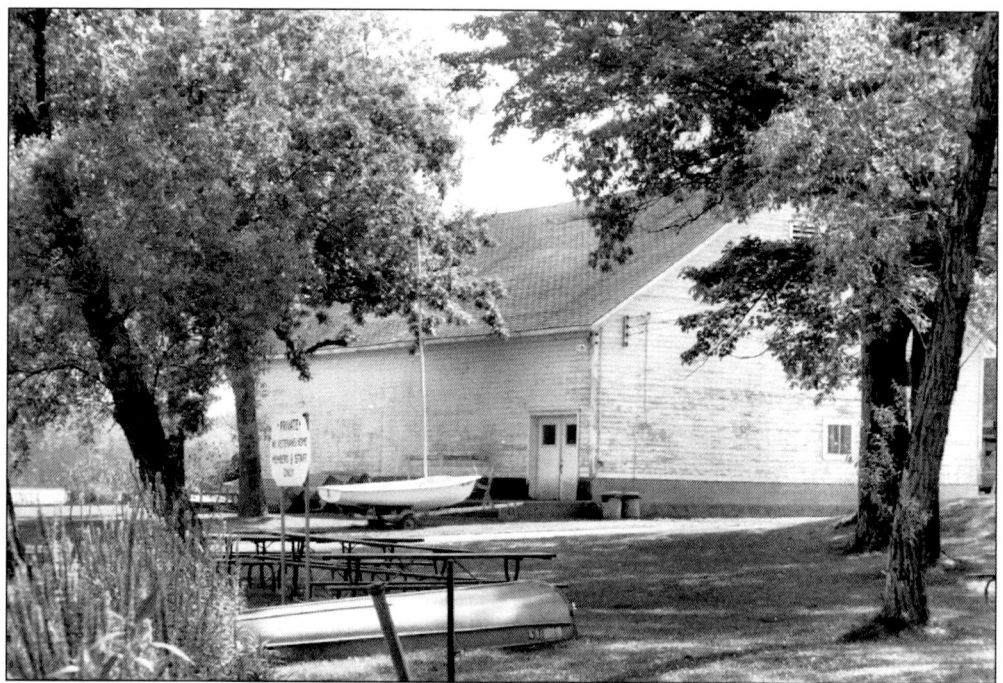

ICE HOUSE. The Ice House, which is still standing, is located on the far north edge of the Home property, on the shoreline of Lake George. With a ramp down to the lake, ice was cut and moved up this ramp to awaiting tongs. Hoisted up to the top opening, the ice block was then released down a roller track and placed in sawdust inside the building.

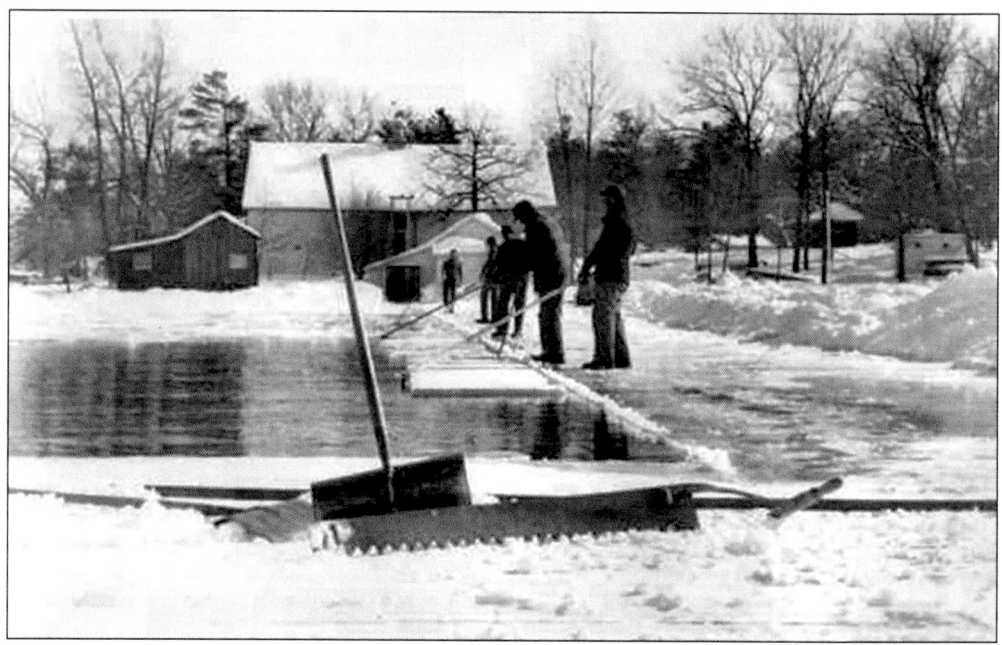

MAKING ICE. Two weeks of the year were set aside to cut and store ice. Home workers are shown moving blocks of ice toward the Ice House. The blocks were lifted to the second floor opening, stacked, and covered with straw.

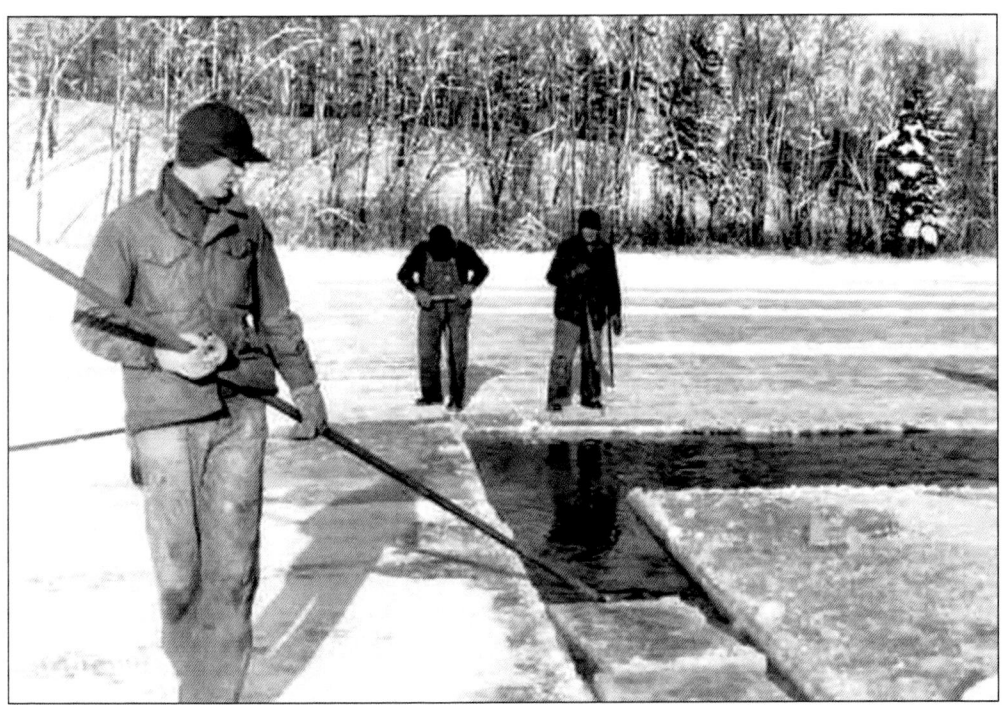

MORE ICE. This is another view of the ice making process.

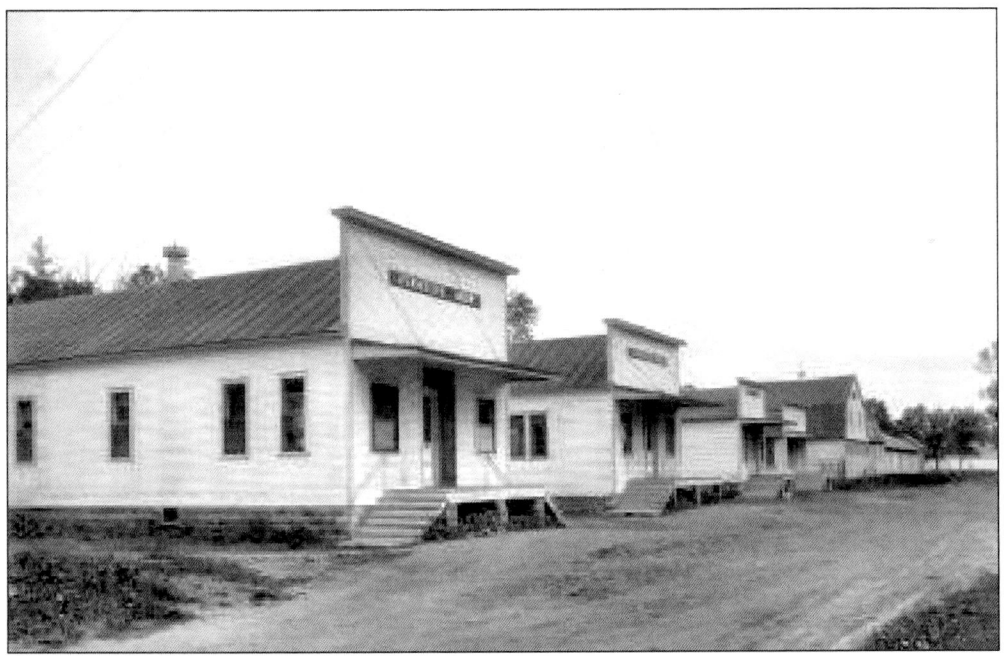

SHOPS. The shop buildings consisted of four buildings that were once the Commissary and Quartermaster Buildings. Moved to Mitchell Avenue just south of the barn, they served as shops for furniture, carpentry, upholstery, and paint. They were located on the site where Ainsworth Hall stands today. Employees worked there, but Home members helped out to stay busy. The Home, if in need of fixing, was repaired in this area when possible.

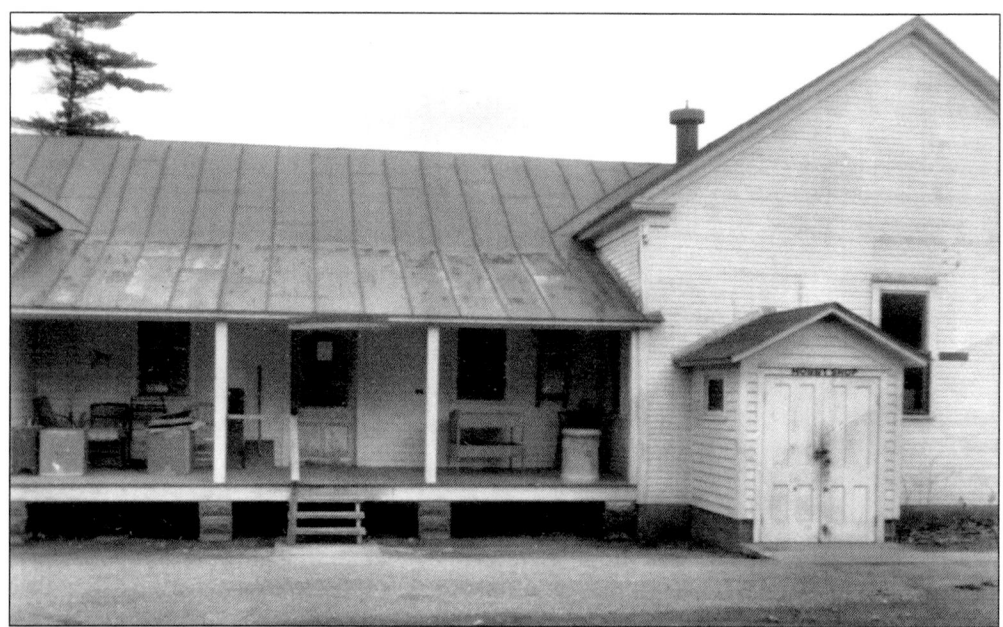

HOBBY SHOP. The hobby shop location might have been Building Number 210, the lumber shed on one of the ground's blueprints. If so, it was used as the furniture shop according to another blueprint. This building would have been located by the other shop buildings along Mitchell Avenue.

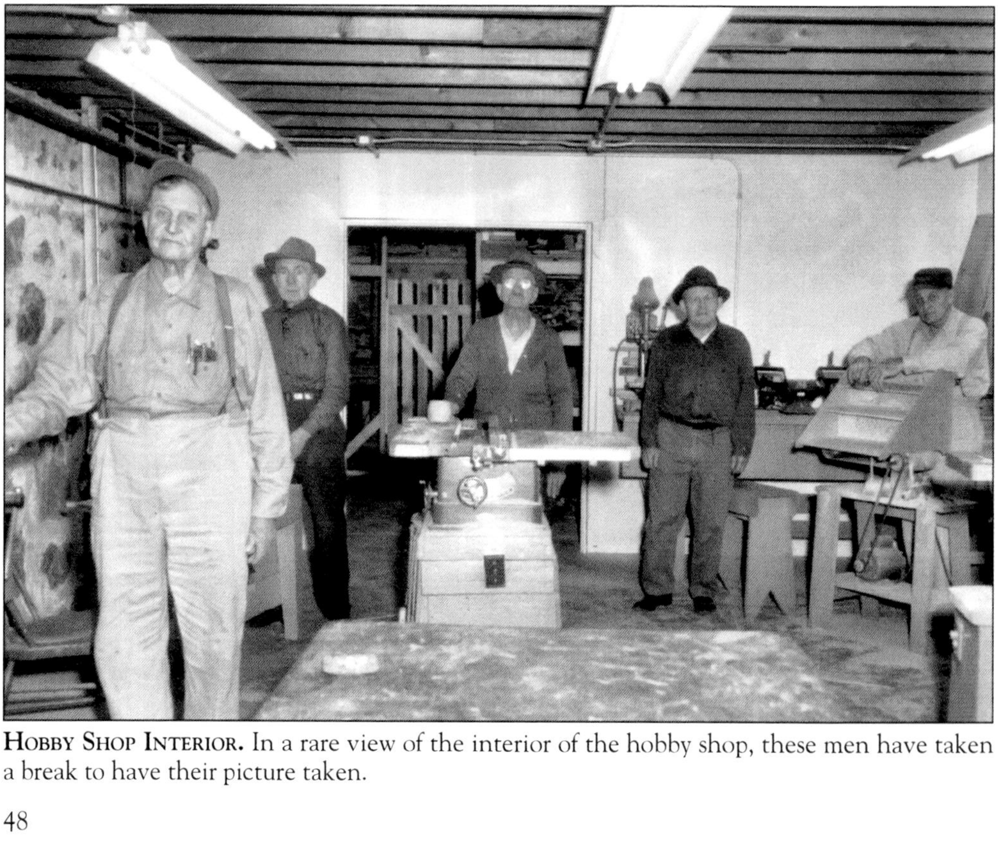

HOBBY SHOP INTERIOR. In a rare view of the interior of the hobby shop, these men have taken a break to have their picture taken.

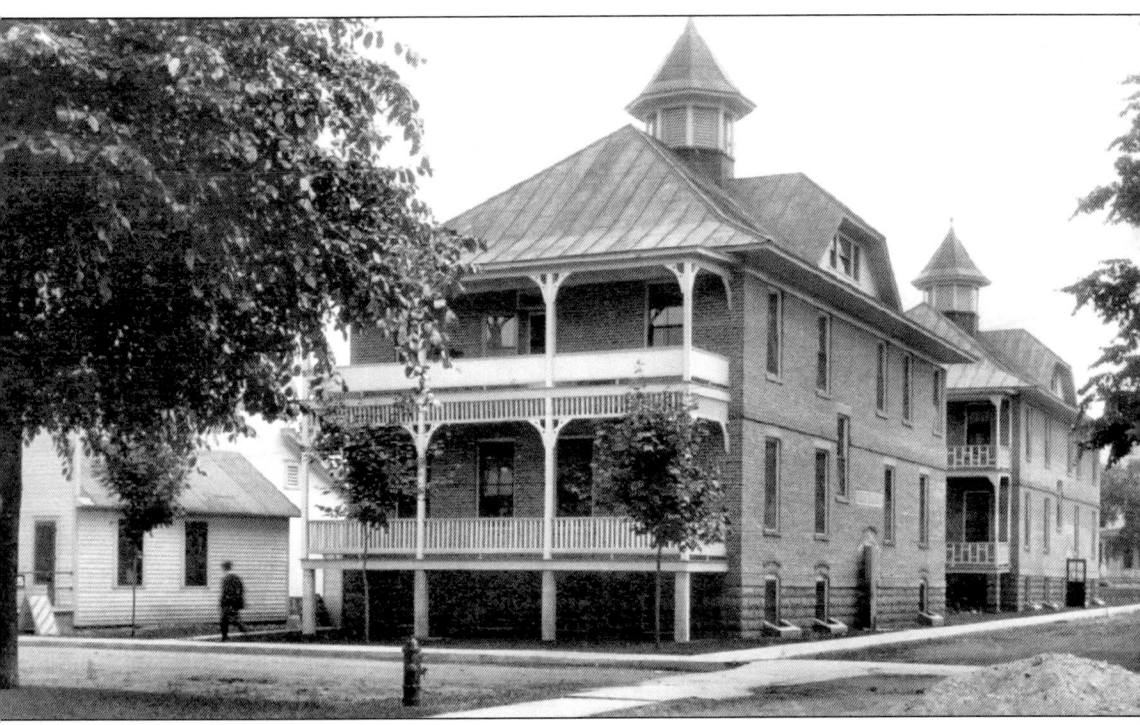

BARBERSHOP ON THE LEFT. This nice view of Roberts Hall and Griffin Hall on Bell Avenue shows the barbershop on the far left. Notice the striped barber sign on the sidewalk. This was Building Number 324.

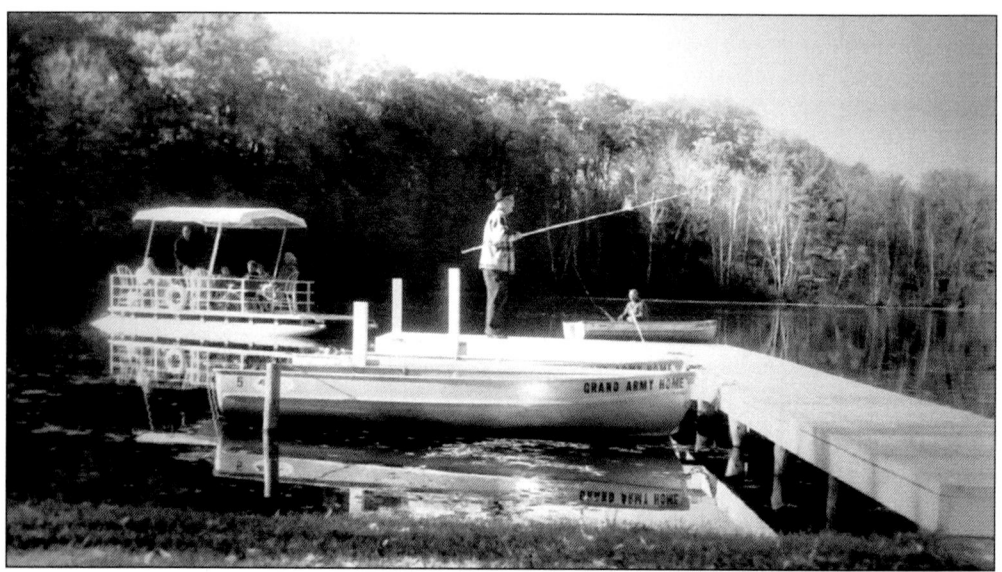

DOCK ON LAKE GEORGE. Members had a dock on Lake George for fishing and to tie up the Grand Army Home boats. Home Island (now Government Island) is seen in the background. This is a peaceful lake and a quiet place for members to relax.

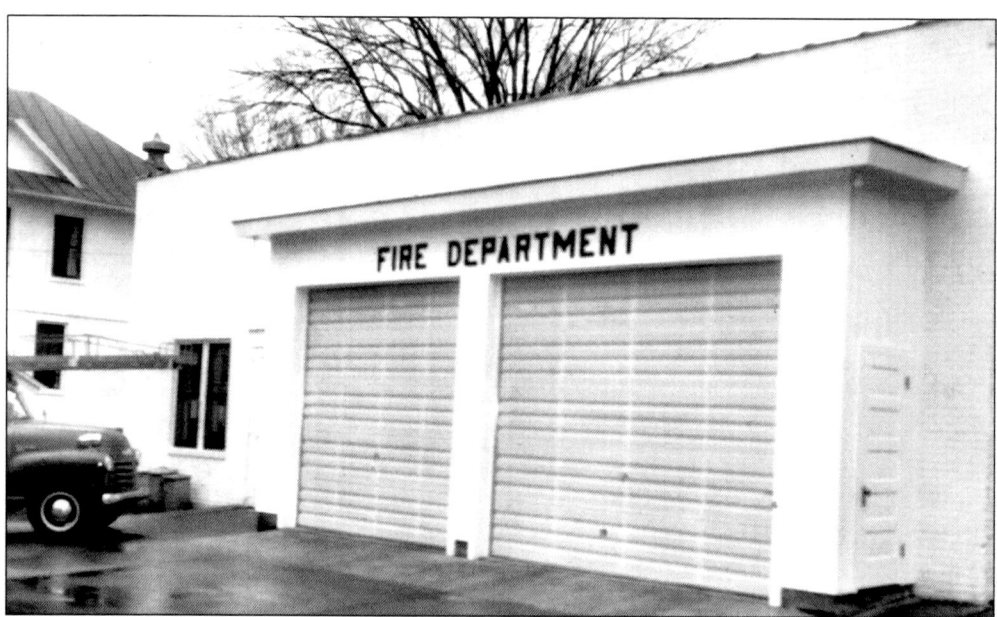

KING FIRE DEPARTMENT. A person could write a book just on the history of the fire department. Early ground blueprints show the Engine House as a separate building just west of Griffin Hall. An arrow on the blueprint indicated a move of the fire department to the Power House at a time unknown. Since the Power House engineers were the ones that had knowledge of pumps, they also had the duties of the fire department. At some point, the fire department became separate from the Power House.

This view of the block building with a 1950s ladder fire truck is the third known location for the fire department on the grounds. Since this photo was taken, the fire department has been moved into another building.

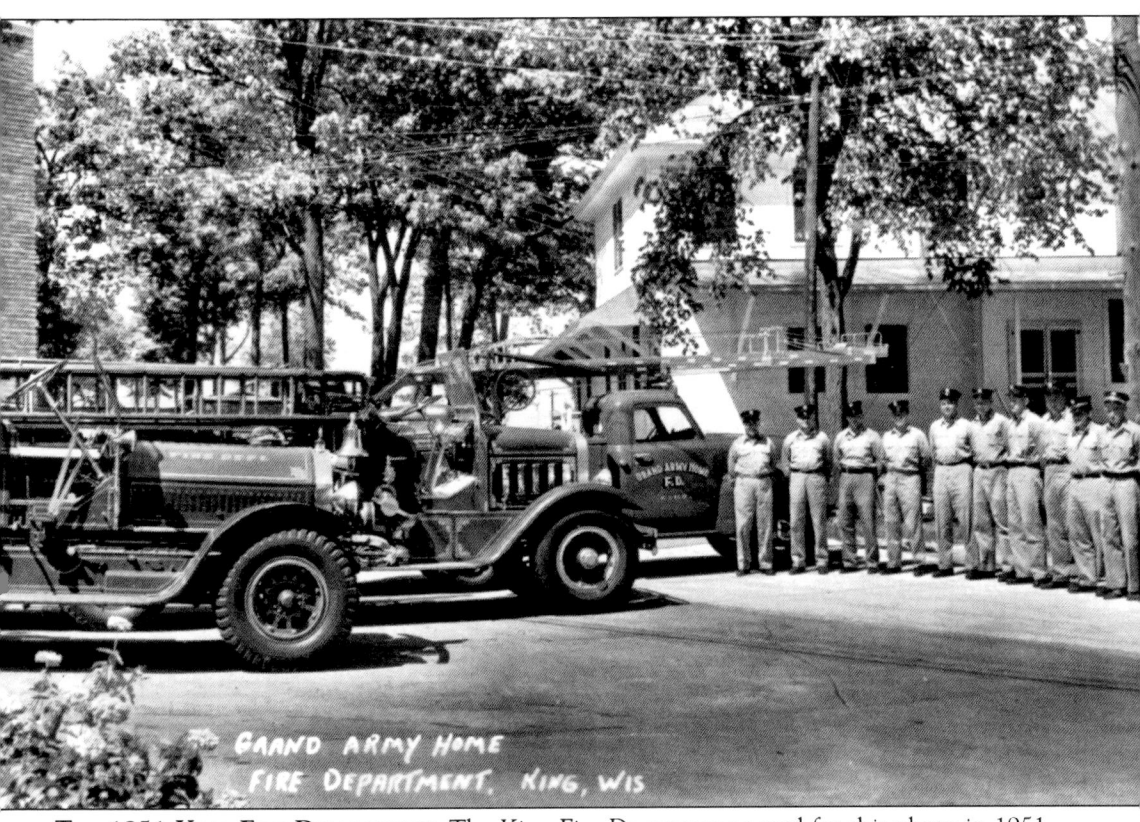

THE 1951 KING FIRE DEPARTMENT. The King Fire Department posed for this photo in 1951 with the ladder trucks and fire truck. The trucks are decorated with Grand Army Home F.D. lettering. The firemen pictured are, from left to right, Erv Hodges, Pete Pitt, Jerry Geiger, Gary Peterson, Dick Glocke, Dewey Bonnell, Bill Cook, Gene Rasmussen, Lt. Pershing Peterson, Lt. Joe Doyle, and Chief Lew Schroeder.

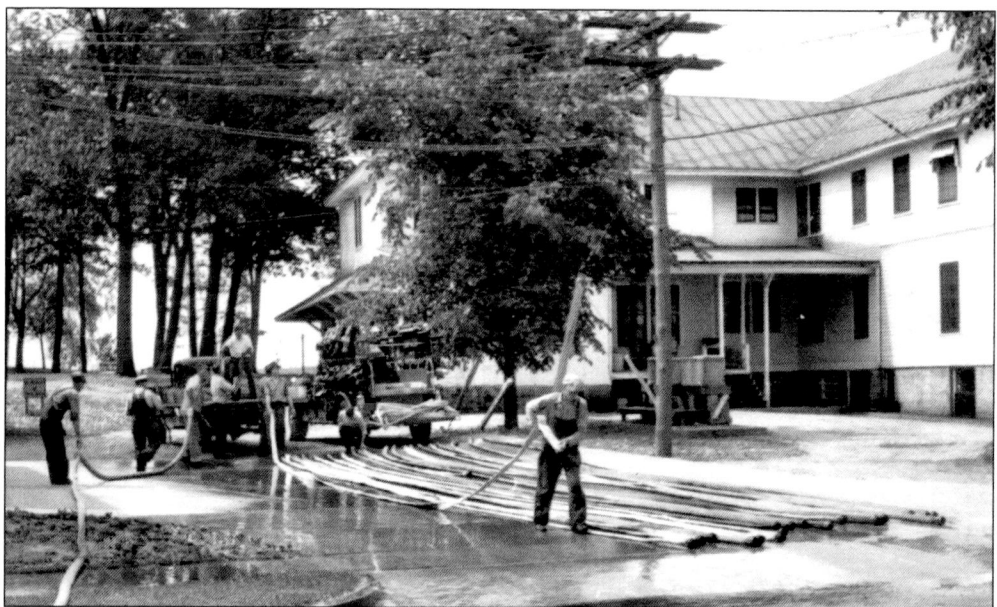

FIRE DEPARTMENT HOSE TEST. The fire department conducted hose tests to be ready for any unexpected fire. This view was probably taken in the early to mid-1950s. The fire department personnel had duties other than just fighting fires. They escorted members to church and back and took care of the movie projection on movie nights. This fire department is the only state institution that still mans its own independent fire department.

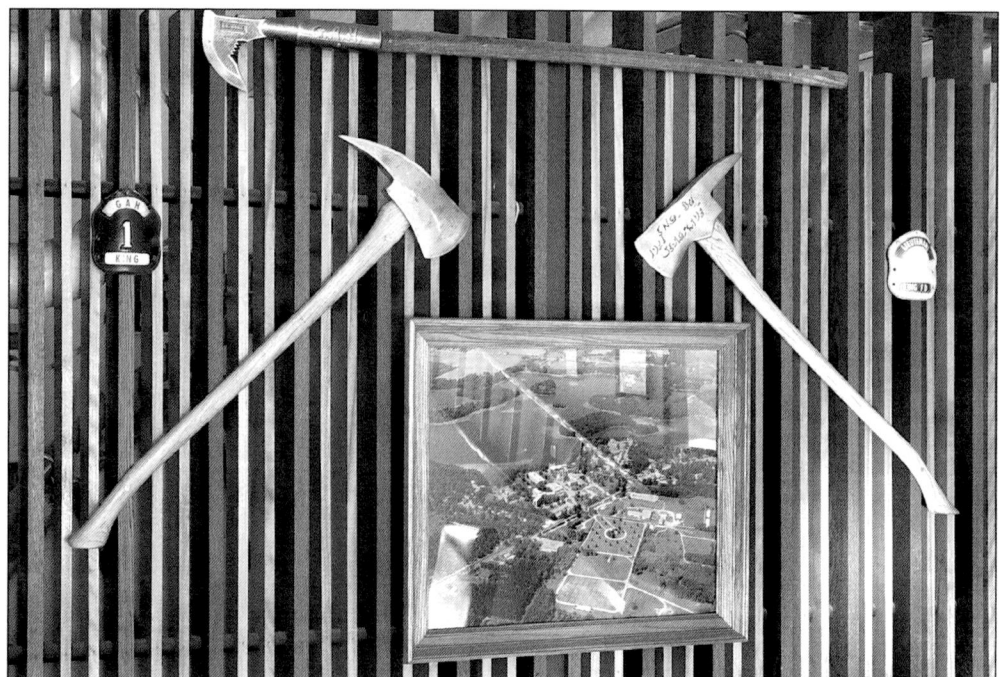

FIRE DEPARTMENT TOOLS. This view shows some of the fire department tools used from the 1920s period to decorate a wall in the present day security office. An aerial photograph of the Home is used as the centerpiece.

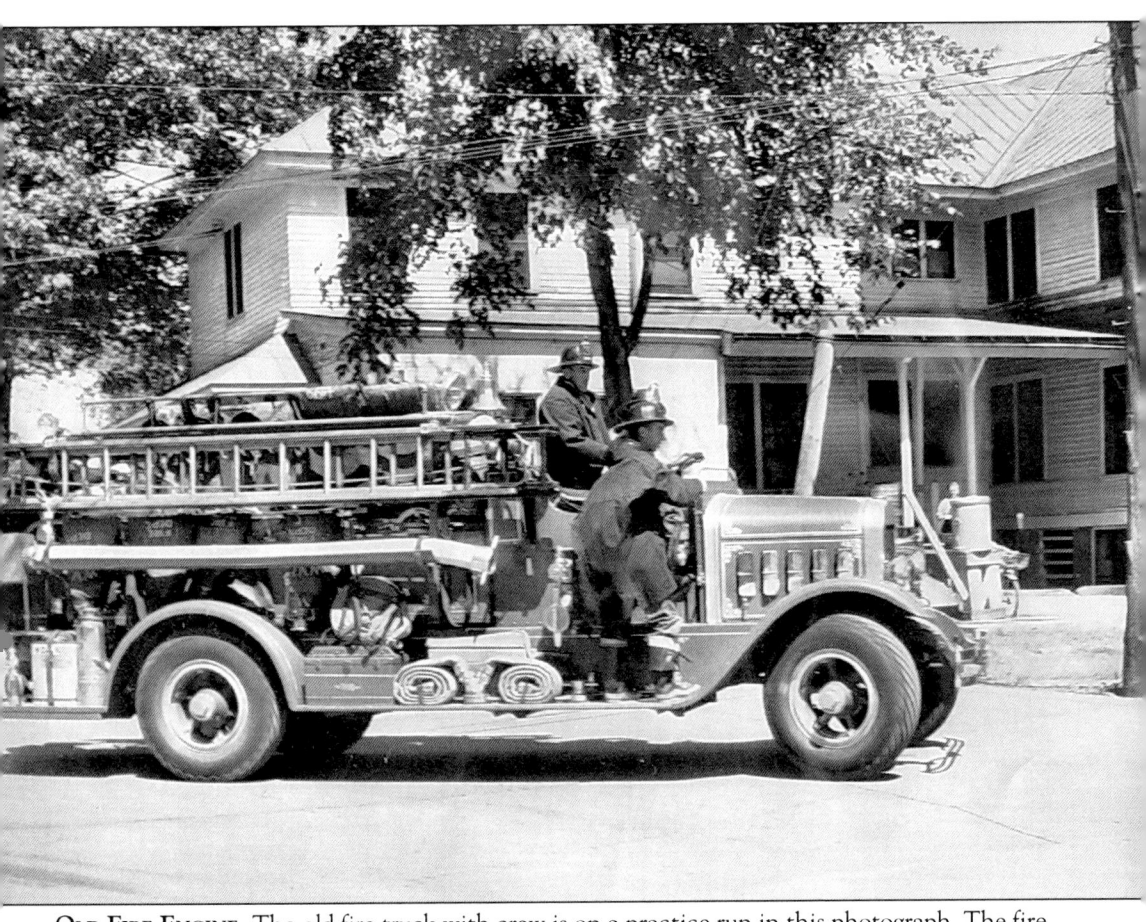

OLD FIRE ENGINE. The old fire truck with crew is on a practice run in this photograph. The fire department ran many practice exercises, including fighting fires from second stories.

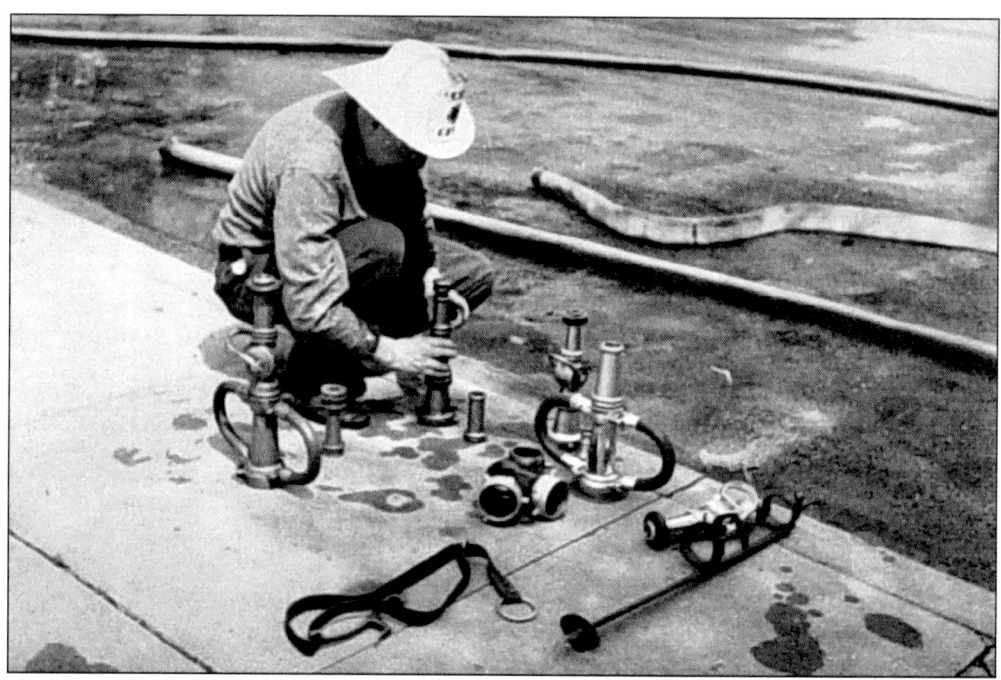

CLEANING THE EQUIPMENT. A member of the fire department cleans nozzles and brass equipment for one of the fire trucks.

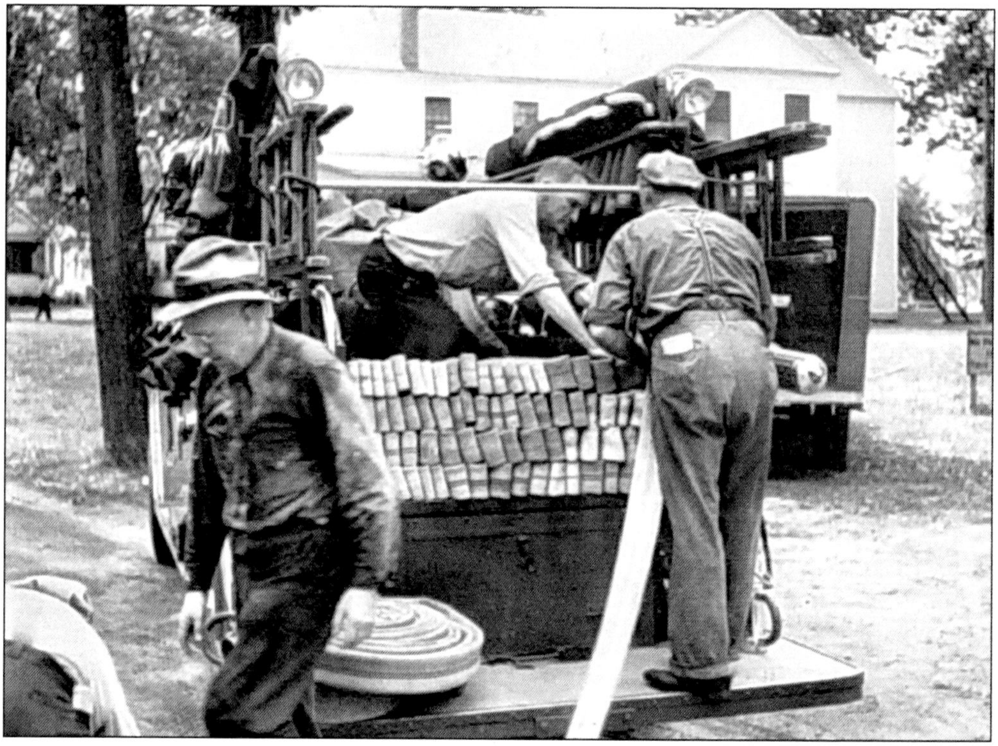

WORKING ON THE FIRE TRUCK. Firemen are shown repacking the hoses and equipment on the fire truck.

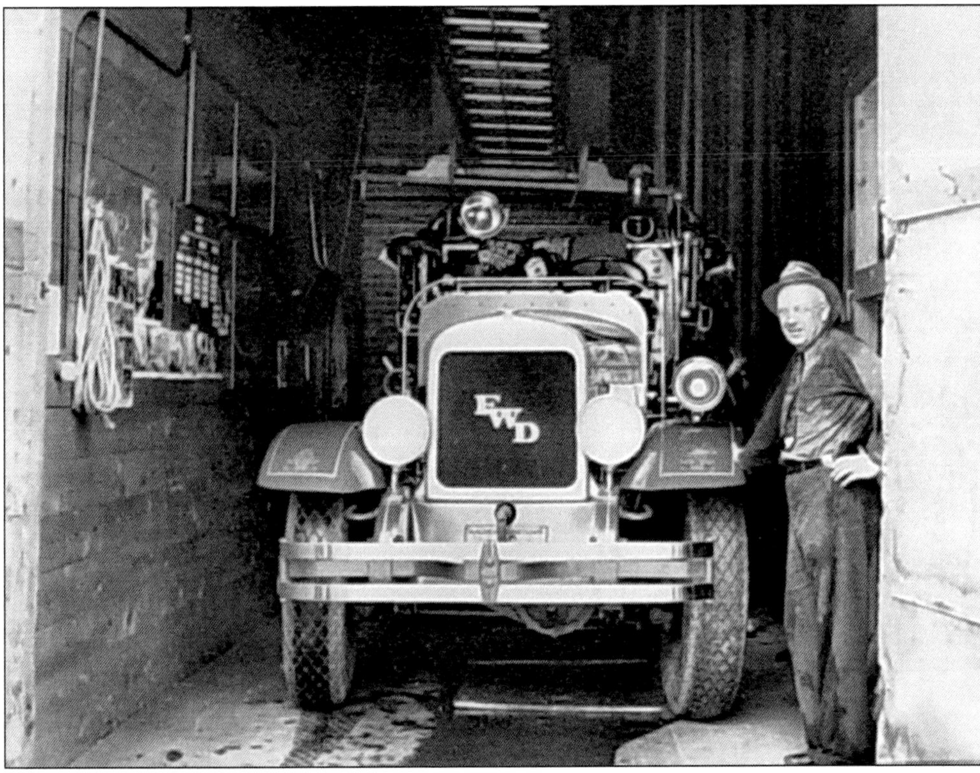

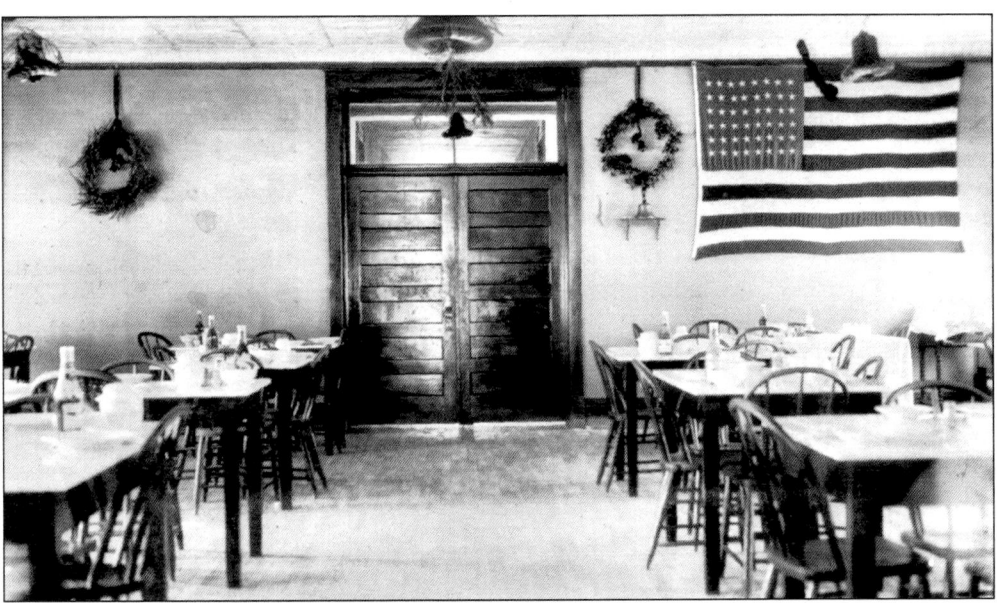

FIRE TRUCK IN STATION. The old fire truck sits in the fire department for its next call.

ONE OF THE DINING ROOMS. This is what one of the dining rooms looked like around 1910. Things were simple, yet clean and presentable. The photograph appears to have been taken about Christmas time, with wreaths hanging on the walls. Notice the hand bell on the shelf under the right wreath. The American flag was present everywhere then, as it is today.

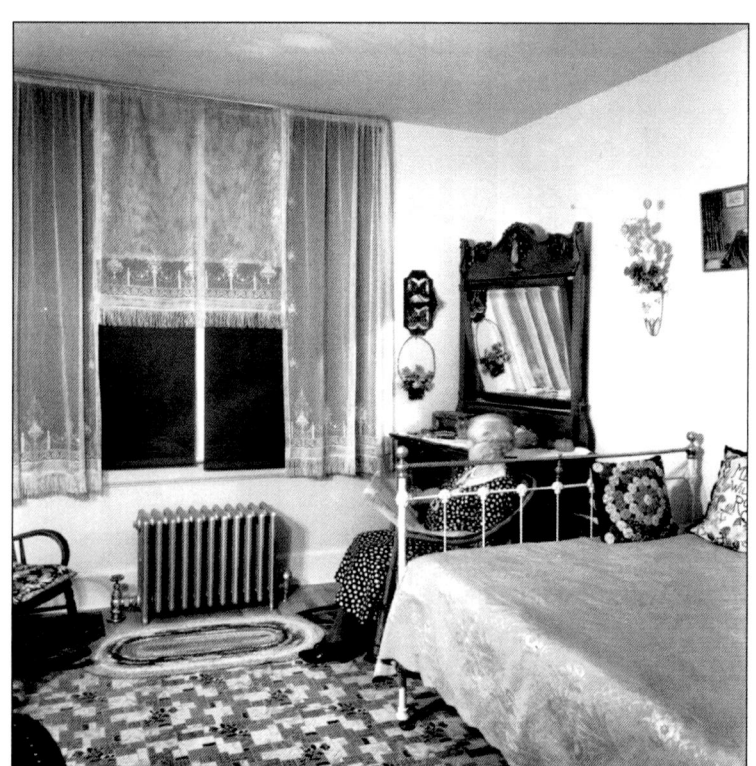

A Typical Room. This is a 1934 view of a member's room. A radiator heater sits in a spacious room that is neat and tidy. There is room for personal items, extra chairs, and tables. Notice Whistler's Mother framed on the wall. It is not known if this was taken in a residence hall or in one of the cottages.

Home Carpenters. This 1936 view of Home carpenters shows a room being redone. They are working on installing a hardwood floor. Notice the lack of power tools.

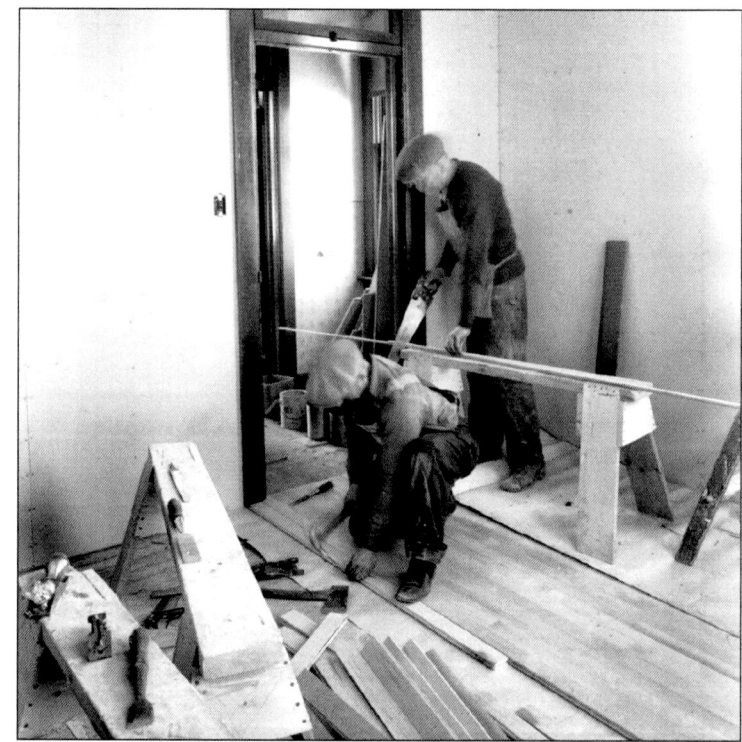

Two

A Walk in the Park

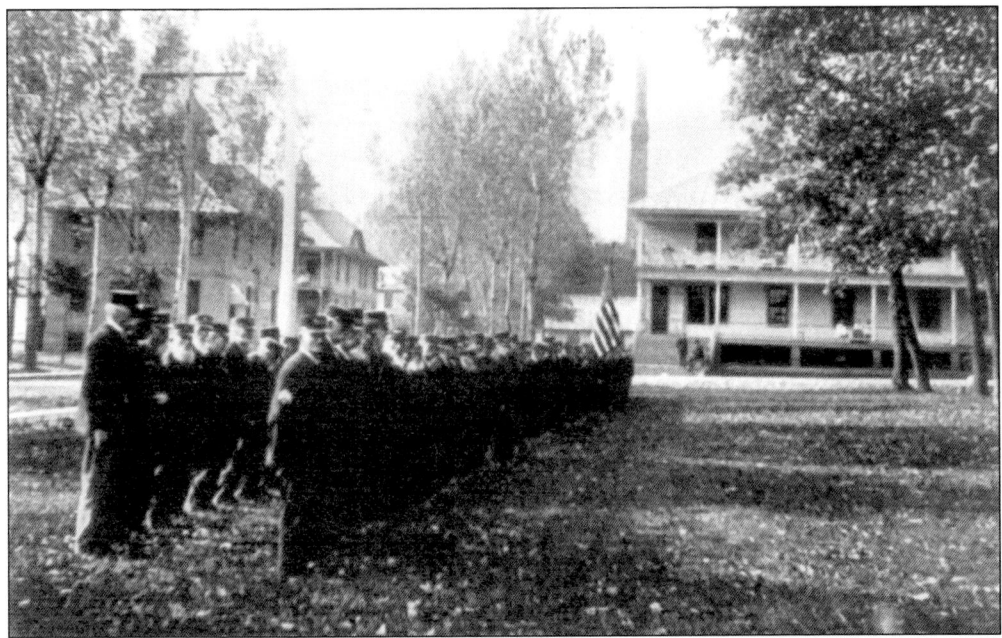

OUR BOYS OF BLUE. Assembled on the park lawn, Home members are dressed in the required uniform of the day. When the Home was established, the uniforms were worn during any function. It was in the late 1920s that members were allowed to dress more casual. On the right is Bryant Hall, while Roberts Hall is seen on the left. Griffin Hall is behind Roberts Hall. In the background, the Power House smokestack can be seen, looking down Manchester Avenue.

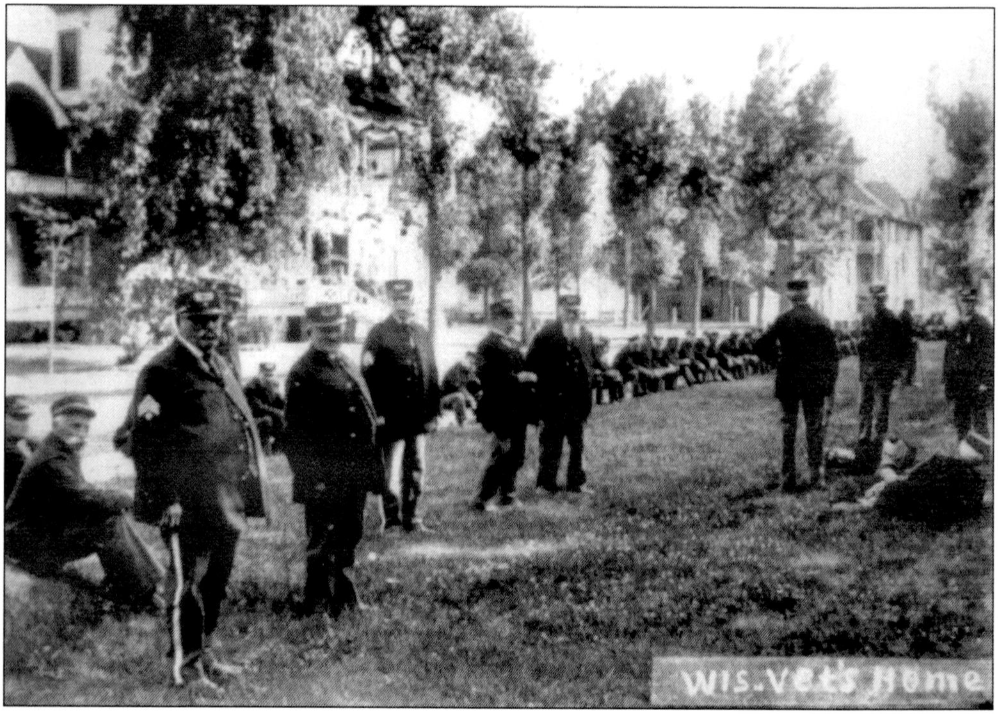

READY FOR ASSEMBLY. The Home members appear to be getting ready for assembly. This was taken at a time when uniforms were standard dress. Fairview Hall is in the background. To the right is Roberts Hall, to the far right is Griffin Hall.

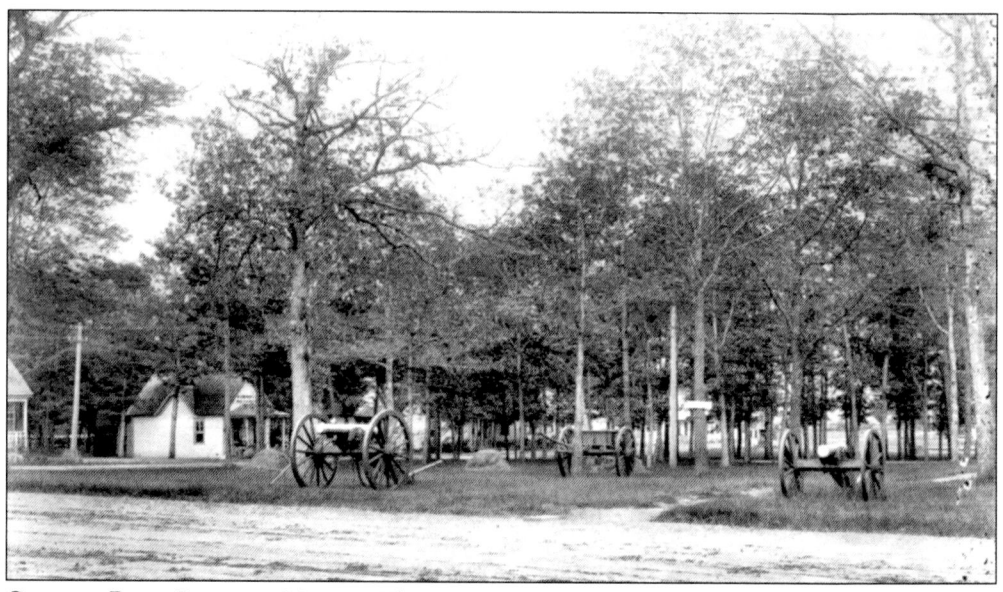

CANNON PARK LOOKING NORTH. This view shows Cannon Park, looking toward Marden Avenue from Woodnorth Avenue. The cottage left of the cannons is Cottage Number 228. The park had several cannons. On the left is a Spanish-American War cannon with the limber in the background. The Home still has the cannon and limber, but they are in need of restoration. These cannons are facing toward Rainbow Lake, which is west of the park.

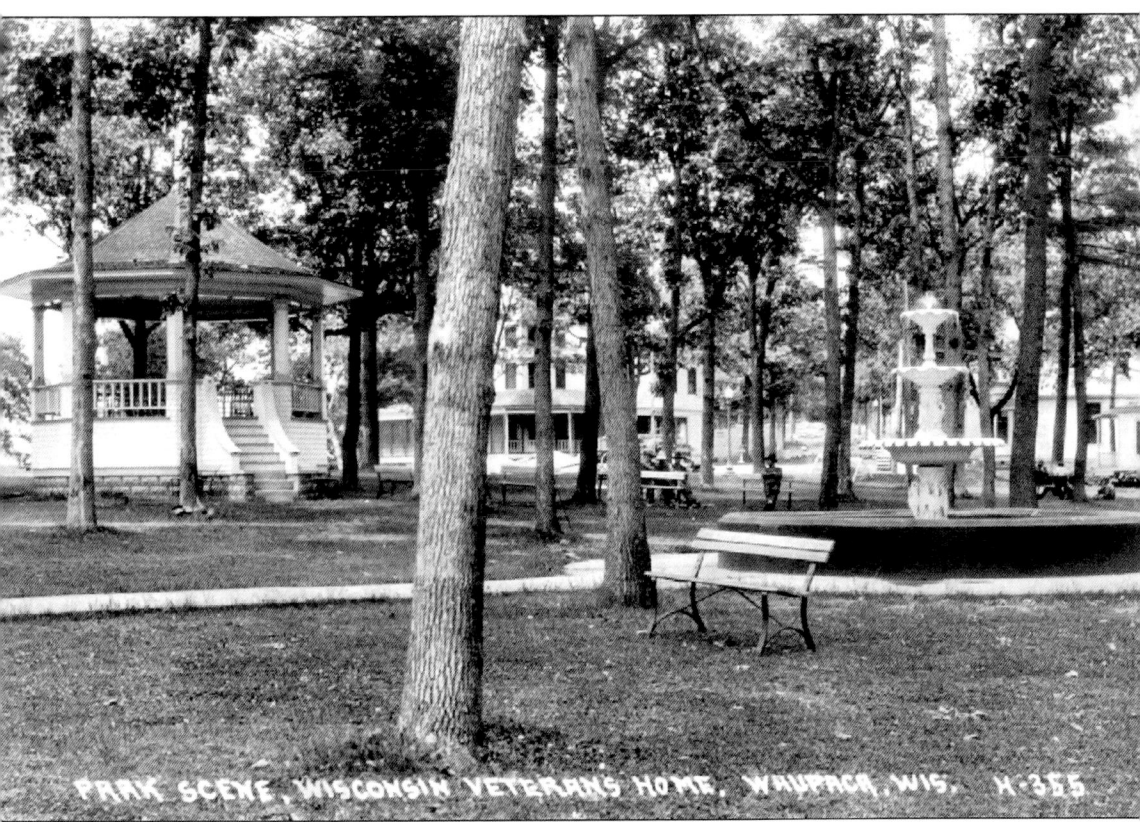

First Bandstand. This is the original bandstand for the Home, located in Cannon Park. A second and a third bandstand replaced it. Note the water fountain in the foreground. The fountain was a gift to the Grand Army Home, dedicated in 1894, from the Sons of (Union) Veterans of the Civil War. In recent years, the centerpiece of the fountain has since fallen into a state of despair and was removed.

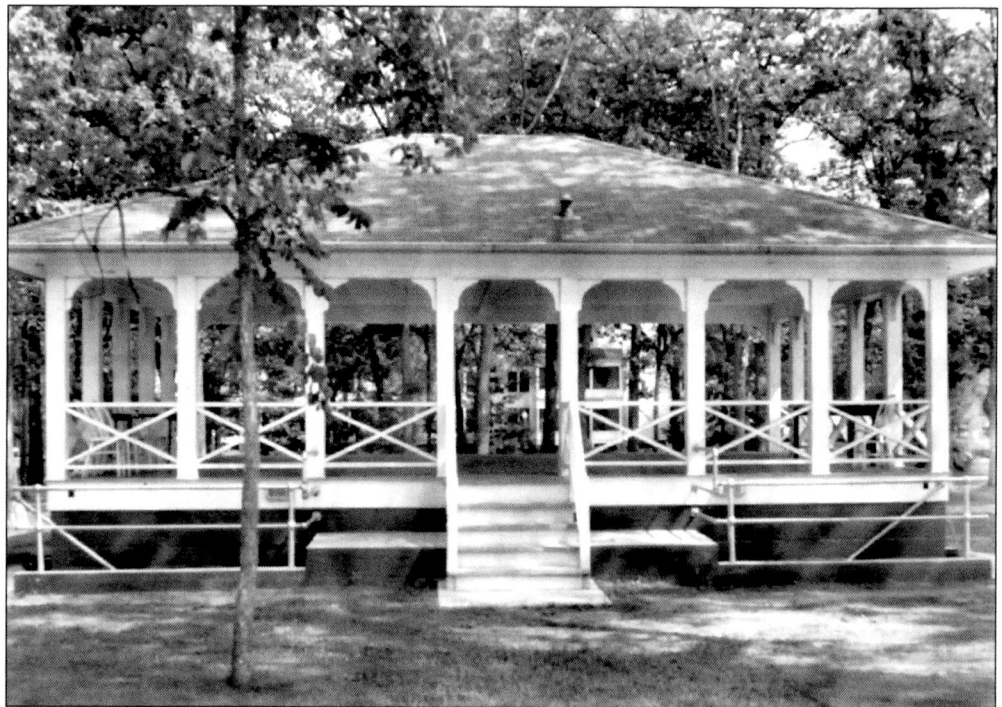

SECOND BANDSTAND. The bandstand, which replaced the original bandstand in 1953, was located in the center of the park. Bands played there and speakers used it as a podium. The piped rails shown in this view guarded the steps to the restrooms located under the bandstand.

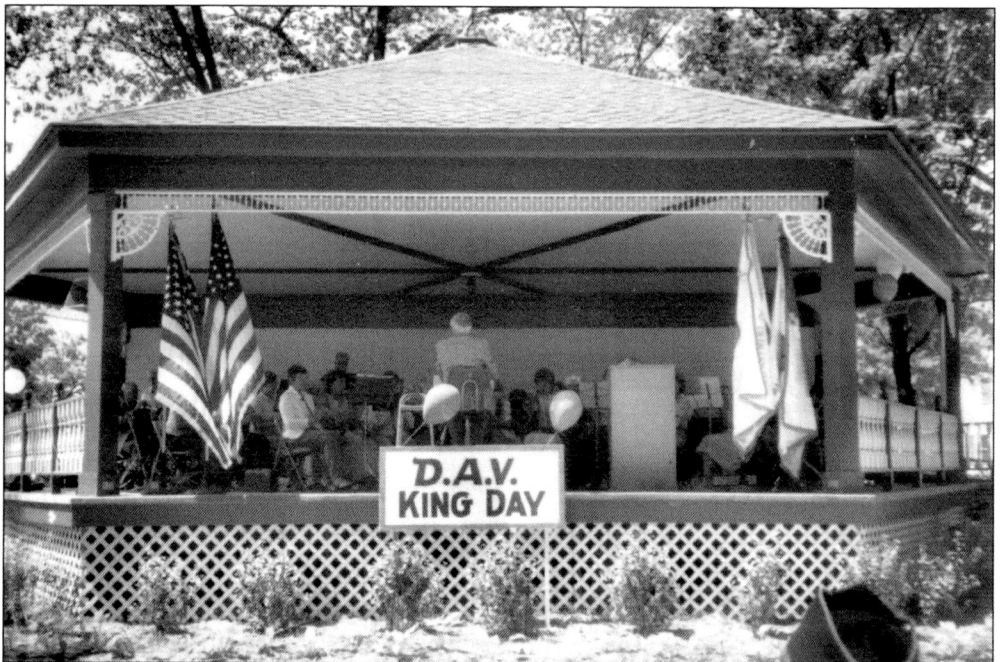

THIRD BANDSTAND. The Home's third bandstand was built in 1987. This building is still there.

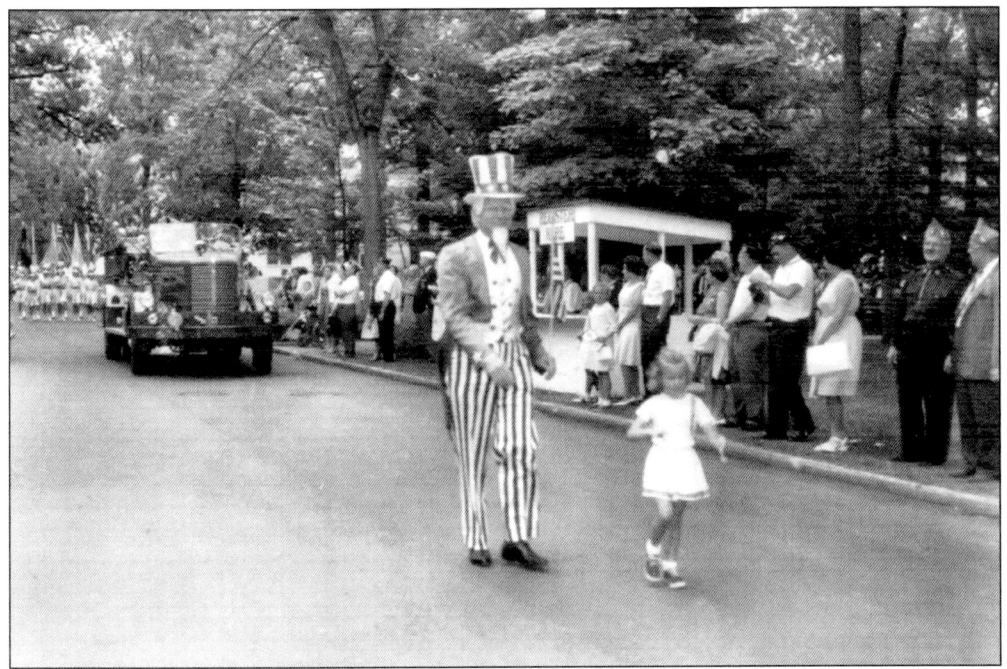

AMERICAN LEGION PARADE. There are several patriotic parades on the grounds each year. This view shows the American Legion marching on the grounds.

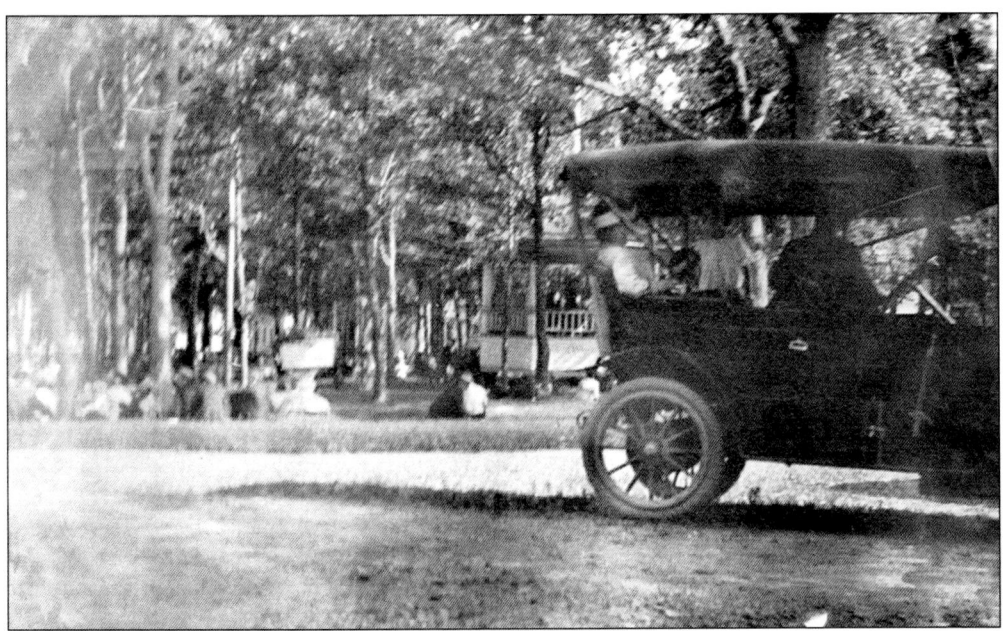

1915 PARK VIEW. This photograph was taken from in front of the commandant's residence, looking toward the park. People are relaxing in the shade of the park while a woman waits in an automobile.

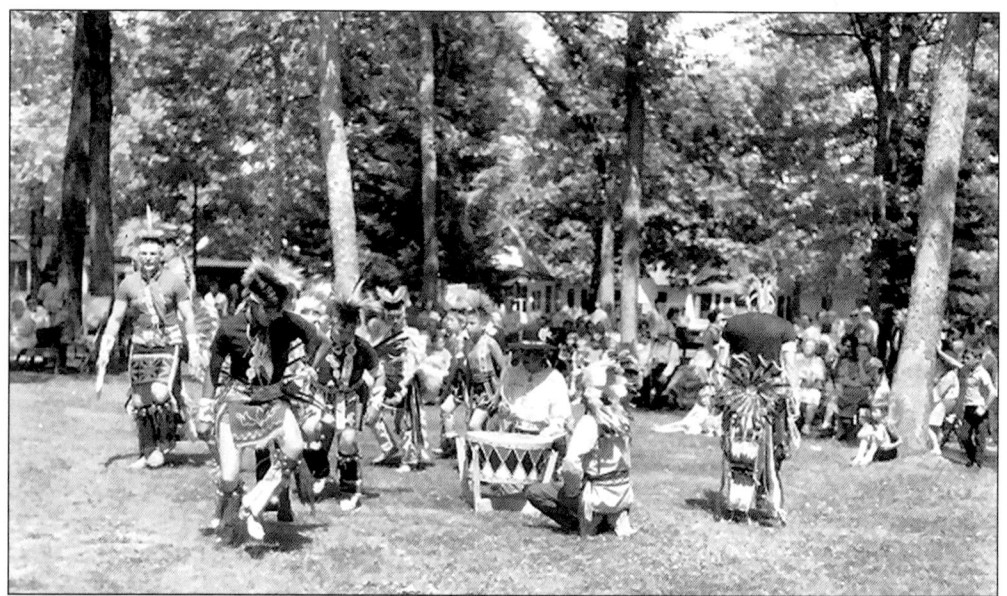

A POWWOW IN THE PARK. It has been said that Native Americans would work at the Home as seasonal workers throughout the years. They would hold a powwow in the park for the members of the Home in order to raise money.

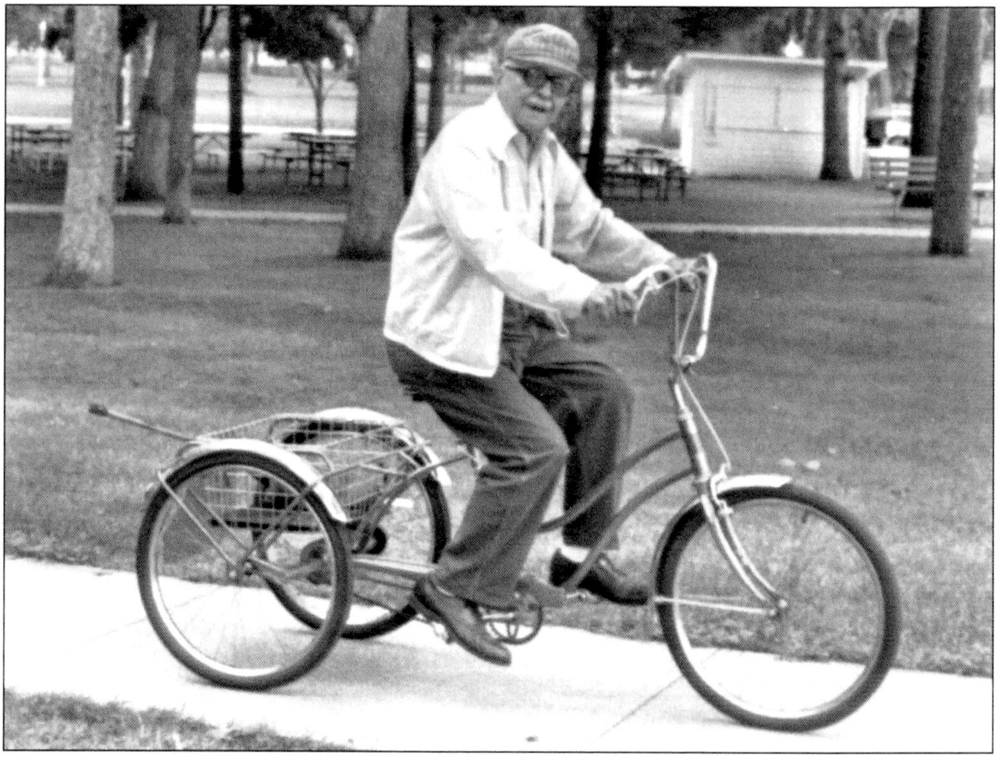

A RIDE ON A BIKE. Home member Ray Skiba is shown riding a bike around the park. Many members ride bikes to get from one building to another. There are several three-wheel bikes available to assist the members that choose to ride them.

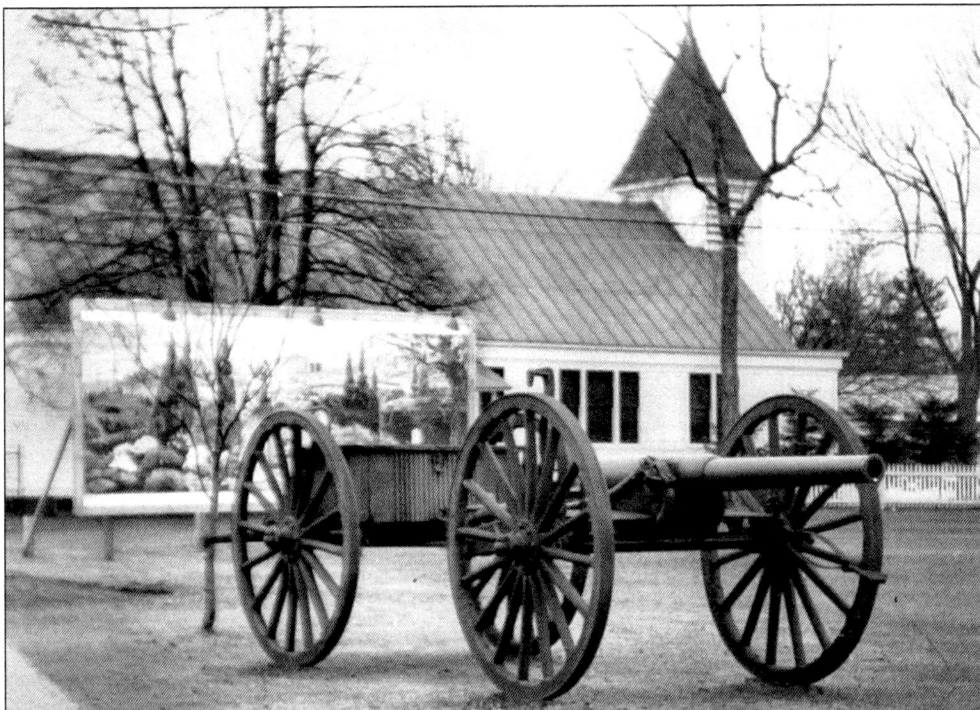

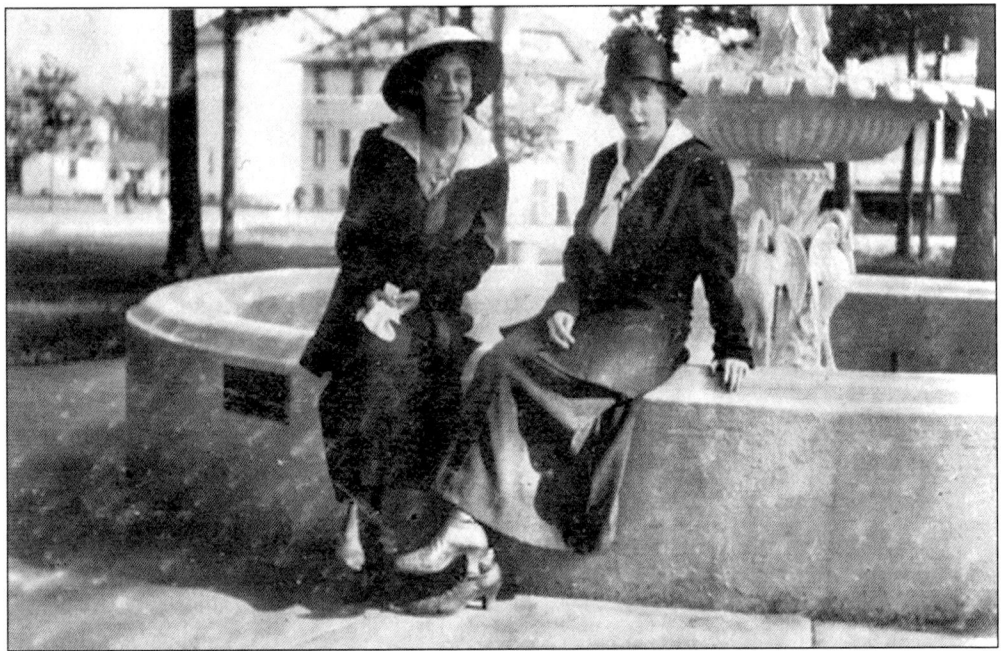

SPANISH-AMERICAN CANNON. This cannon has been moved several times within the park. Here, it is shown near the Amusement Hall. The wheels on the cannon had since become decayed and it was moved to storage.

WOMEN AT THE FOUNTAIN. Many photographs were taken with the fountain. This is a 1915 view of visitors enjoying the fountain.

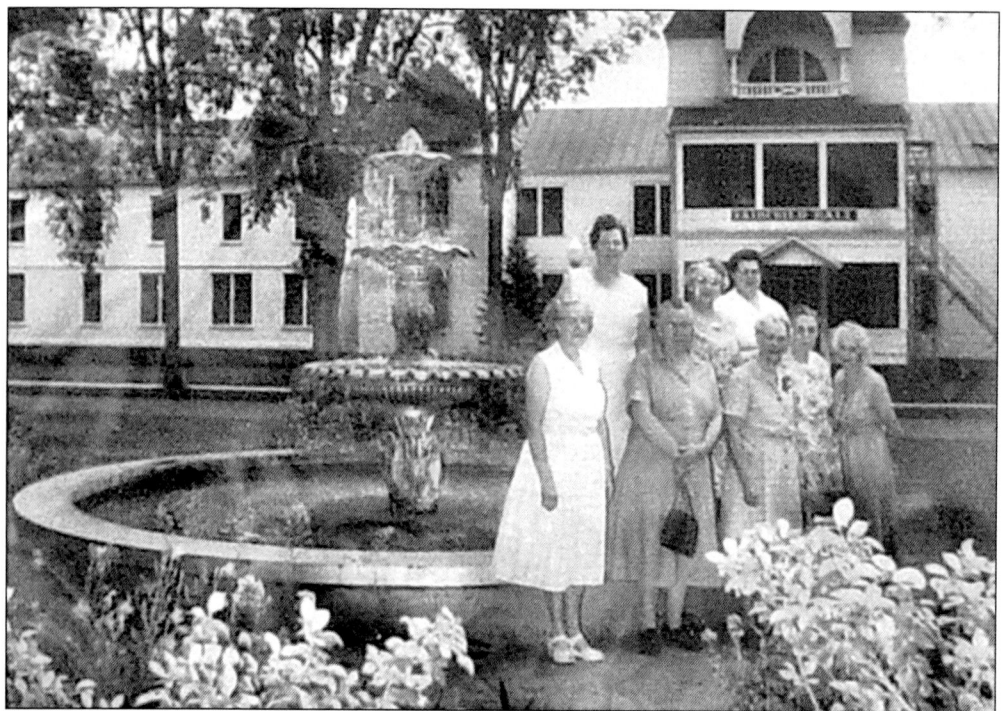

WRC AND THE FOUNTAIN. These women from the Women's Relief Corp. are posed for a photograph by the fountain with Fairchild Hall in the background.

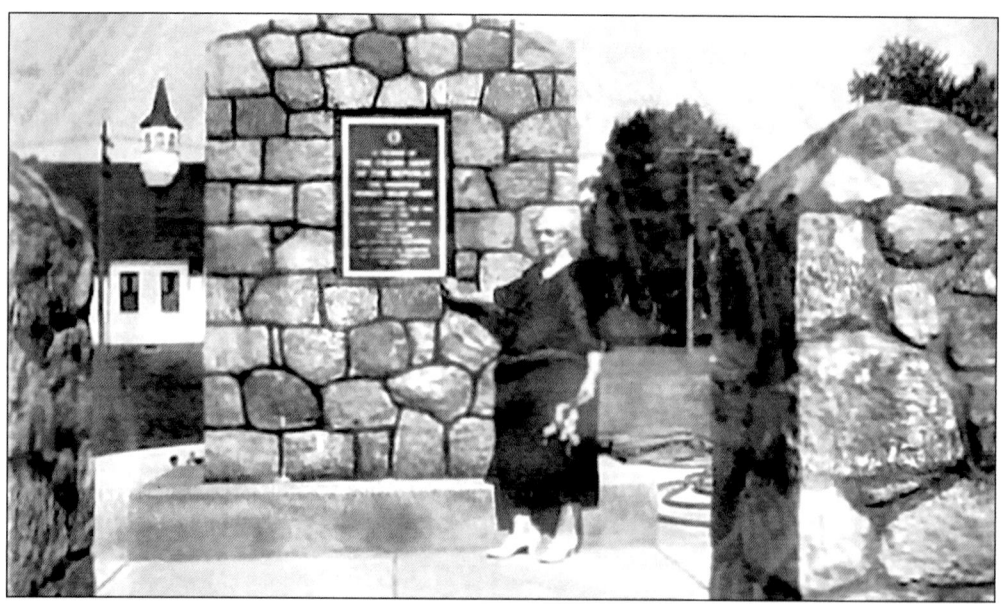

WRC MONUMENT. The WRC has helped the Home in many ways. This plaque tells of being instrumental in the building and upkeep of the chapel and ten cottages on the grounds. The monument is located in the center of a stone fence that guards the front of the Home.

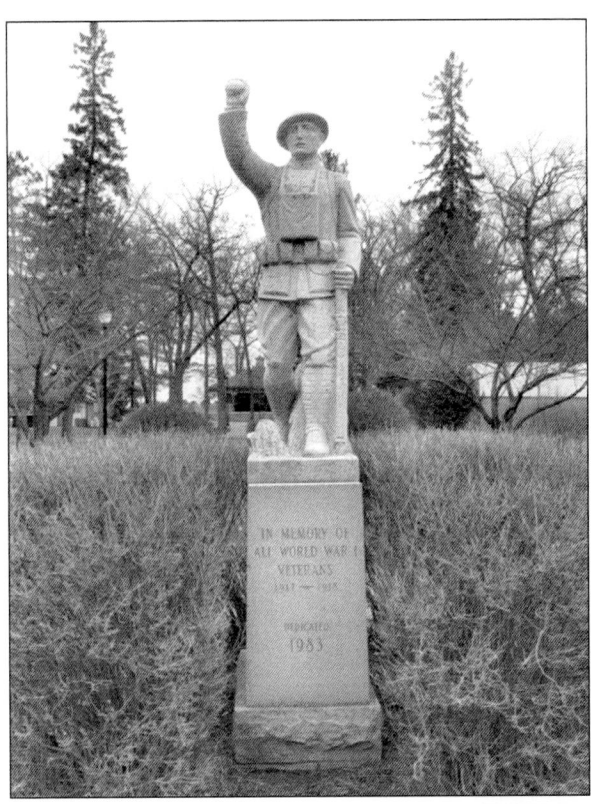

WORLD WAR I MONUMENT. This monument is located in the center of the park.

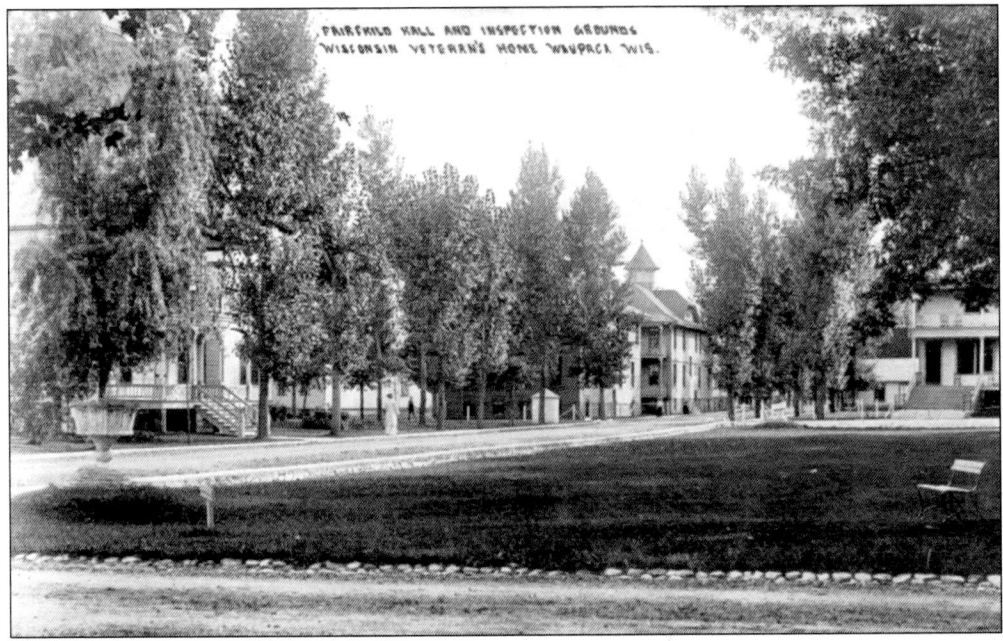

FAIRCHILD HALL AND INSPECTION GROUNDS. This 1911 postcard view shows some of the park and the surrounding buildings. This was taken from Marden Avenue looking south down Manchester Avenue. Fairchild Hall is on the far left, Roberts Hall and Griffin Hall are in the middle, and the edge of Bryant Hall is on the right.

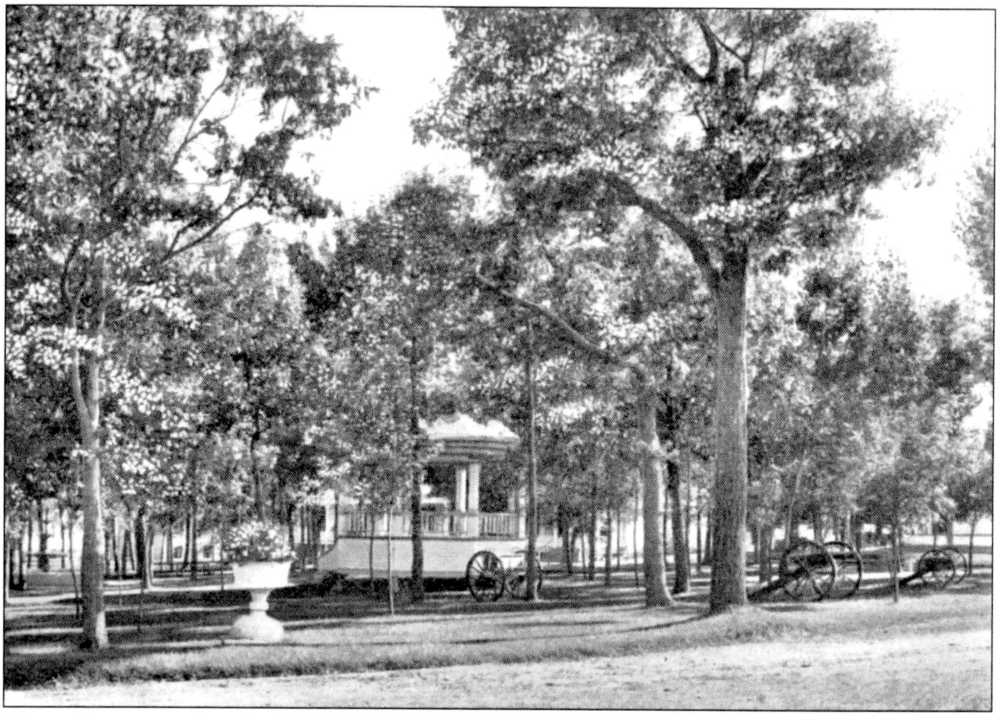

HOME GROUNDS. Another early 1907 view of the park shows the cannons and the bandstand. This view was taken from the commandant's residence.

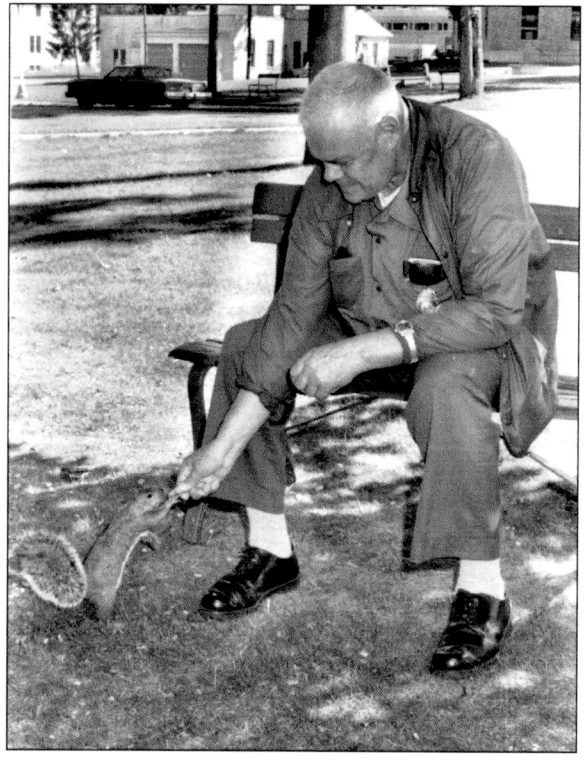

FEEDING SQUIRRELS. Employee Walter Ledder feeds a squirrel in the park. Some of the photograph albums used for this publication had pages filled with photos of members feeding the squirrels.

Three
STREET SCENES

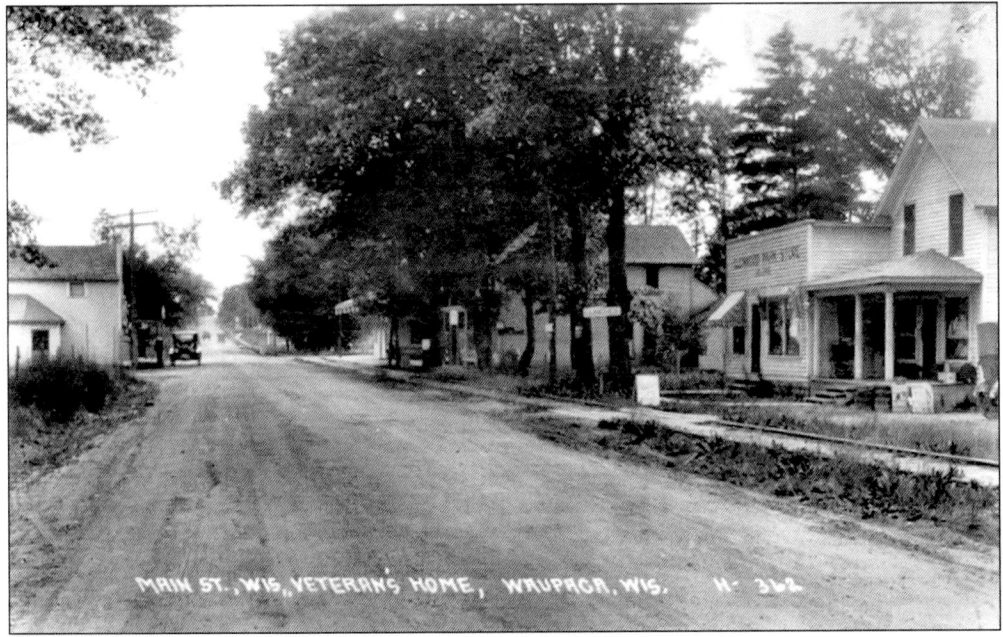

HIGHWAY LOOKING SOUTH. Most photographs show the King area from the Home grounds. This rare view shows how the Home started to look when traveling in from Waupaca. The above postcard shows the surrounding buildings just outside the Home. The stone fence can be seen on the far right side of the roadway. The trolley tracks lead to the Interurban Depot, the fourth building from the right with the overhang.

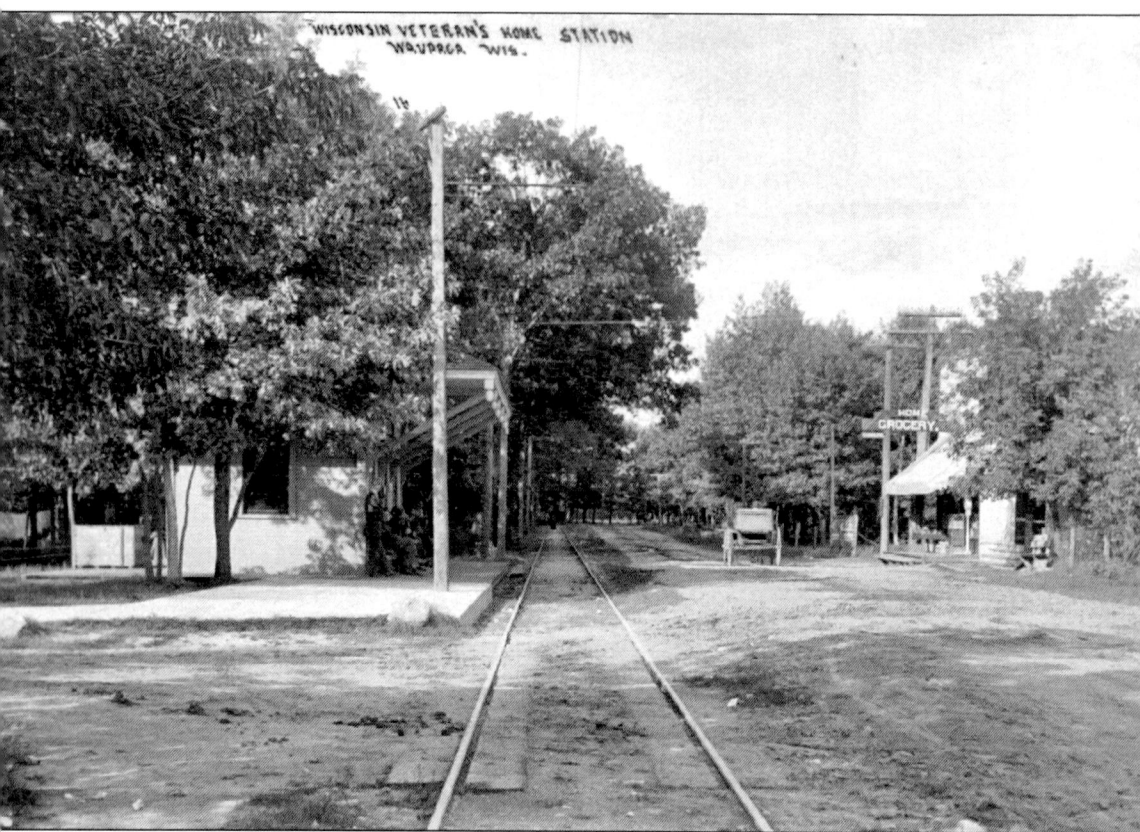

HIGHWAY LOOKING NORTH. The view is taken just as Marden Avenue adjoins the highway. Looking north from the Home entrance, the depot was on the left side of the trolley tracks. The buildings barely shown on the right are the Home grocery store and restaurant. The trolley ran from downtown Waupaca to the Grandview Hotel just south of the Home, making the Home an ideal location for travel. The grocery store was torn down recently, the restaurant was torn down years ago. This photo shows only horse and wagon travel, making it a very early photo of the front of the Home. Marston Hall would have been to the right of the photographer of this photo as it was taken.

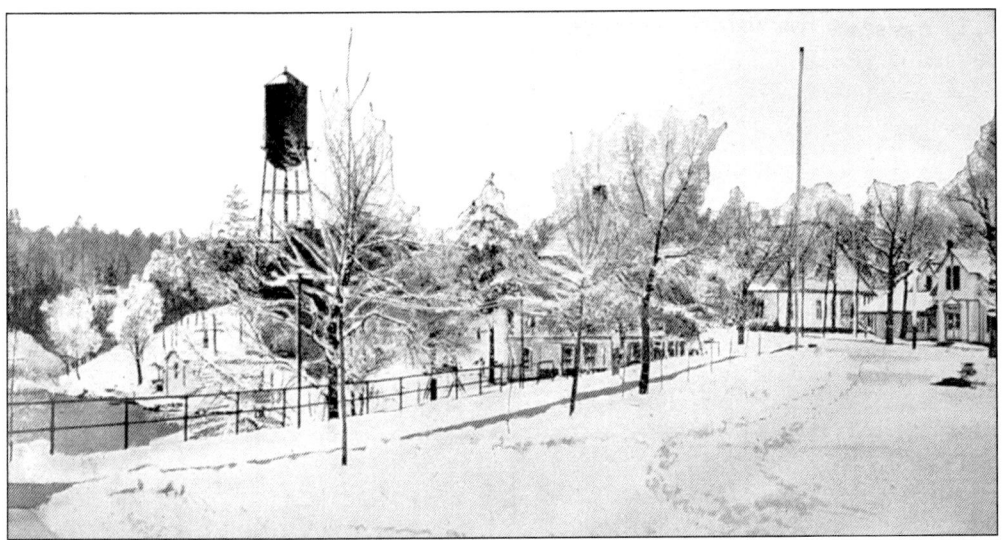

WOODNORTH AVENUE IN THE WINTER. For some reason, there were not many photographs taken of the Home during the winter months. This photograph shows Woodnorth Avenue from the nurses' residence looking toward Marden Hall. The road overlooked the lake frontage.

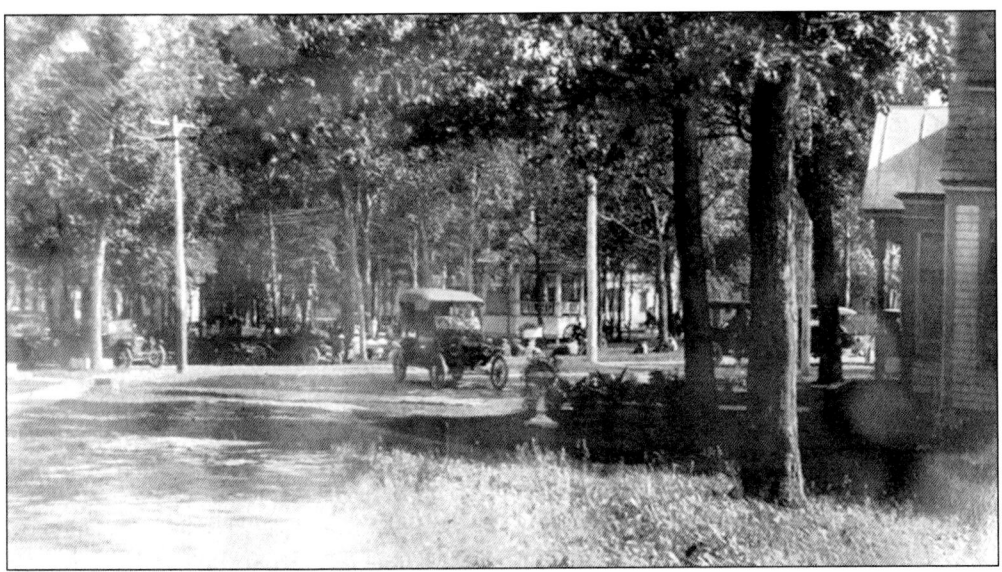

LAKE STREET AND WOODNORTH AVENUE. In this 1915 photograph, Lake Street, Marden Avenue, and Woodnorth meet in front of the commandant's residence. The park with the bandstand is on the left while the commandant's residence can barely be seen on the right.

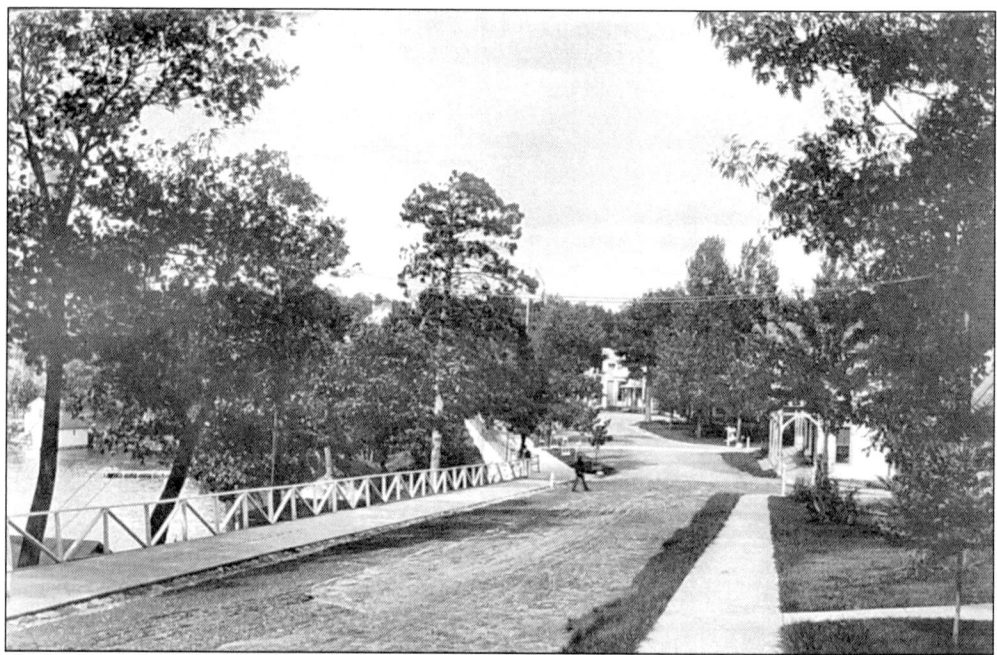

WOODNORTH AVENUE. This is Woodnorth Avenue as it looked in front of Marden Hall. Woodnorth Avenue was built along the shoreline of Rainbow Lake, making it one of the most picturesque viewpoints of the Home. Just past Marden Hall is the park.

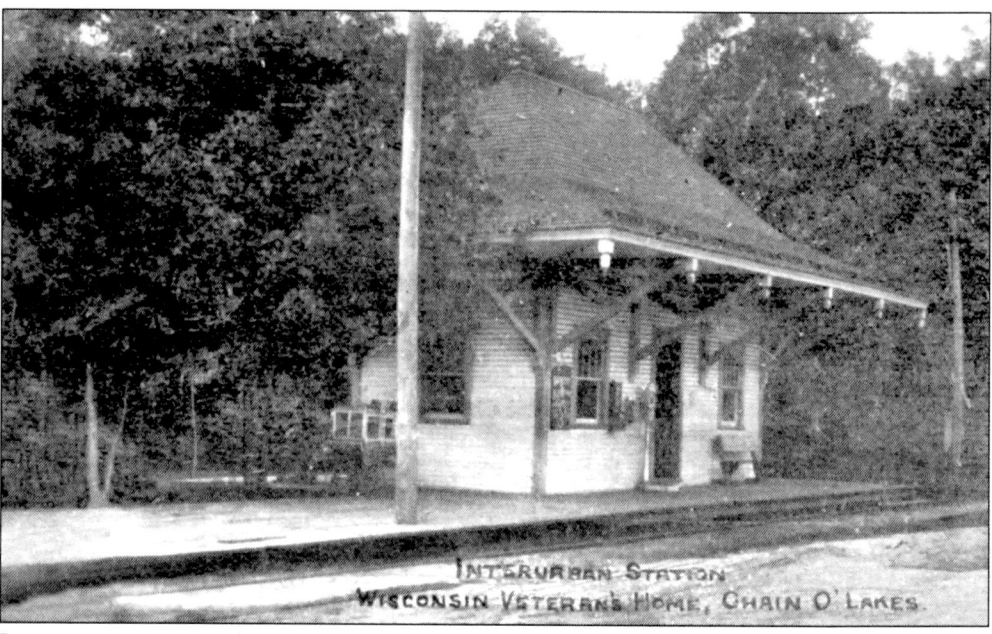

INTERURBAN DEPOT. This is a rare view of the depot at the front of the Home. The depot made it easier for visitors to stay in Waupaca and still visit members at the Home during the daylight hours. The road to the Home was just a dirt road, which got muddy and rutted up from the rain. The trolley to the Home made the trip more pleasant. The present-day Farmers State Bank is located on the other side of the trees in the background of this photograph.

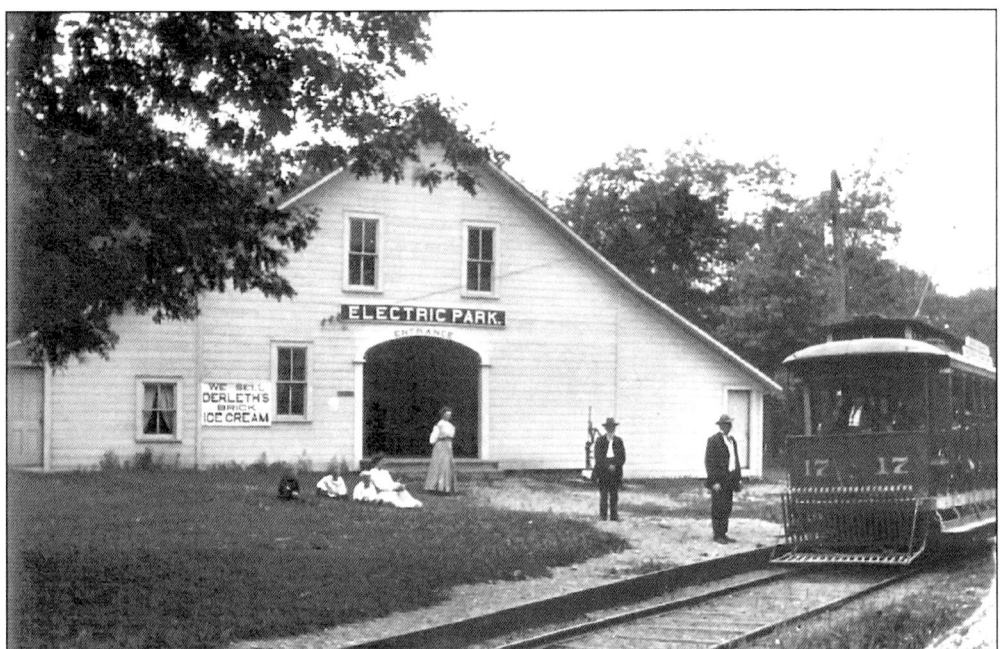

TROLLEY AND ELECTRIC PARK. Although not officially part of the Home, this scene was familiar for Home members. The Electric Park was located near the Grandview Hotel, south of the Home by the lake.

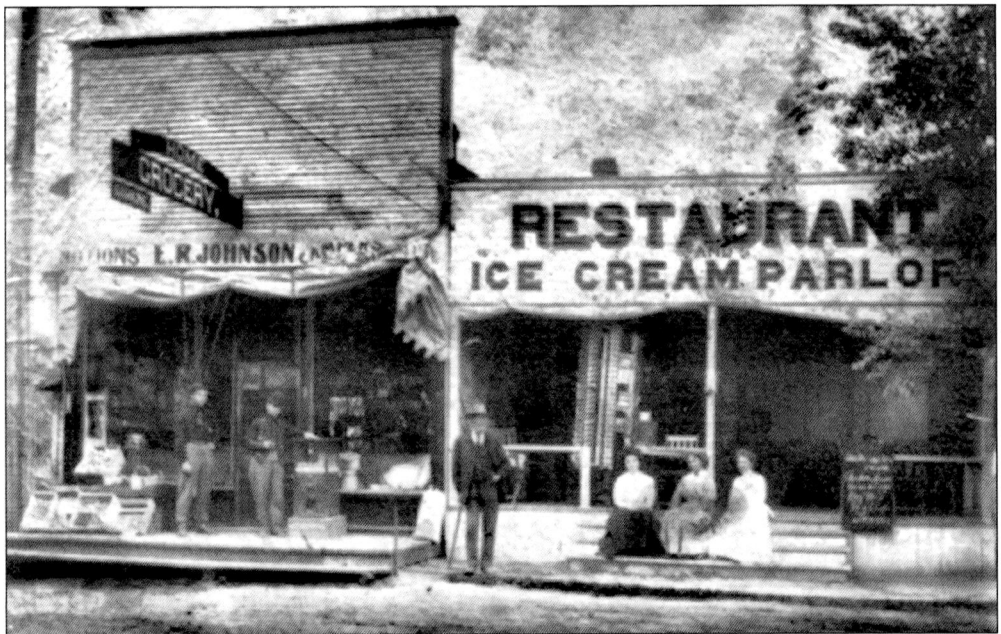

HOME GROCERY. The Home Grocery, as it was earlier known, was located across from the highway at the Marden Avenue entrance. There was a restaurant next to the grocery store. Not formally part of the Home, it was a gathering place for members, as well as a place to pick up odds and ends. The grocery store was owned by several different people throughout the years, and was torn down within the last couple years.

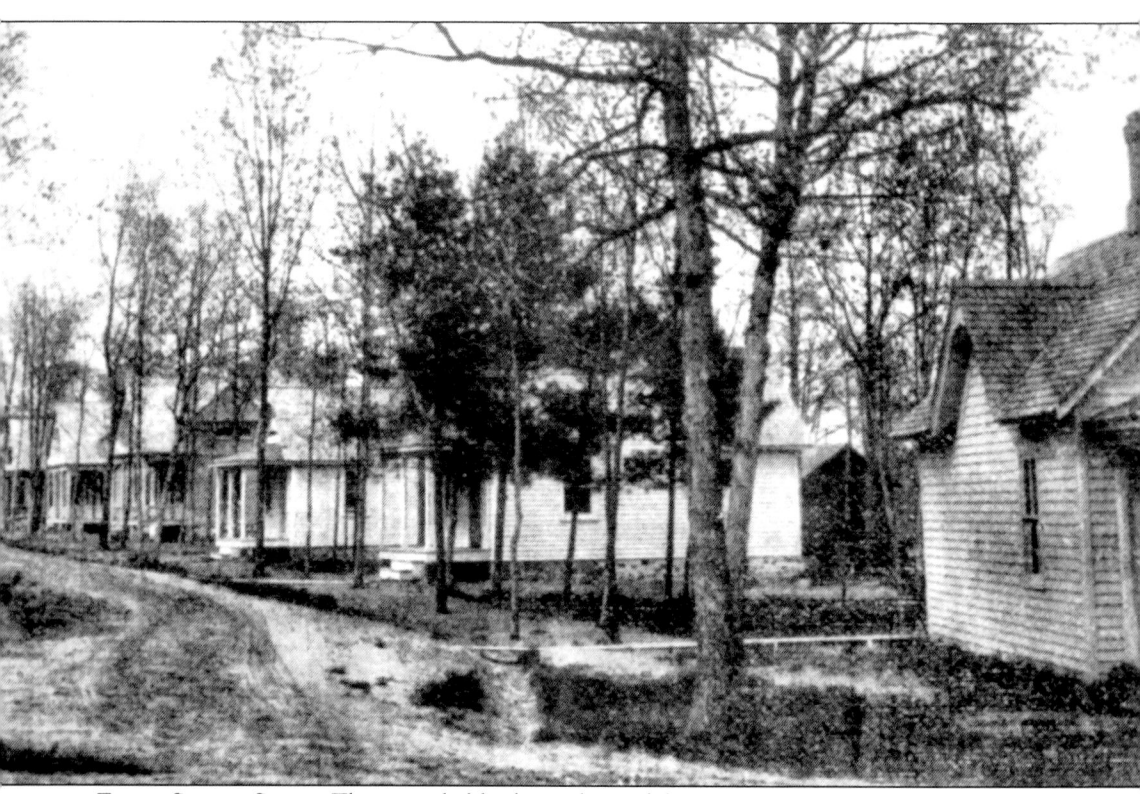

EARLY STREET SCENE. This is probably the earliest of the street scenes at the Home. The roads are roughly traveled. Members walked wooden planks to the cottage entrances. It is hard to visualize a Home member trying to go to dinner at one of the halls after a steady rain or Wisconsin blizzard.

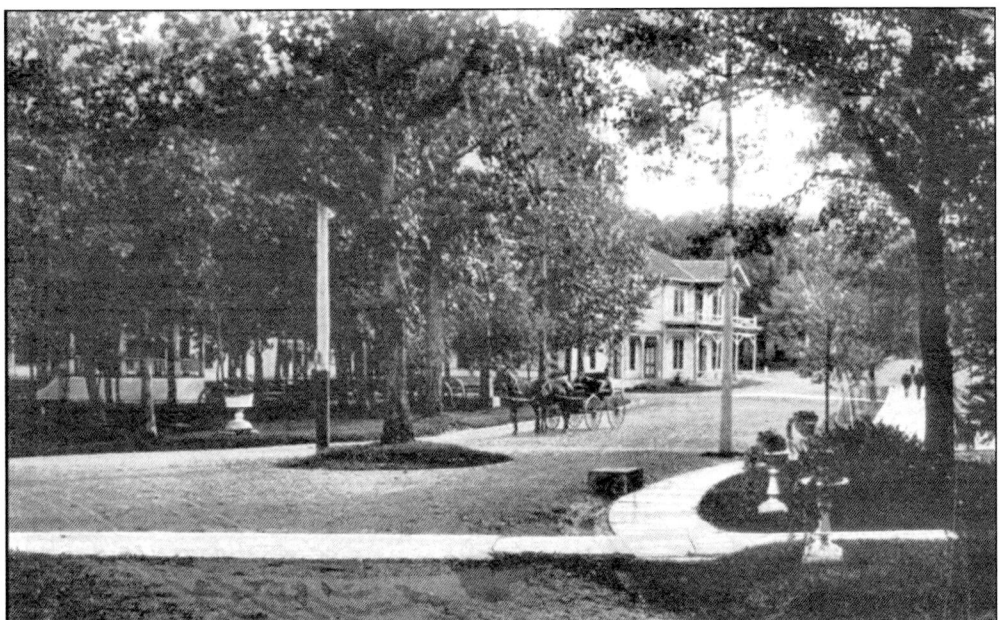

LOOKING SOUTH FROM HEADQUARTERS. This 1912 postcard has Marden Hall in the background and Bryant Hall past the trees of the park. This is the corner of Marden Avenue and Woodnorth Avenue. The sidewalk was a boardwalk. The front yard of the commandant's residence has the flower pots along the boardwalk. The main flagpole was located at this intersection.

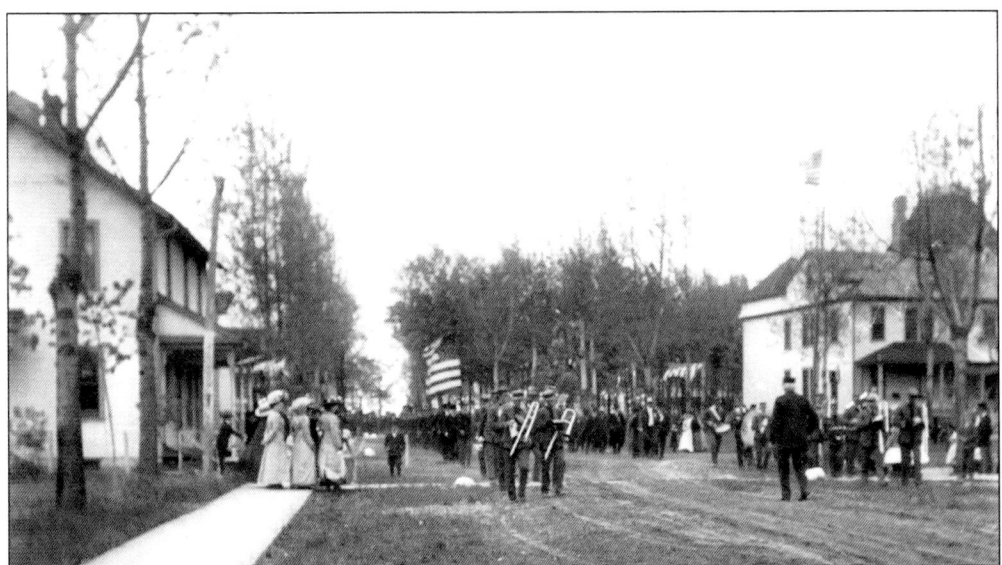

PARADE ON MARDEN. This scene was of one of the many parades held at the Home. The back of Fairchild Hall is shown on the right. At first glance, it was hard to locate where the photograph was taken. The park is on the right hand side past Fairchild Hall. Building Number 310 is on the left.

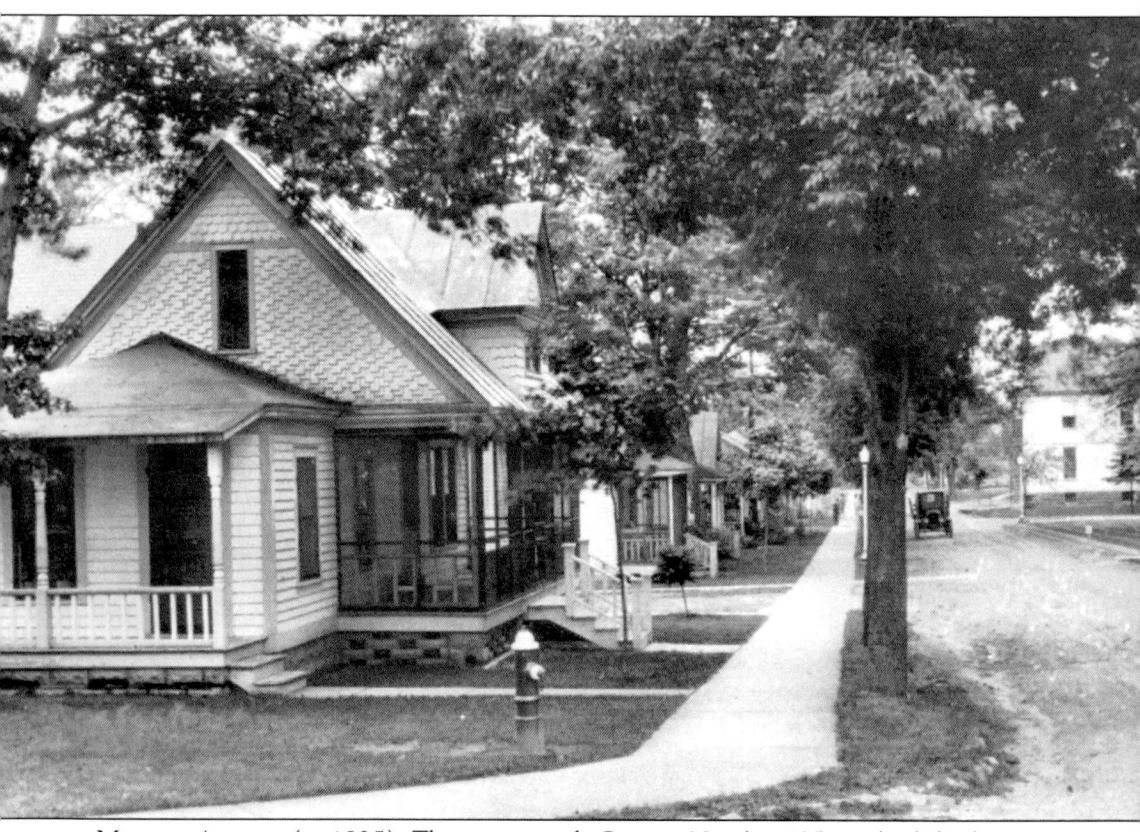

MARDEN AVENUE (c. 1925). This scene, with Cottage Number 125 on the left, shows some of the peacefulness that the members enjoyed. The park is on the right. This view would have been taken from the commandant's residence looking east.

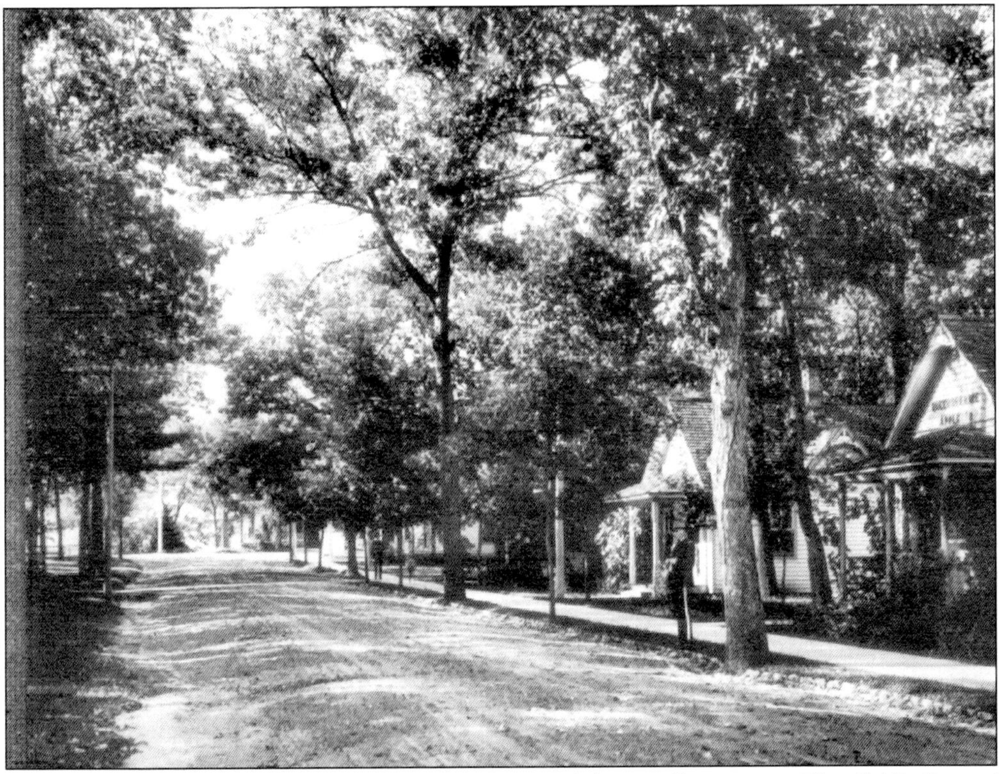

STREET SCENE (c. 1925). This view shows some of the small cottages. The GAR Post of Appleton, Wisconsin sponsored the building on the right.

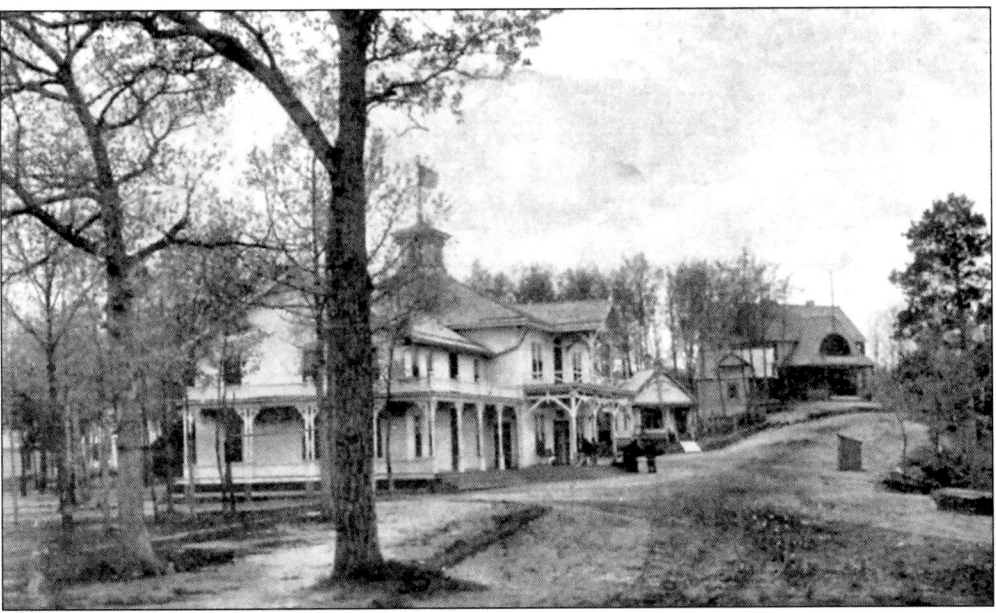

MARDEN HALL AND THE 21ST REGIMENTAL BUILDING. Marden Hall is on the left when looking south on Woodnorth Avenue. Taken during the early days of the Home, this photograph shows the 21st Regimental Building on a small hill in the background.

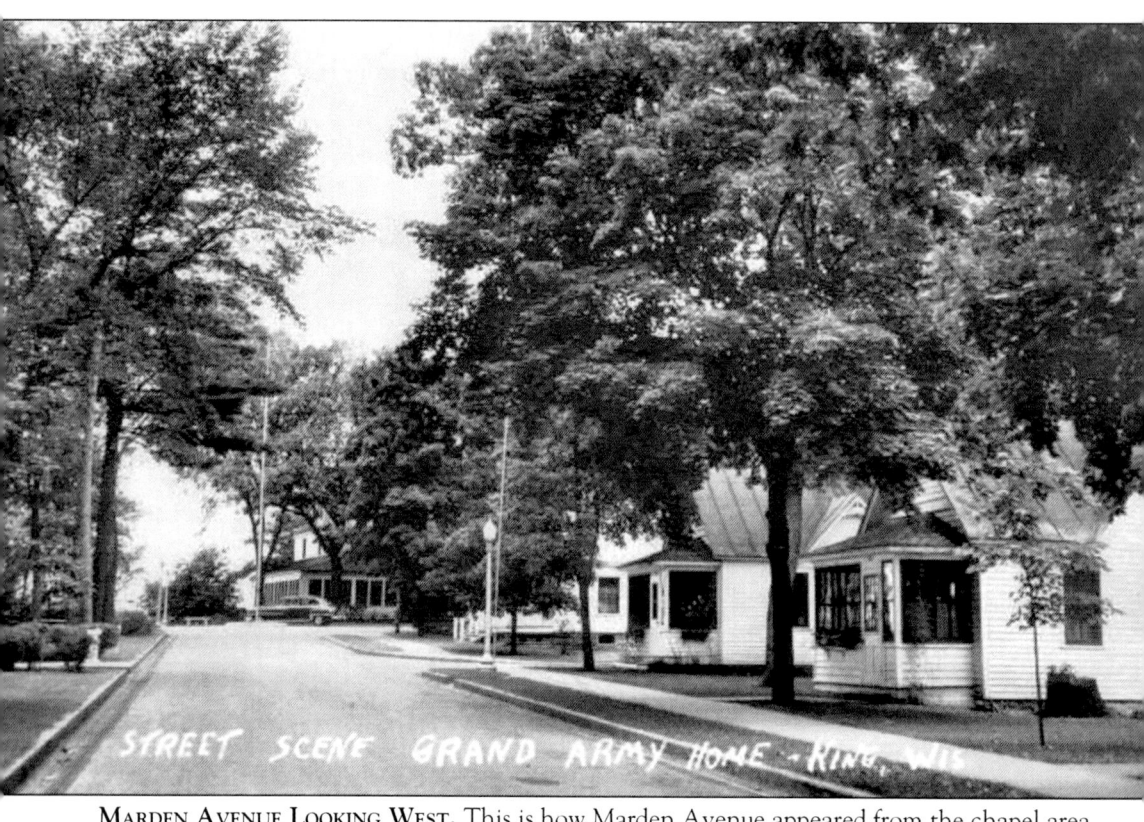

MARDEN AVENUE LOOKING WEST. This is how Marden Avenue appeared from the chapel area as one looked toward the commandant's residence.

Four

ACROSS THE ROAD

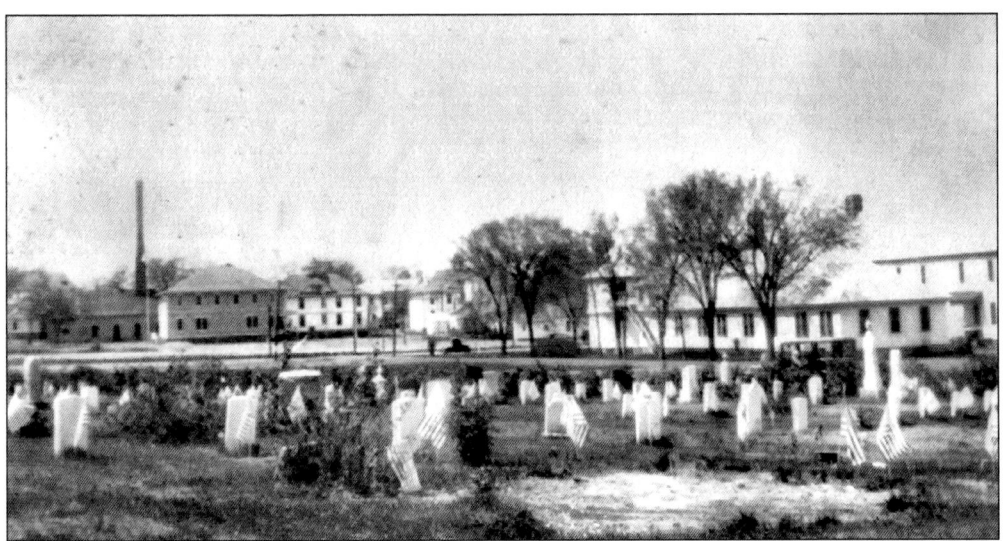

HOME CEMETERY 1920. The Home Cemetery is located across Main Street (present day Highway QQ) from the Home. Located next to Marston Hall, the cemetery pictured here is from 1920, looking back toward the Home. Across the street is pictured, from left to right, the Power House, the Law Building, Griffin Hall in white, and Roberts Hall in white. Marston Hall, from the back, is in the foreground behind the grave markers.

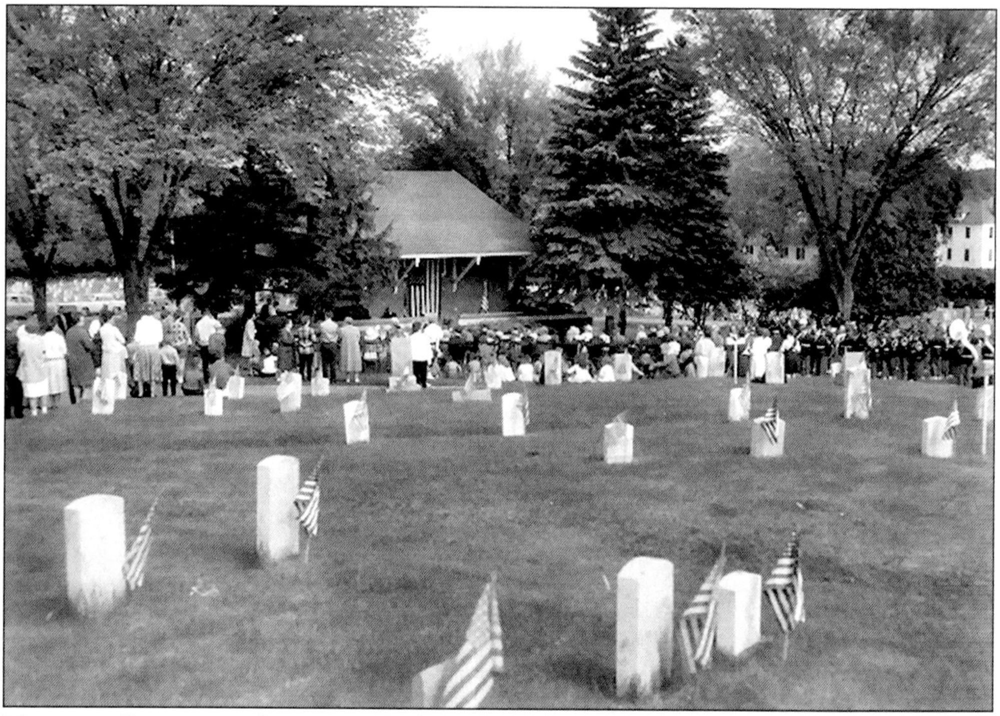

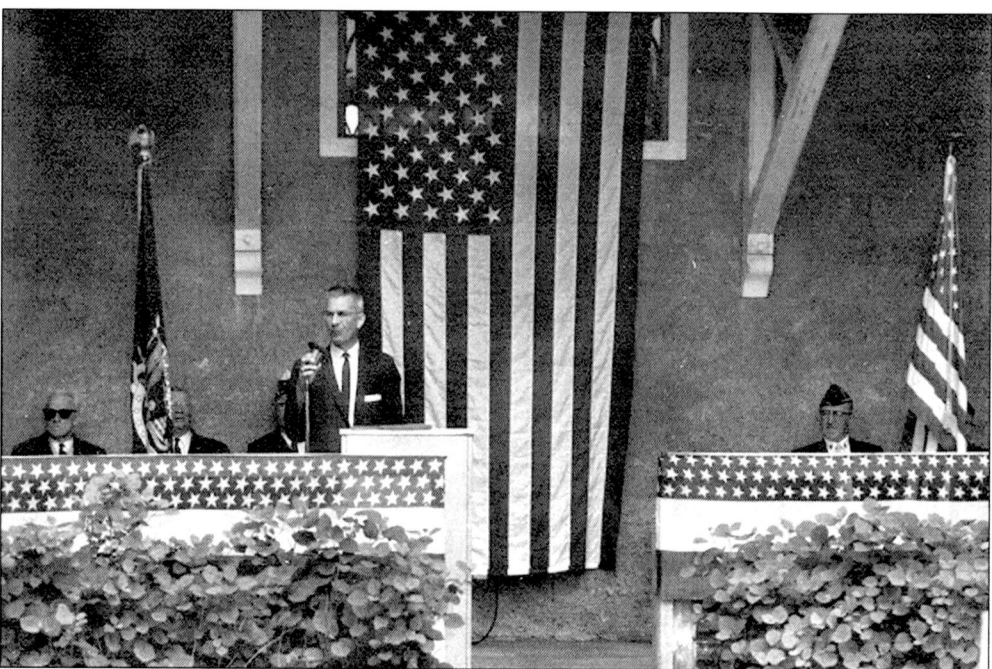

MEMORIAL DAY IN THE CEMETERY. Each year on Memorial Day, the day is set aside to honor this country's veterans, living or dead. The American flag is honored as well as the veteran. Memorial Day is still celebrated this way today at the Home.

MEMORIAL DAY 1964. A guest speaker is the guest of honor each year at the Home on Memorial Day. The deeds of our veterans are praised by a series of speakers, honor guards, and the public.

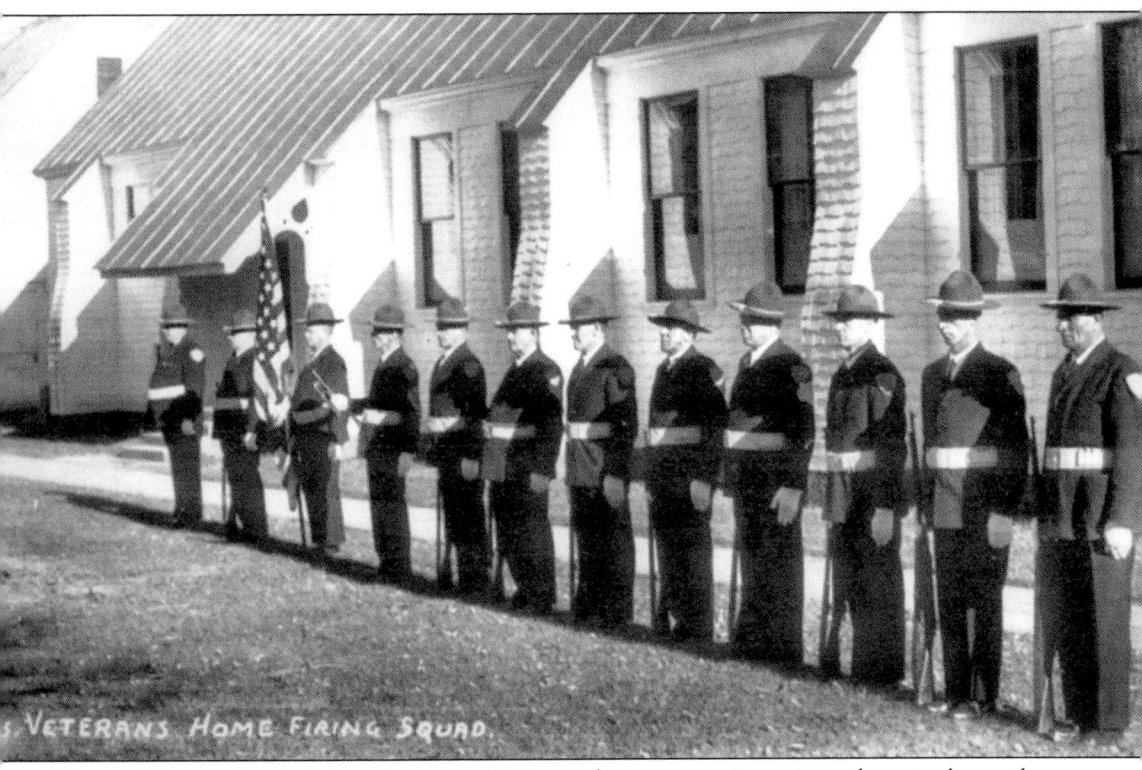

HONOR GUARD. As the Home has up to 800 members at any given time, there is always the aspect of a death of a veteran. Military funerals are almost a daily event. The Honor Guard escorts the caskets of their fellow members, helps perform in the military rites at the gravesite, and serves as the Color Guard for the flag during parades.

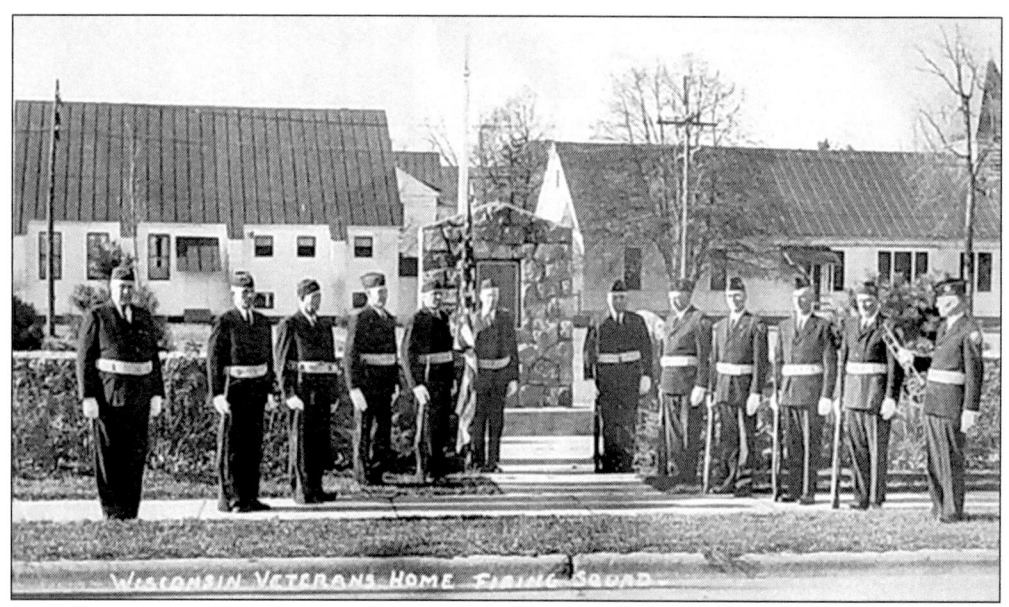

ANOTHER HONOR GUARD. These men serve with pride as Honor Guards for their fellow members. It is a job taken very seriously.

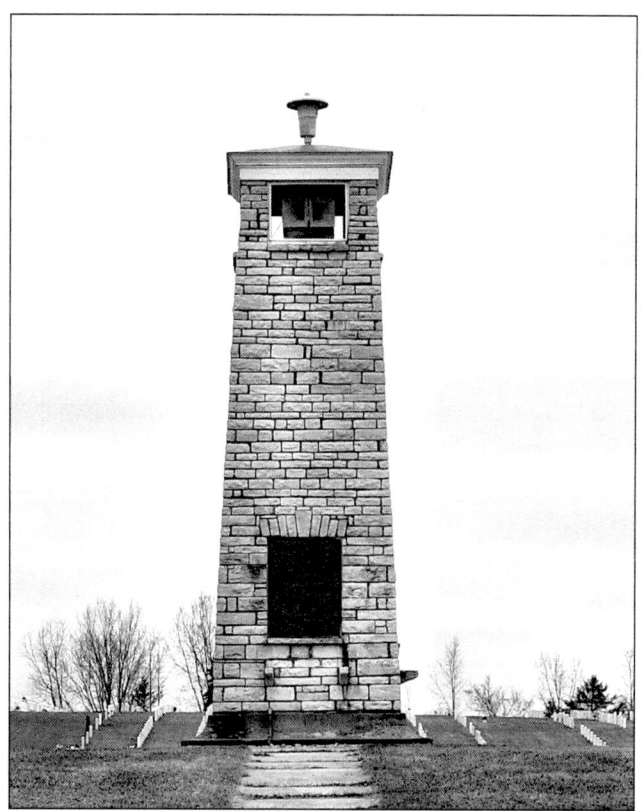

CEMETERY TOWER. This monument was build as a monument to all that served this country. It also includes the mothers of the veterans. The monument is on the highest ground of the cemetery and is still there today.

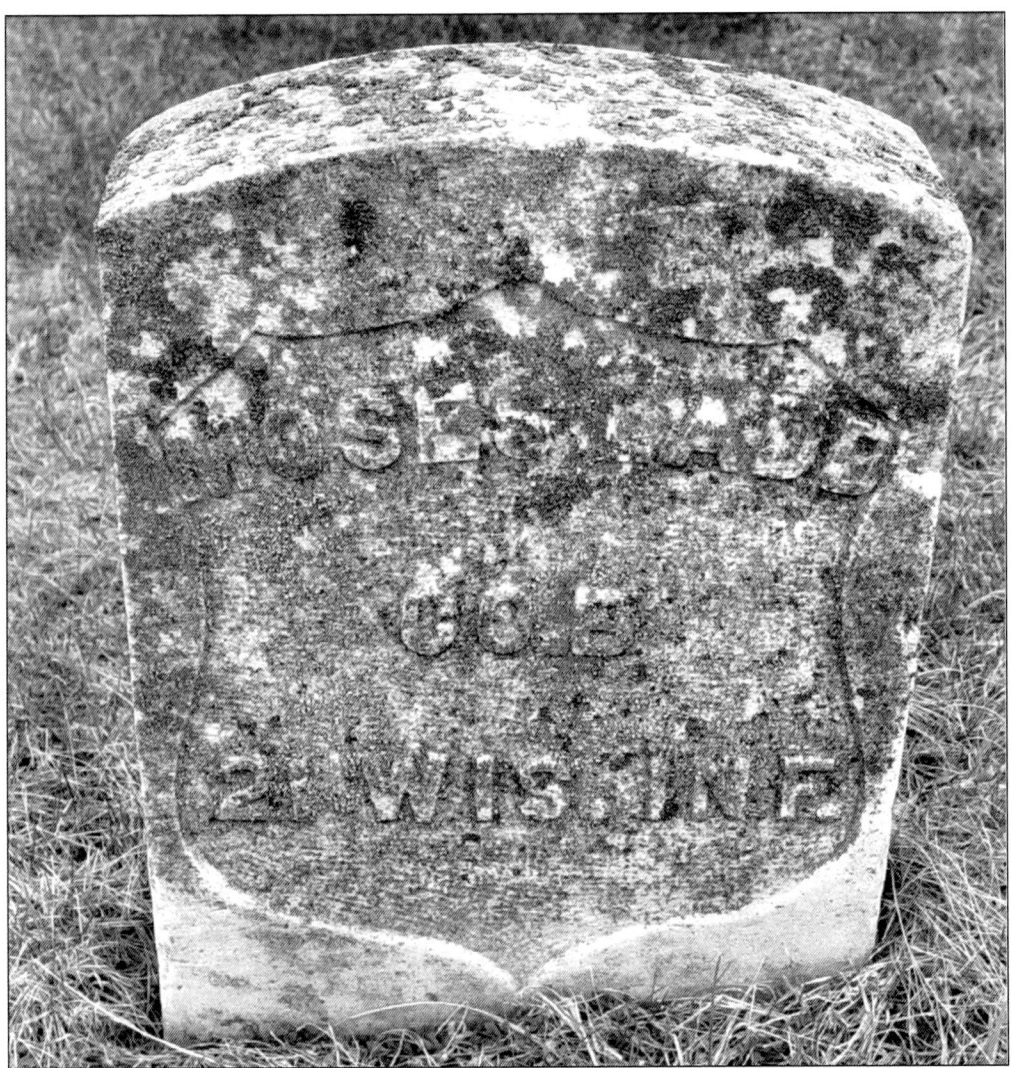

SOME ARE FAMOUS. This is the headstone marker for Moses Ladd, Company B, of the 21st Regiment of the Wisconsin Volunteers. A Menominee Indian, Moses served as the Chief Scout for General William T. Sherman during the March to the Sea. He scouted the right flank. He performed his job so well that General Sherman came to Omro, Wisconsin in 1870, just to offer him a house in Washington D.C. as a reward for his service during the Civil War. Moses turned the offer down, saying he could not leave his hunting and fishing grounds in the town of Poygan. He went on to become a chief for the Menominee tribe in the late 1870s and was part of the delegation that was sent to Washington D.C. There were four photographs taken of Moses while he was in D.C. The Smithsonian Institute retains those photographs. He died in 1923 on his third stay at the Home and was honored at the 1923 Reunion of the 21st Regiment for his heroic deeds and good disposition. He is credited with saving the lives of several soldiers during battle.

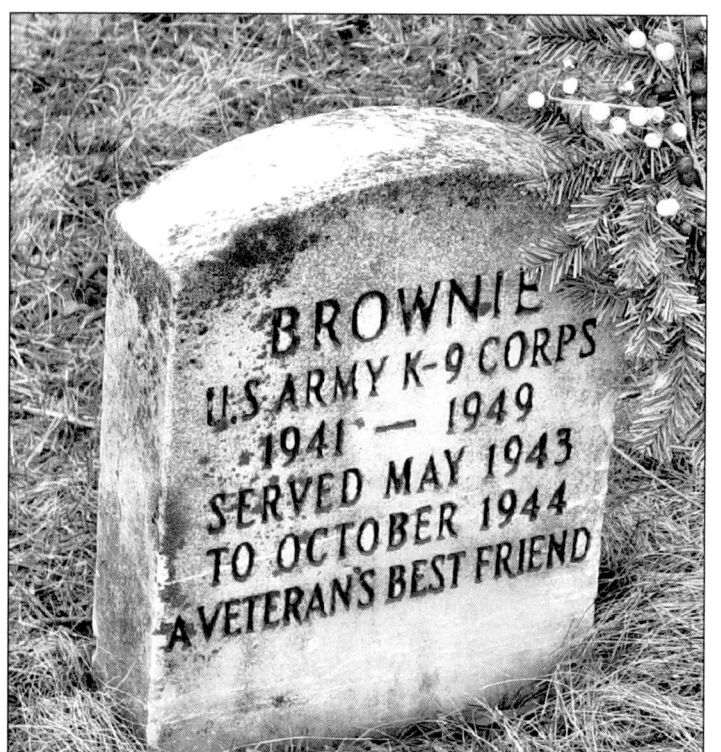

Brownie's Gravesite. Brownie's grave is shown here, the only animal buried in the cemetery. Brownie was a sentry dog in the Pacific during World War II and lost an eye while in the Army.

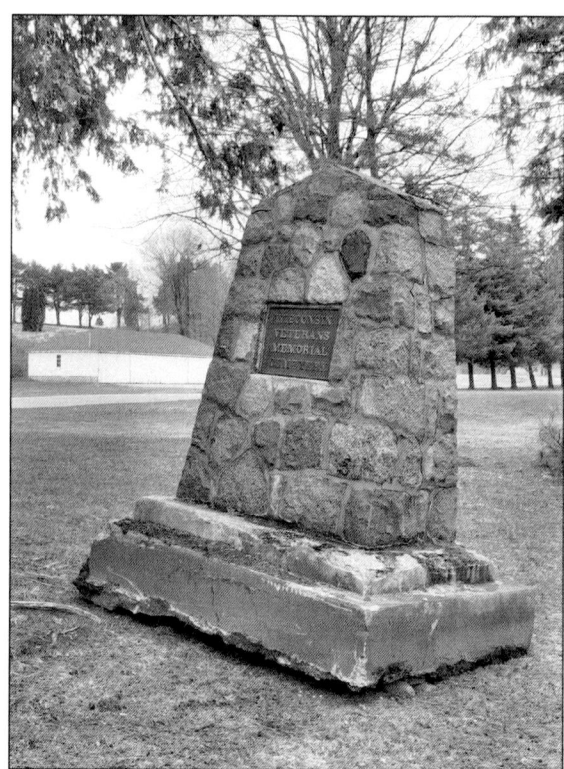

Cemetery Entrance. Stone posts greet the visitors to the cemetery. They were removed last year during a street widening.

Five

THE WATERFRONT

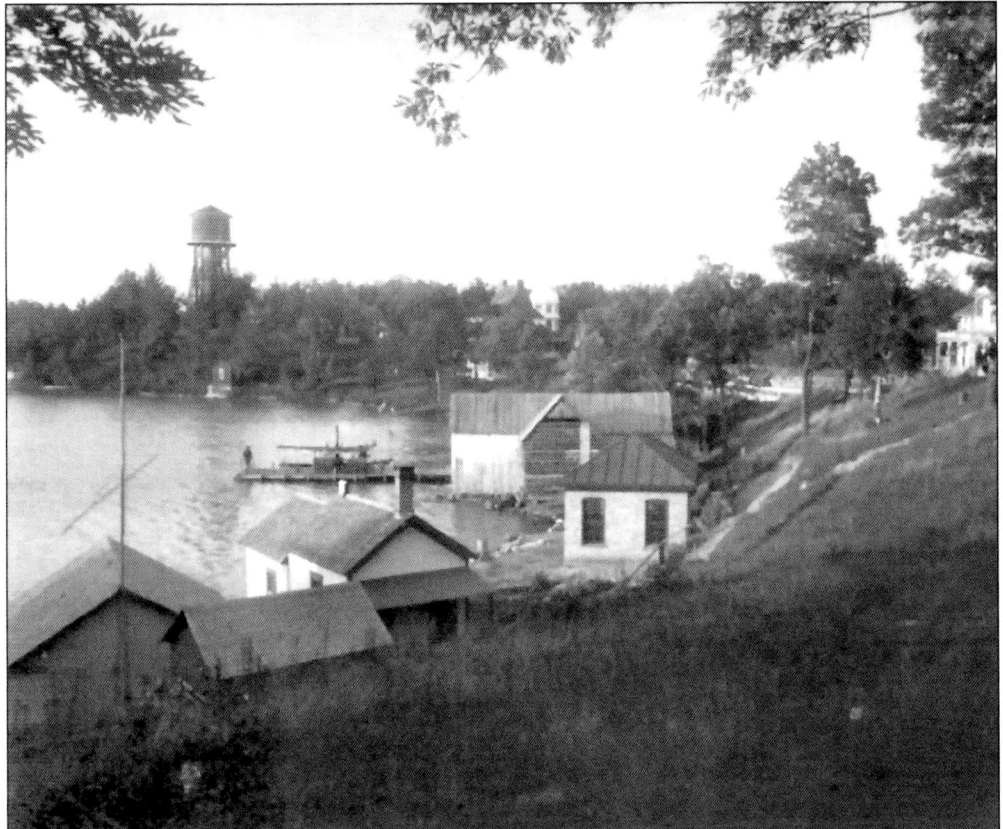

EARLY LAKESIDE (c. 1910). This photo was taken in the first decade of the 20th century or in 1910 from the shoreline of Rainbow Lake. It shows the Pump House, boat houses, Marden Hall on the far right, the commandant's residence in the middle with its white tower, and the first water tower of the Home. This view also shows the slope from Marden Hall to Rainbow Lake. The photo would have been taken from in front of the nurses' residence area.

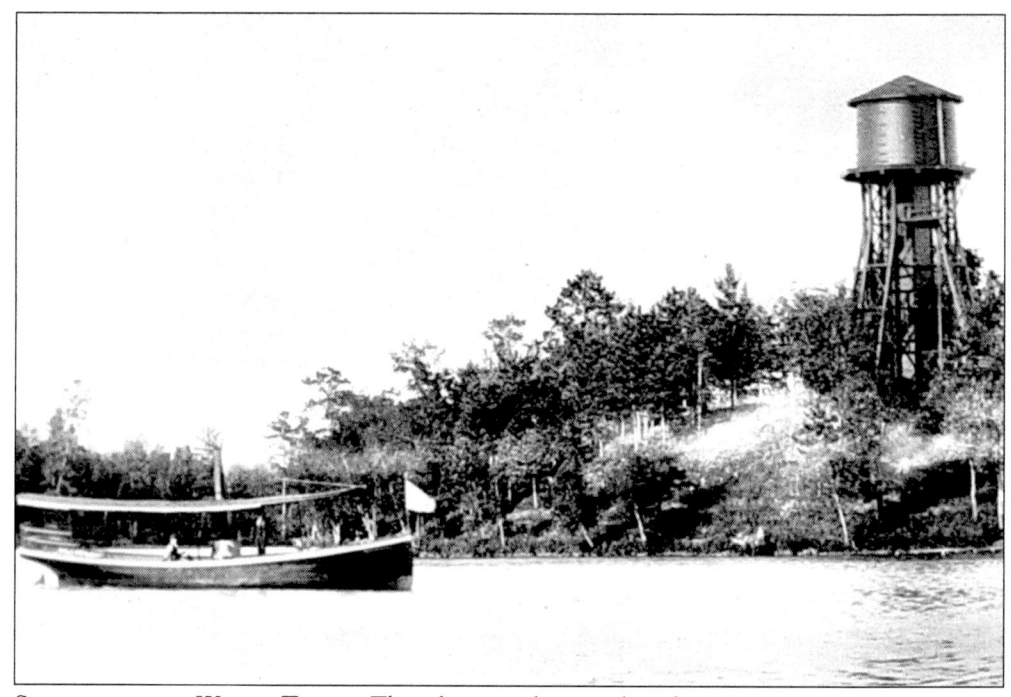

STEAMBOAT AND WATER TOWER. This photograph was taken from a 1915 album. There were several of the small steam-powered boats on the Chain O' Lakes during the early 20th century. The rivets on the water tower are visible in this photograph. It was once thought that the tower was wood. This photograph cleared that up.

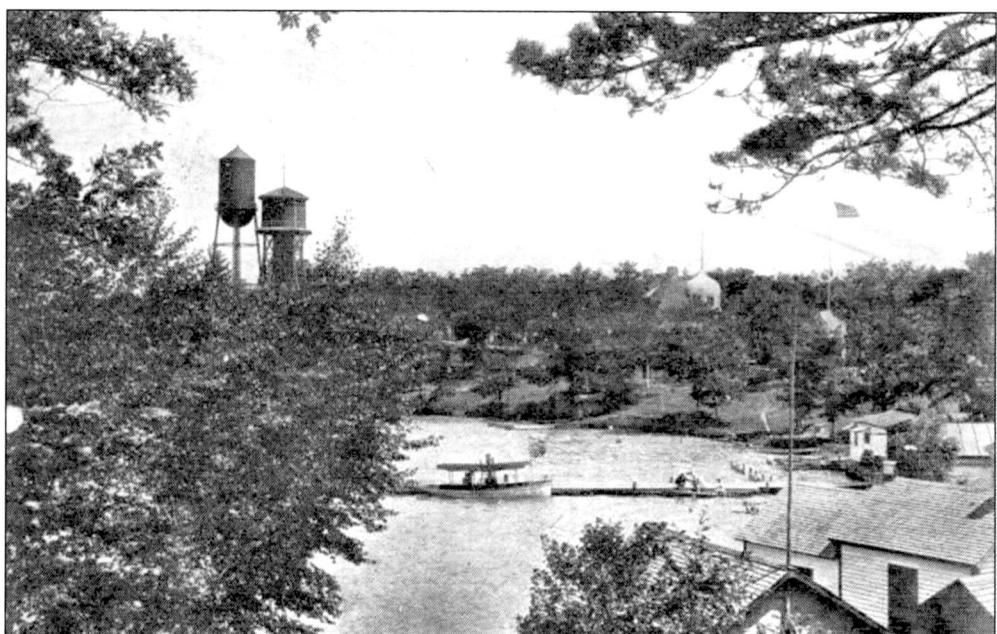

TWO WATER TOWERS. This 1911 post card view shows a rare photograph of two water towers. The smaller water tower was later torn down. Most of the other views from this angle only show one or the other water tower.

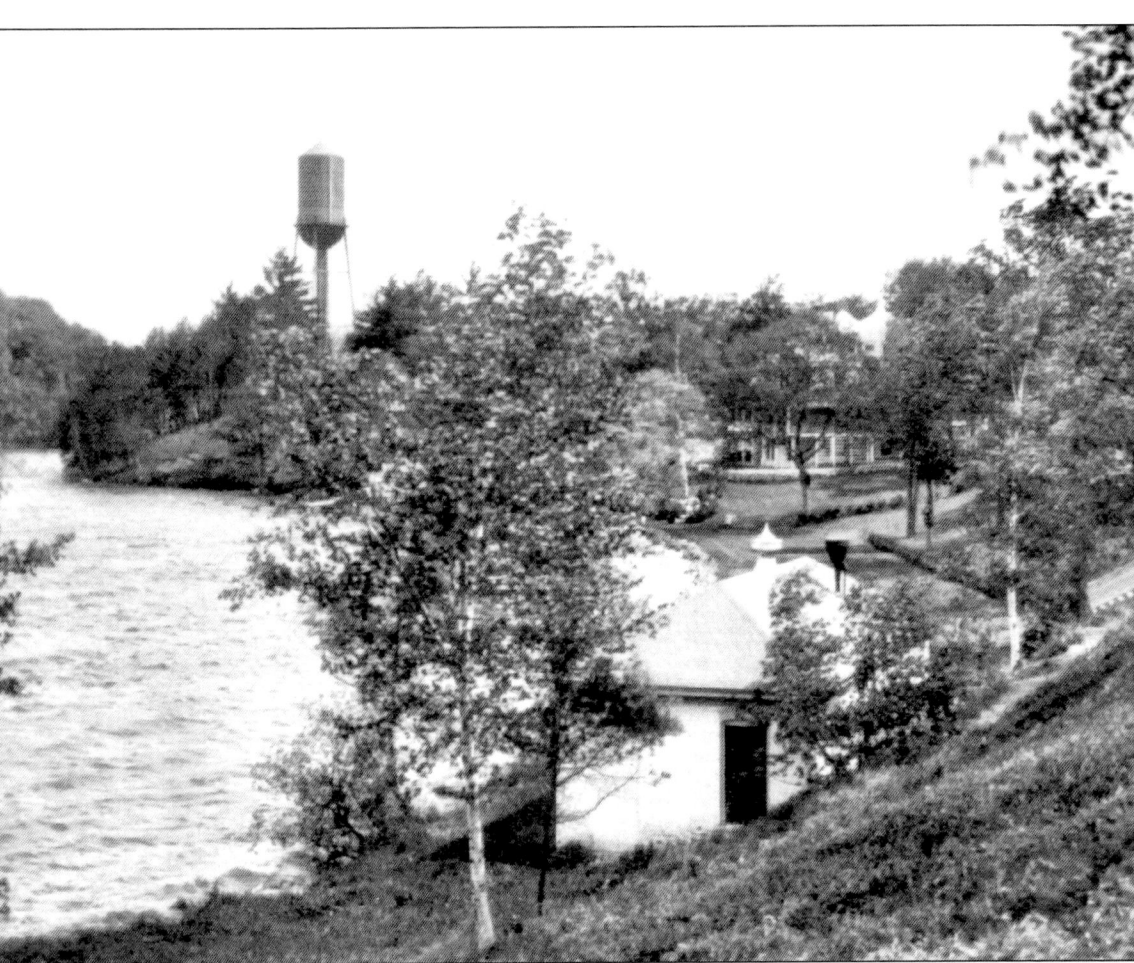

LAKESIDE VIEW OF THE HOME. Taken from the shoreline of Rainbow Lake, this picture shows the Pump House and the second water tower at the Home. The water tower had a 30,000-gallon capacity to supply the needs of the Home. It replaced the tower as seen in one of the other lakeside views. The commandants residence can be seen in the middle of the photo.

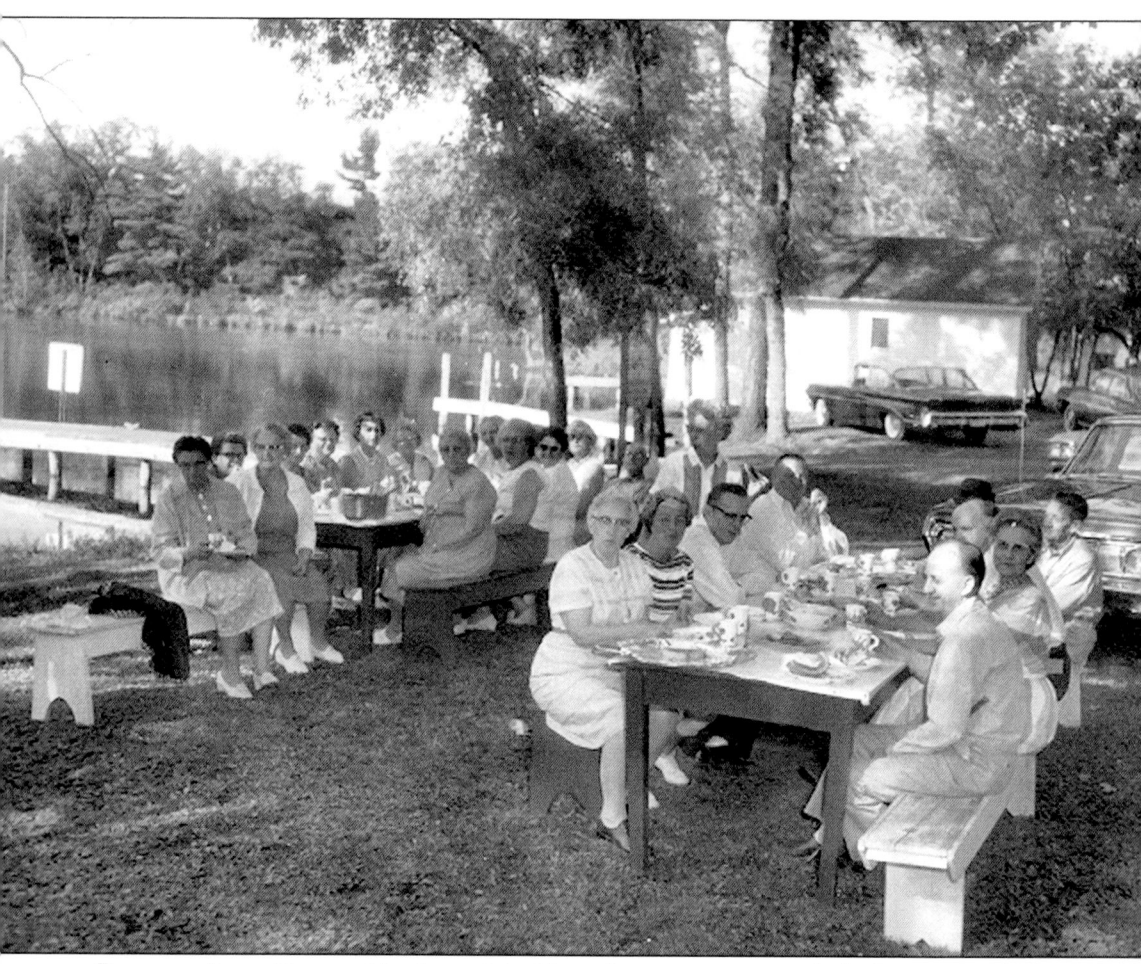

PICNIC ON LAKE GEORGE. Members of the Home have an area set aside for boat use and fishing. Located near the Ice House, the picnic tables are being used for a small get together. Lake George is located north of Rainbow Lake between the Home and Government Island (once called Home Island).

Six
NATIONAL HISTORIC DISTRICT AND COTTAGES

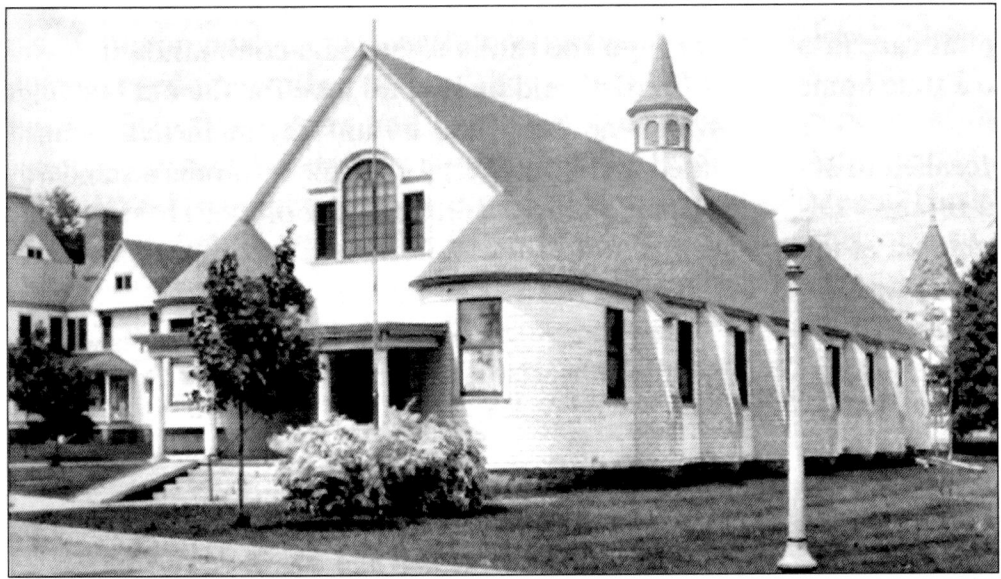

AMUSEMENT HALL. The Amusement Hall, a wooden-framed structure built in 1895, was the entertainment arena for the Home. Made up of a main floor with a stage on the north end, the building also had dressing rooms. The main area could seat 500 people if needed. The building had a balcony and a movie projection room above the first floor. The basement had a kitchen and dining room.

Dances were popular, as were plays and movies. As television got to be more popular, there was a decline in people going to the movies at the Amusement Hall. Soon the community was using the hall more than the Home members.

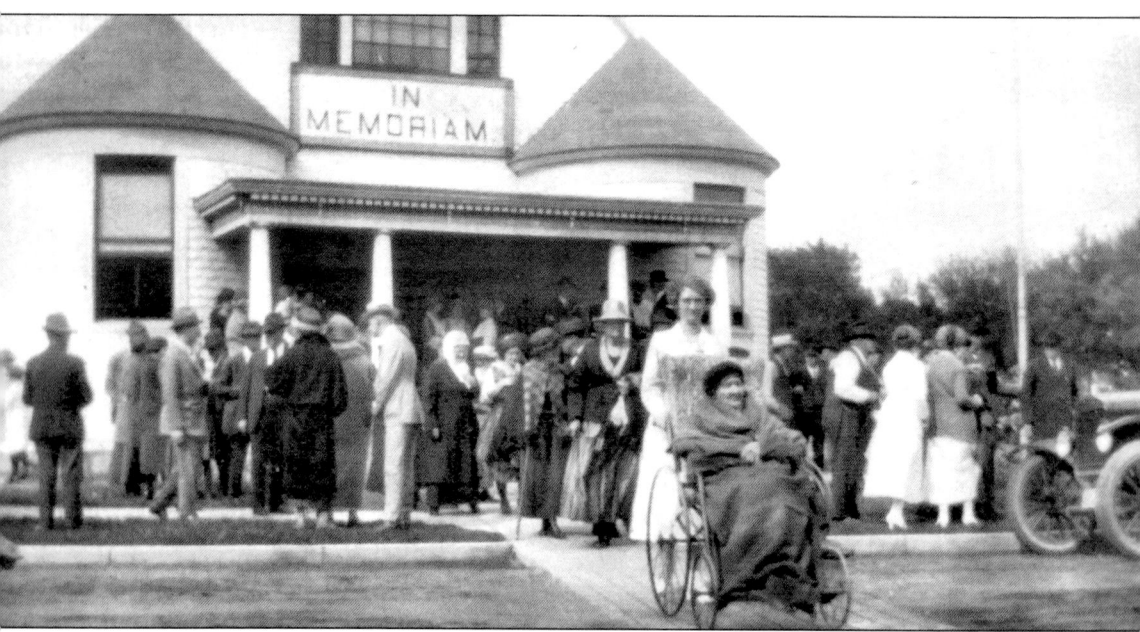

AMUSEMENT HALL MEMORIAL DAY 1923. This is a view of members gathered in front of the Amusement Hall, which is decorated for Memorial Day 1923. A nurse pushes a member in a wheelchair, while a Model T is parked on the right. Notice the cobblestone for the walkway across the street.

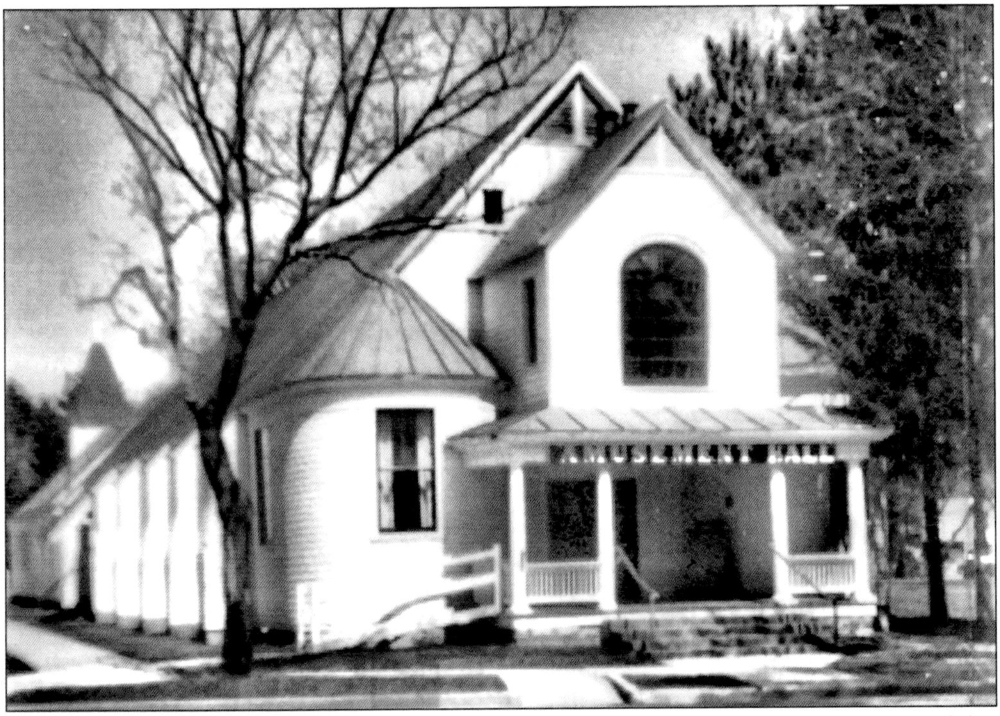

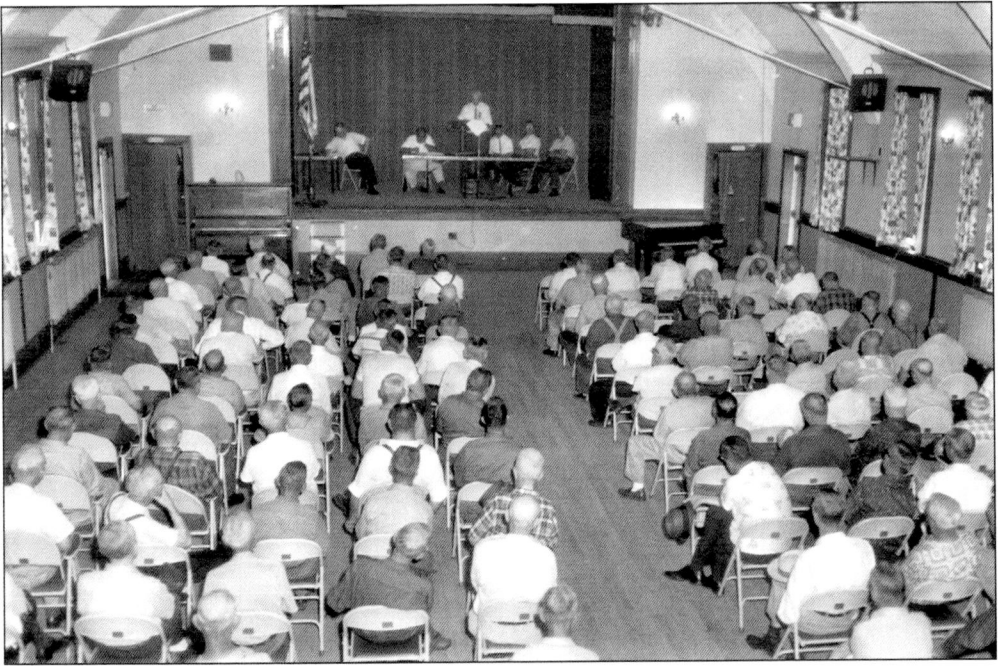

AMUSEMENT HALL WITH SIGN. There were several changes to the outside appearance of this hall. Here, the building is identified with the nameplate above the entrance.

AMUSEMENT HALL INTERIOR. The interior was used for parties, plays, movies, etc. Notice that the members are sitting on portable chairs. They can be put away and the floor can then be used for dancing.

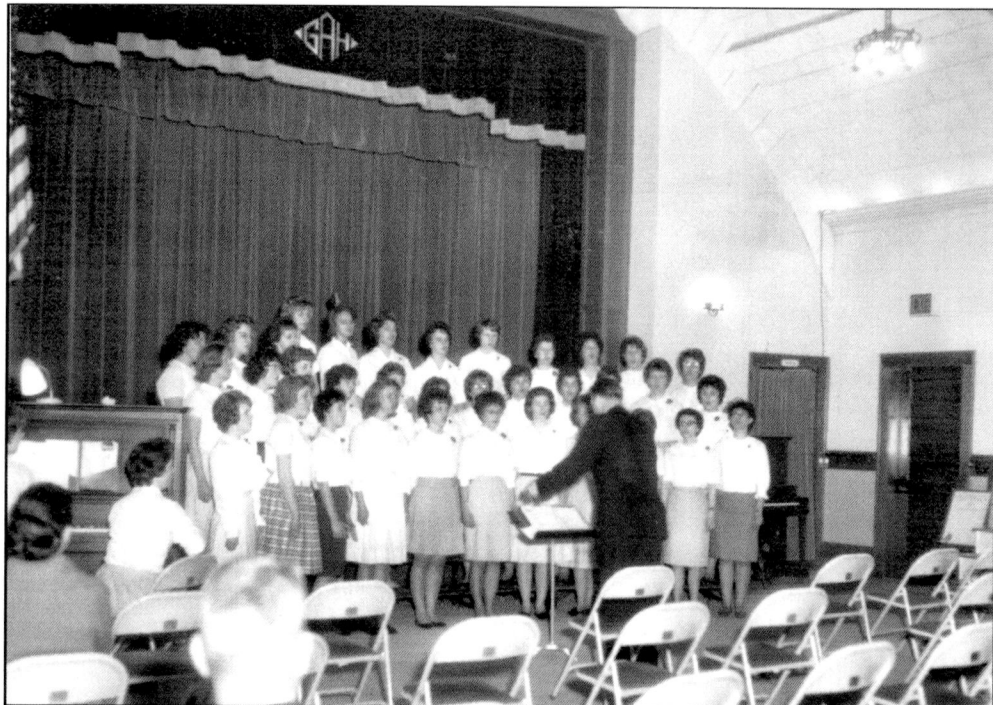

ANOTHER INTERIOR VIEW. The Amusement Hall was used for numerous events. Here, the girls practice for one of the shows. Notice the stage area and the curtain. GAH, which stands for Grand Army Home, is on the curtain above the girls.

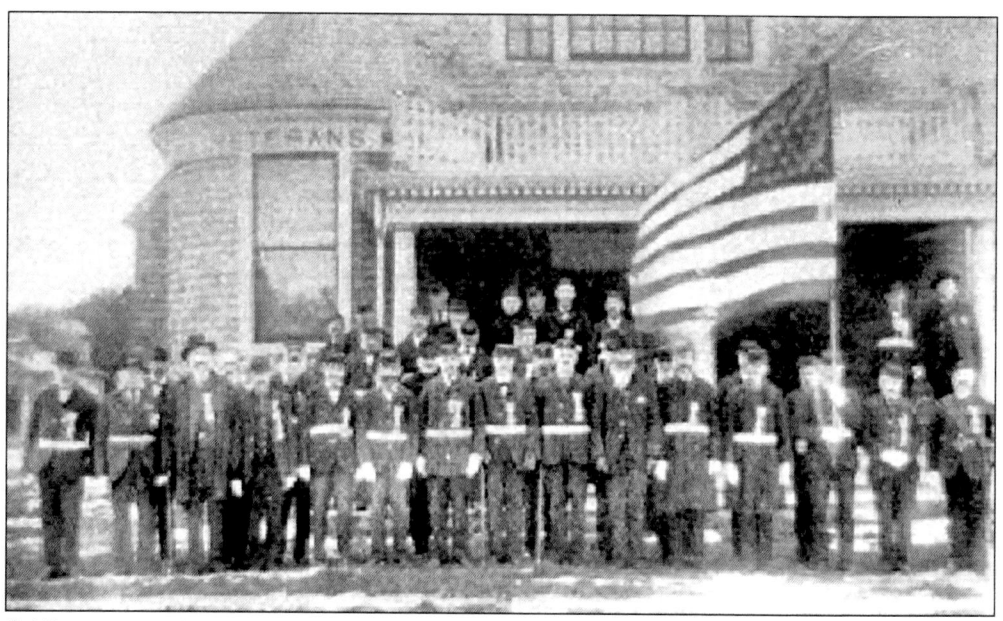

GAR AND THE AMUSEMENT HALL. Either a reunion of one of the Wisconsin Regiments or a Memorial Day was celebrated at the Home in this image. The soldiers are standing in front of the Amusement Hall wearing ribbons and badges. As always, the 36-star American flag is waved proudly, a flag they helped preserve.

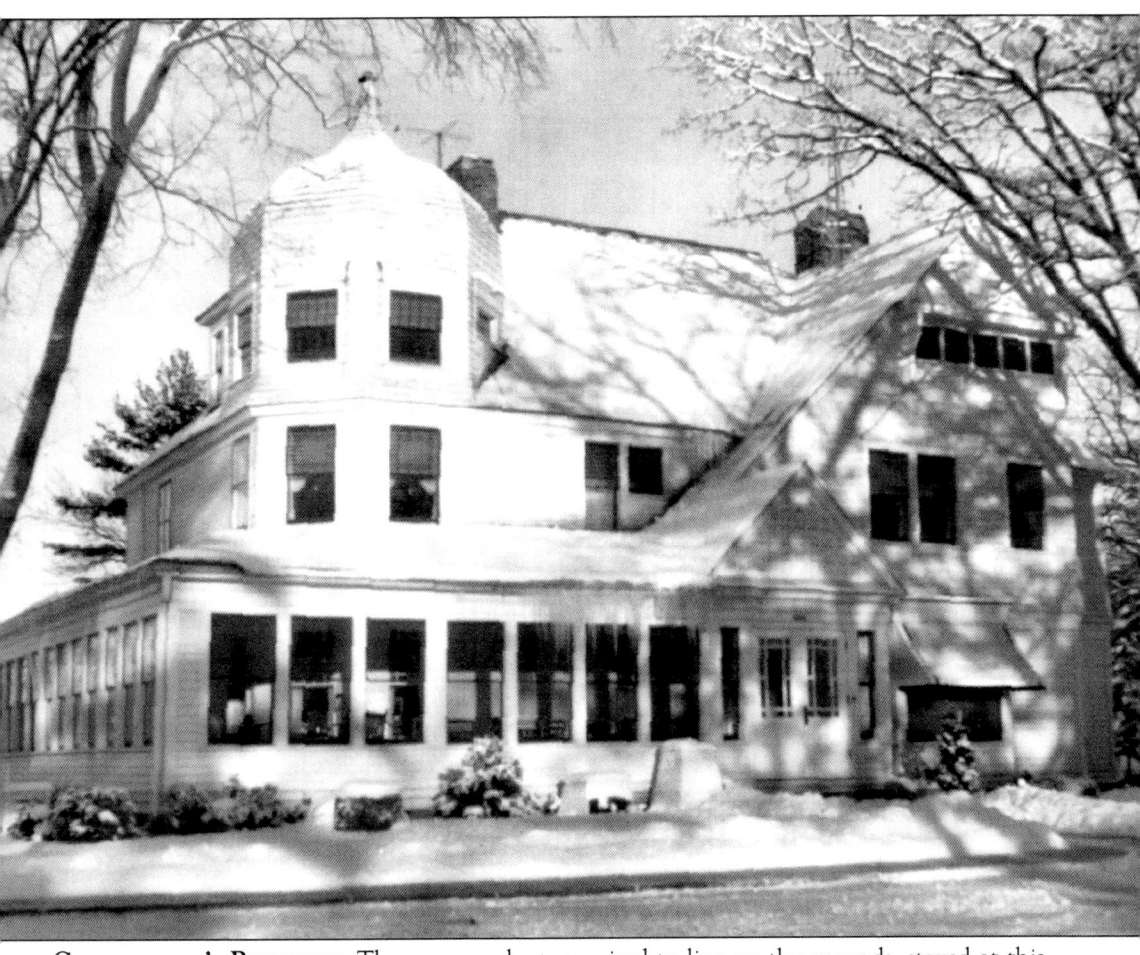

COMMANDANT'S RESIDENCE. The commandant, required to live on the grounds, stayed at this building. It is located on the raised shoreline of Rainbow Lake, with one of the nicest views of the lake from this location at the back of the house. The front overlooked the Headquarters office and the park. The building was located at the corner of Marden Avenue and Lake Street. The wrap-around porch was originally open.

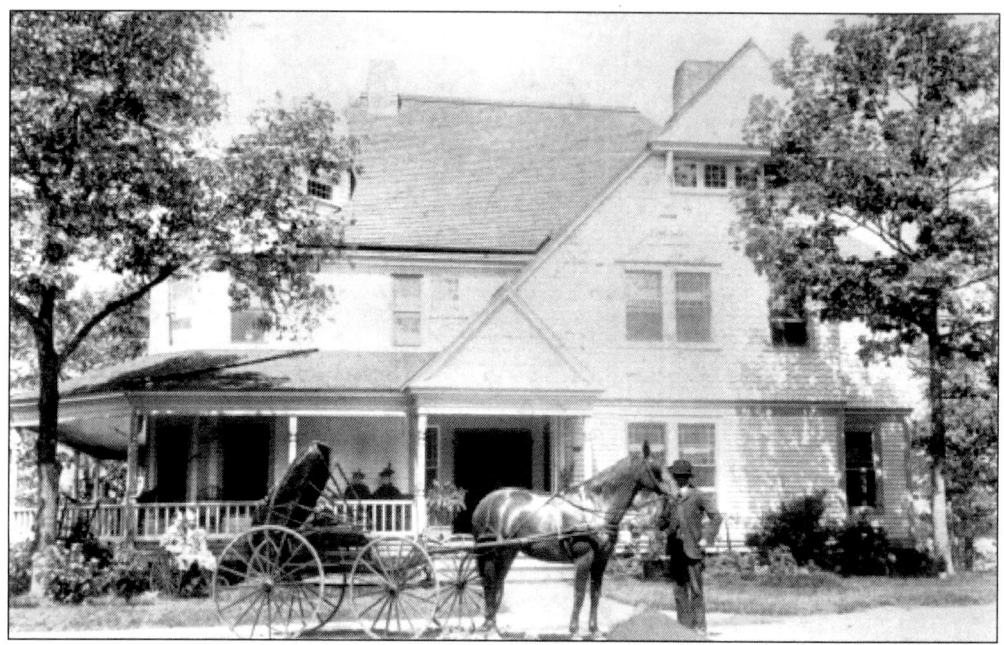

COMMANDANT'S OPEN PORCH. This is an early view of the commandant's residence while it had an open porch. Barely visible is the third-floor tower on the house. One large room was used for board meetings. There were also sleeping rooms for board members while on business at the Home.

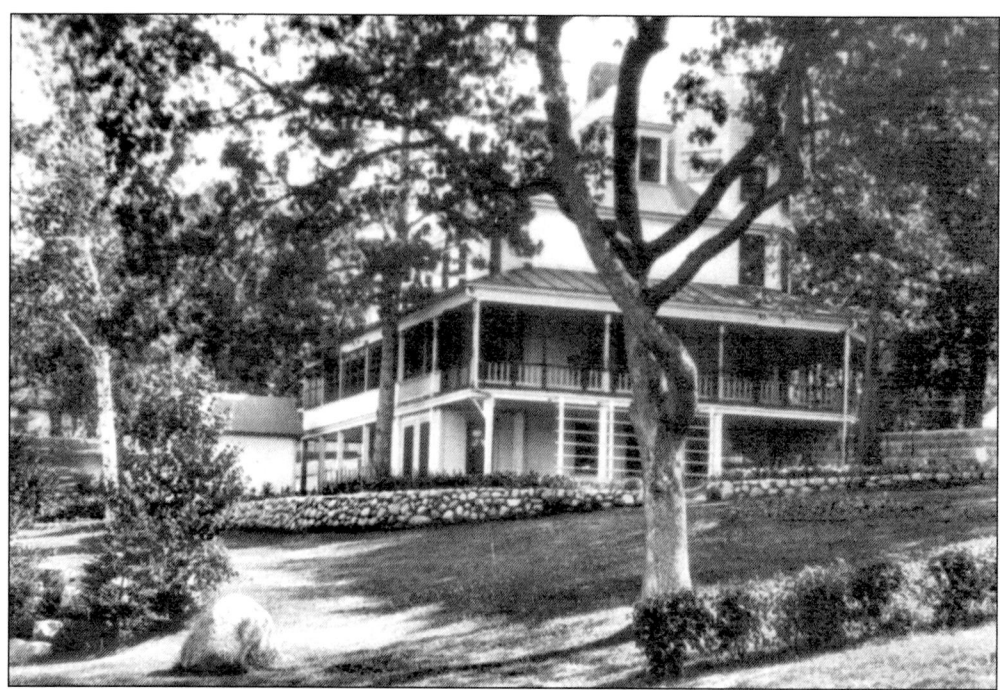

COMMANDANT'S RESIDENCE FROM THE LAKE. This view shows the back yard of the commandant's residence with the stonewall ledge tapering to the front of the building. As the back yard slopes down to Rainbow Lake, the ledge is not only decorative but also functional. Always well groomed, the commandant's residence still remains impressive.

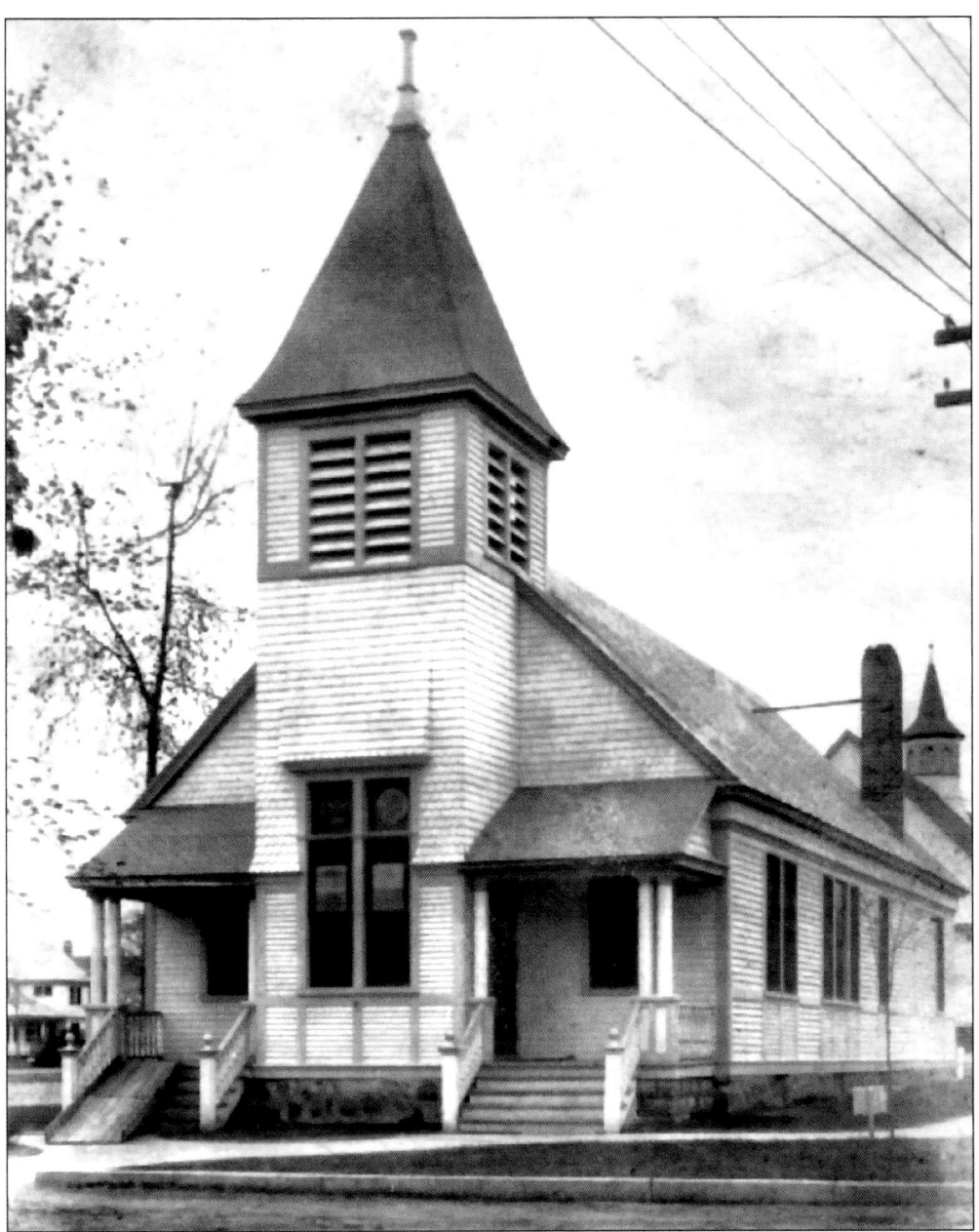

HOME CHAPEL. A gift in 1890 from the Women's Relief Corp, Wisconsin Department, the chapel was constructed at a cost of $3,256.50. This building was basically taken care of by the WRC alone. In 1914, they gave the gift of a "very fine communion service, individual glasses to the number of eighty." In 1915, they donated 50 folding chairs. 1918 was the year they installed indirect lighting and two electric fans. Later, stained glass windows were installed in the front windows. When the front porches were removed and the new entrance was made, the bottom sections of the windows were removed. The upper sections of the stained glass windows above the entrance are still there. The fire department had the duty to pick up the members and give them a ride to the chapel on Sundays. The building was built on Marden Avenue, a short way into the Home grounds. The building still stands today.

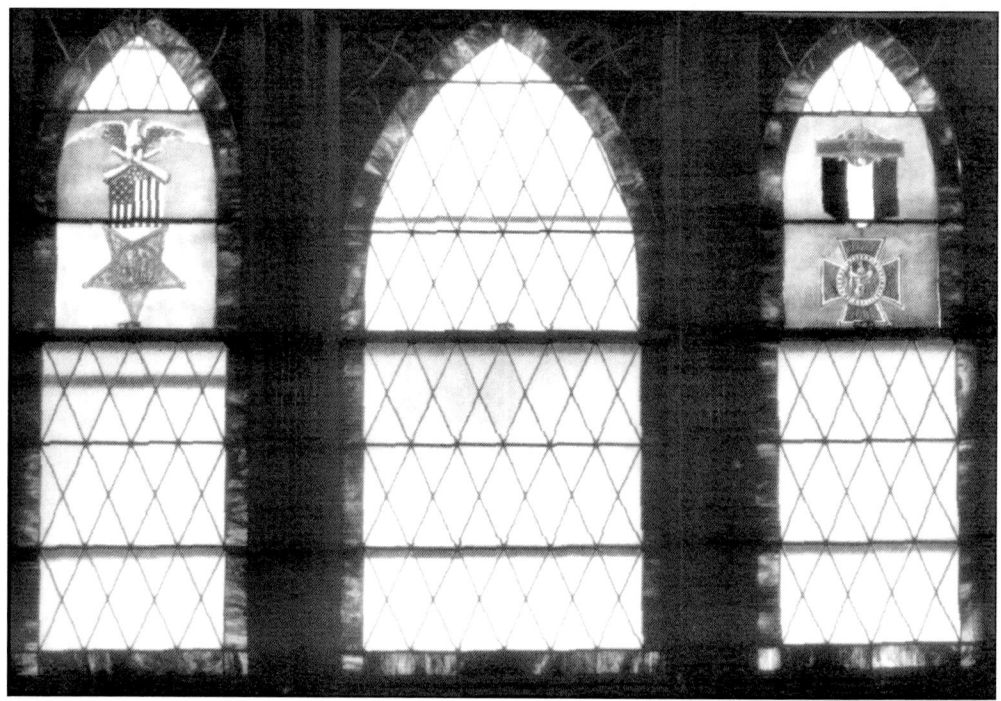

GAR AND WRC WINDOWS. The chapel, a gift from the Women's Relief Corp., has numerous stained glass windows. This window assembly, with both windows dedicated to the veteran groups, is rare. There are only about four other GAR windows in the state of Wisconsin. To have the WRC window aside the GAR window in the same building makes it extremely rare.

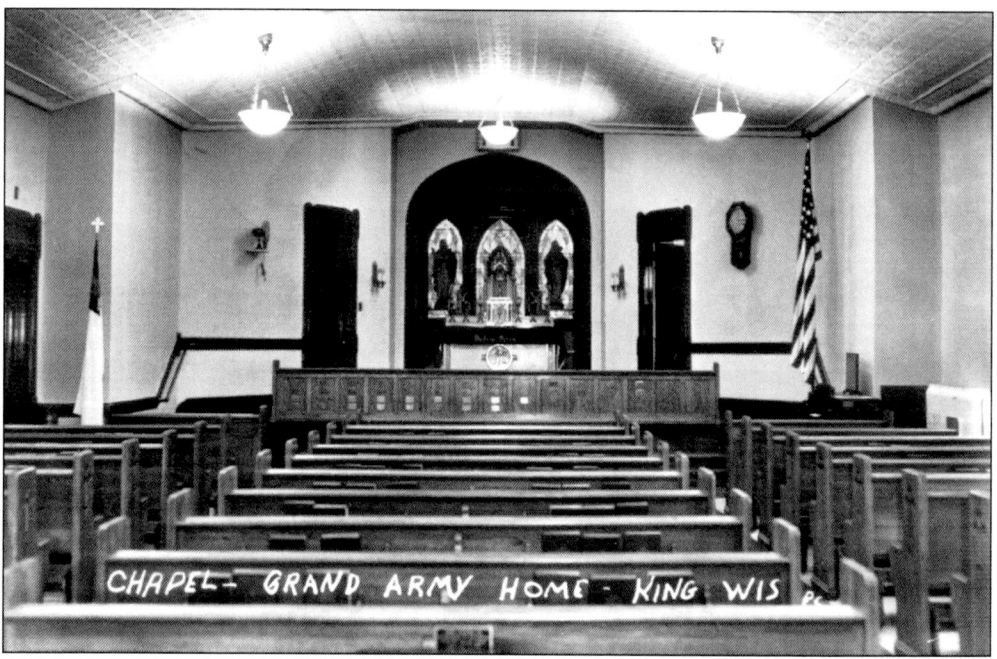

CHAPEL INTERIOR. This is a post card view of the Chapel. Hanging from the ceiling are the lights from the Women's Relief Corp.

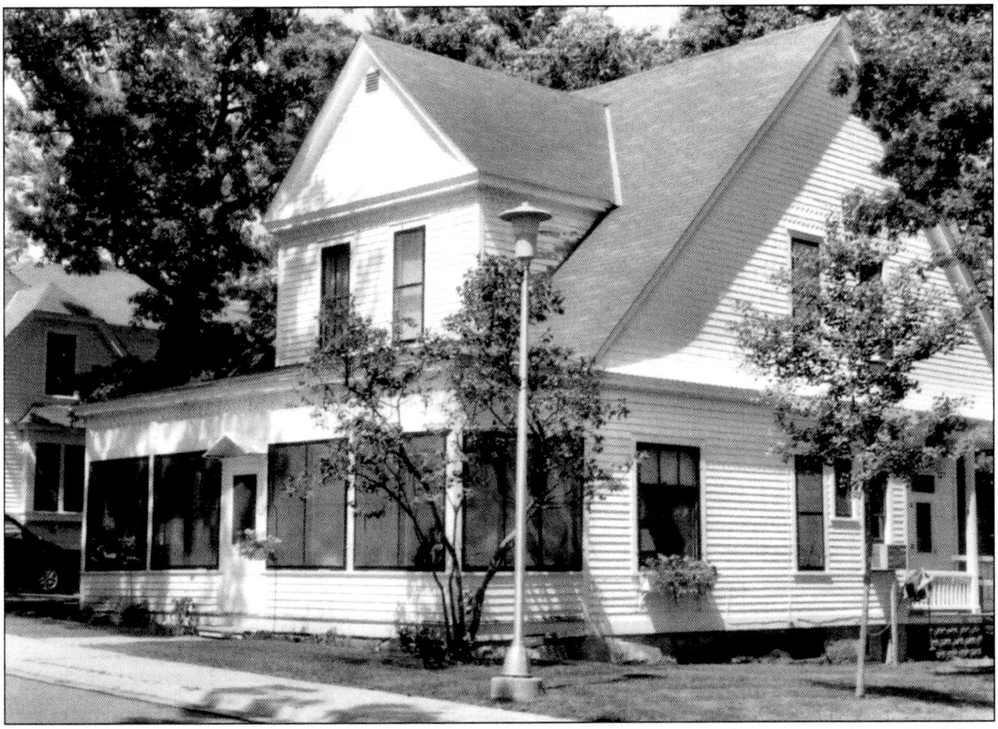

ADJUTANT'S RESIDENCE. The adjutant's residence was next to the Headquarters. This is Building Number 104. Later, at various times, the adjutant lived in different buildings.

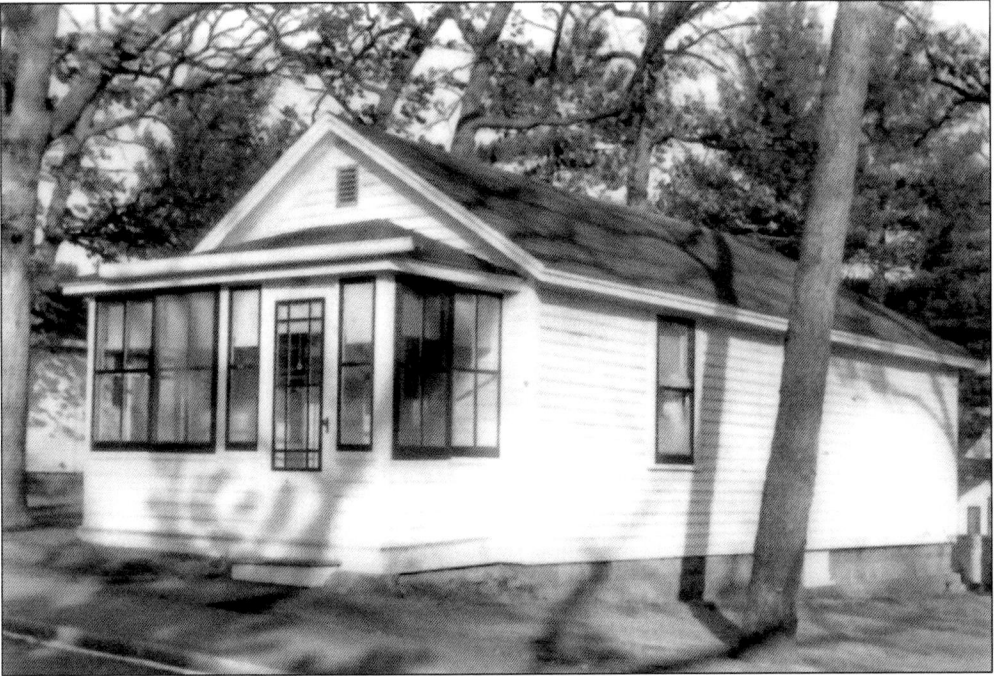

COTTAGE NUMBER 105. This building was removed. It once stood north of the adjutant's residence on Lake Street.

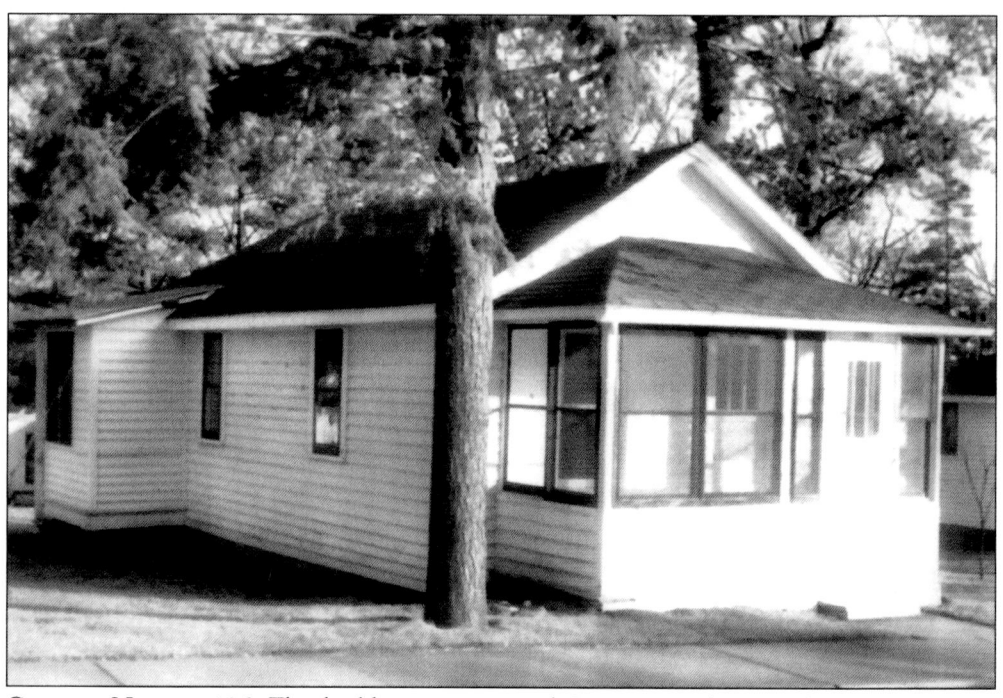

COTTAGE NUMBER 106. This building was removed. It once stood north of Cottage Number 105 on Lake Street.

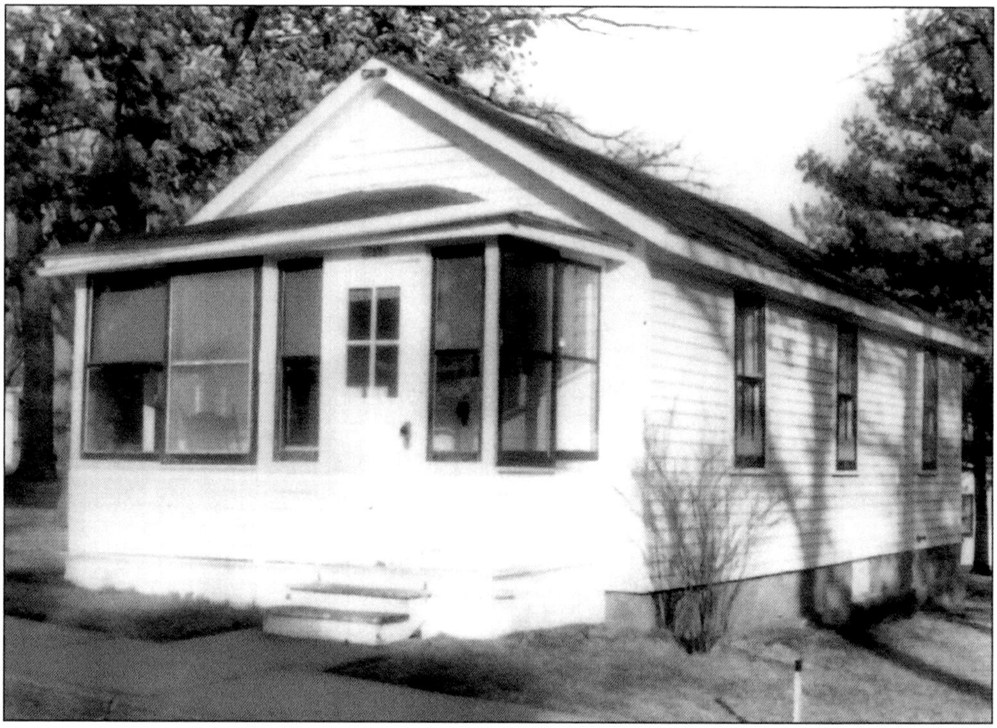

COTTAGE NUMBER 107. This building was removed. It was located north of Cottage Number 106 on Lake Street.

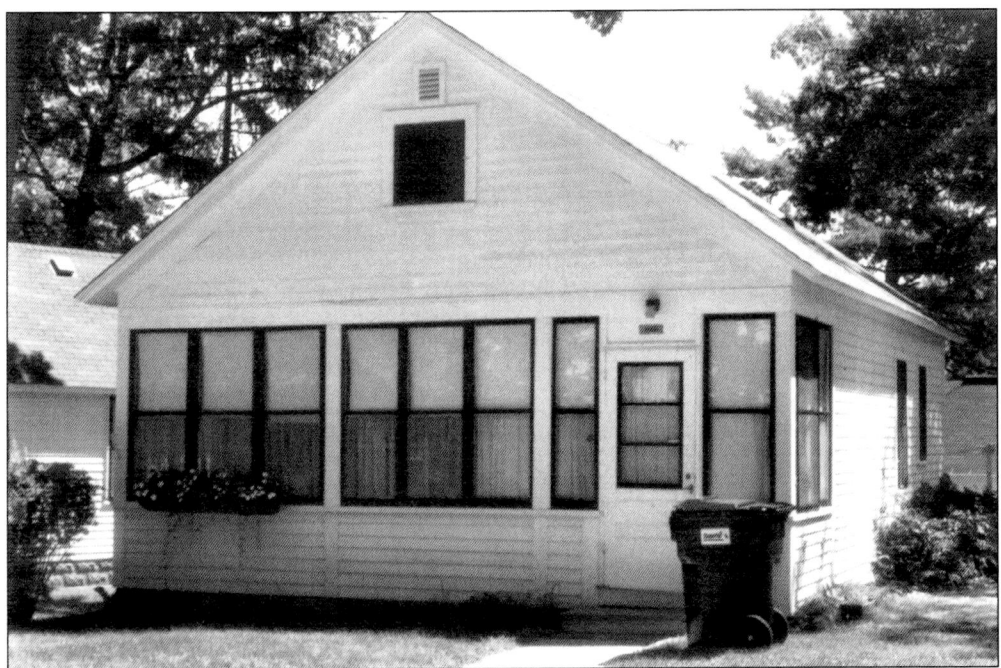

COTTAGE NUMBER 110. This cottage is located on present day Wright Avenue. It was not originally built there. It was moved there and saved from destruction.

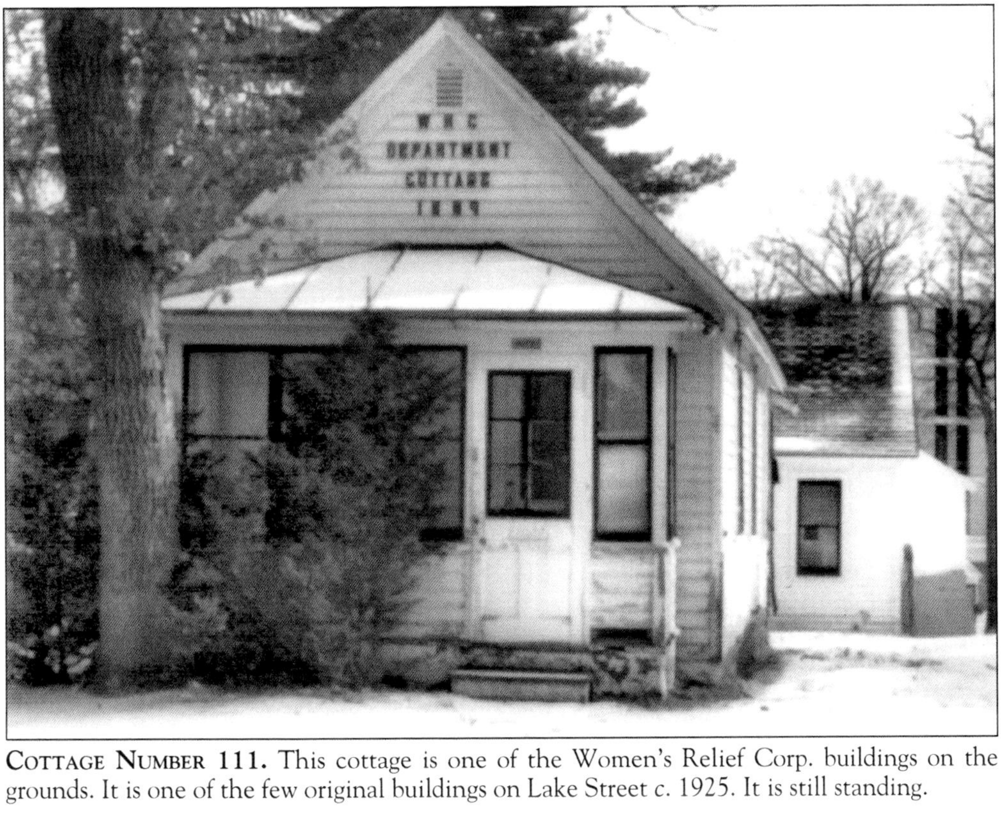

COTTAGE NUMBER 111. This cottage is one of the Women's Relief Corp. buildings on the grounds. It is one of the few original buildings on Lake Street c. 1925. It is still standing.

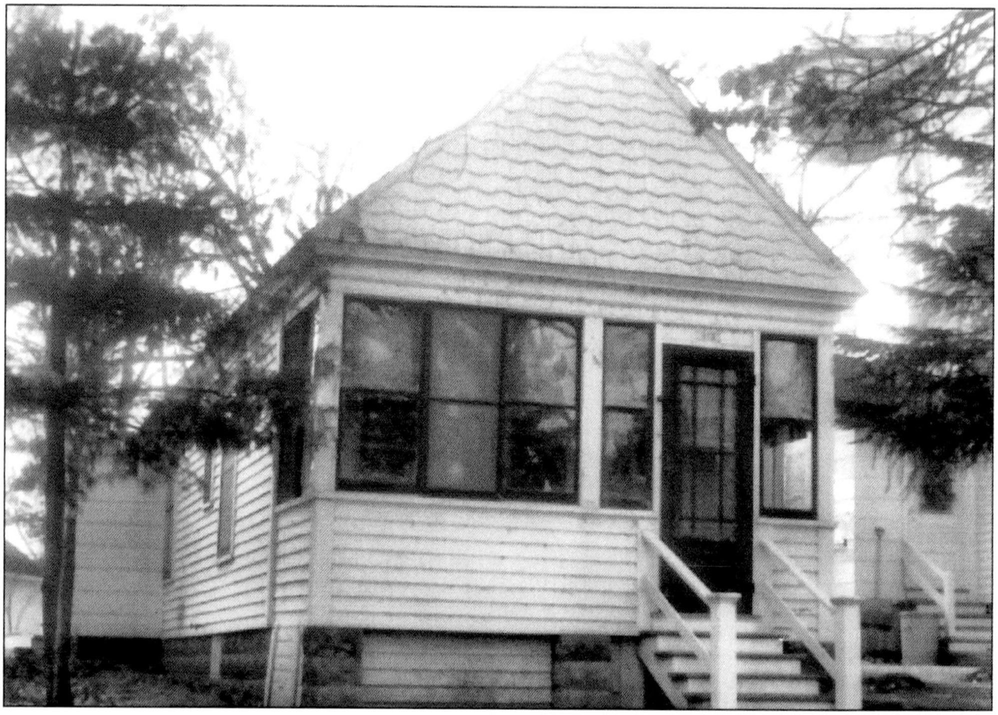

COTTAGE NUMBER 113. Cottage Number 113 was around the corner from Cottage Number 111, the WRC Cottage. It was on Wright Avenue and was torn down or removed. Cottage Number 414 is in that location now.

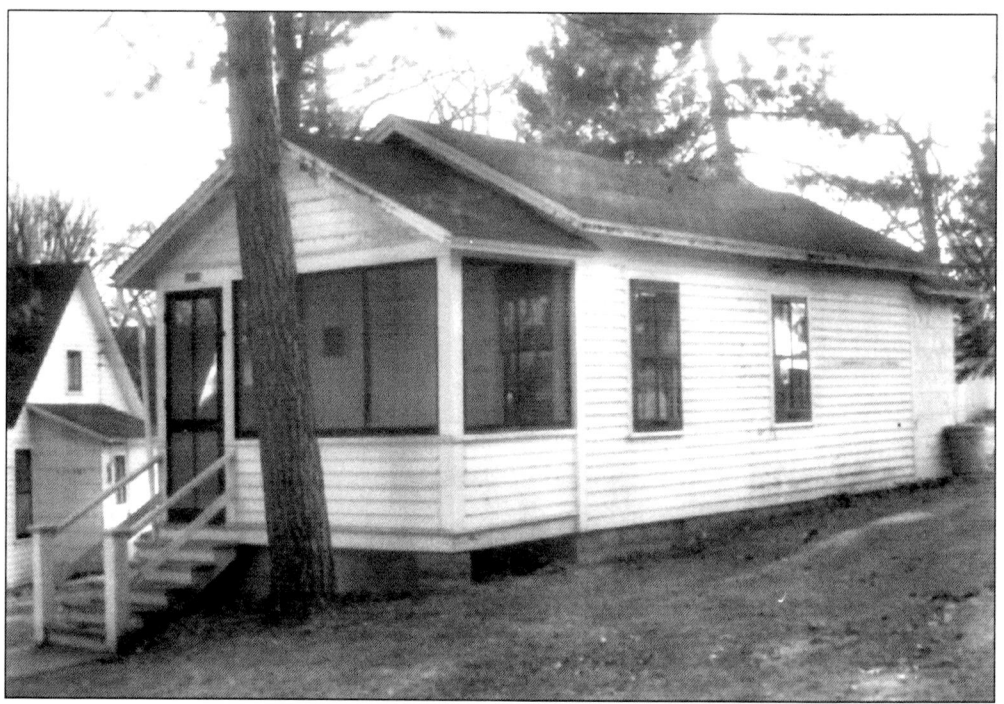

COTTAGE NUMBER 115. Cottage Number 115 was located on Wright Street. It has been removed.

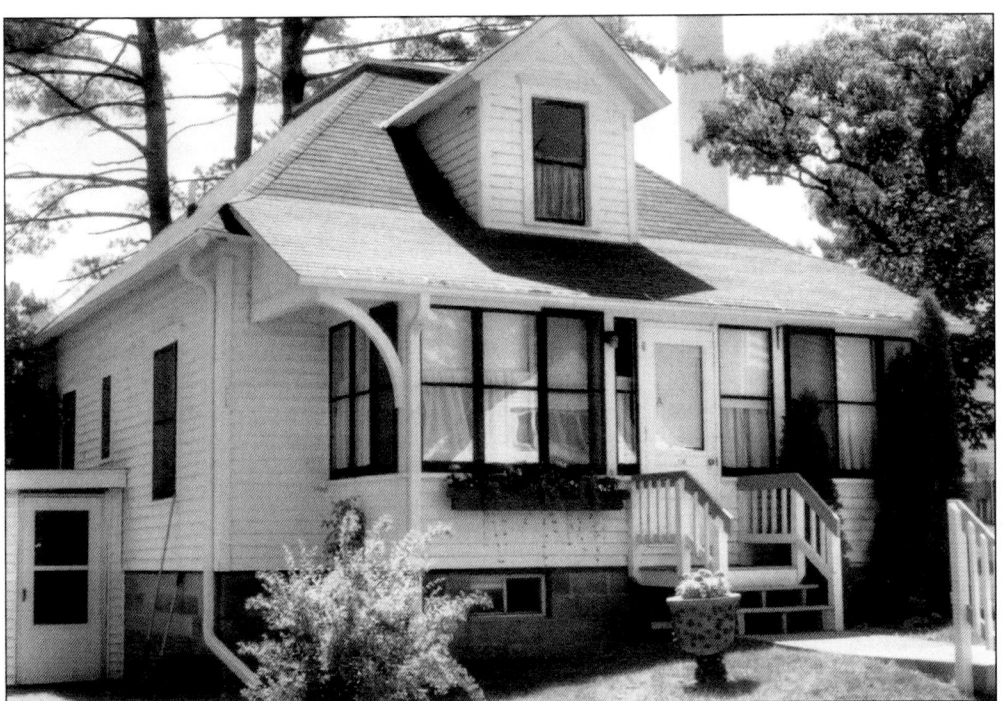

COTTAGE NUMBER 116. Cottage Number 116 was first located on the end of Milwaukee Avenue, where it met Lake Street. Later, the building was moved to Wright Street.

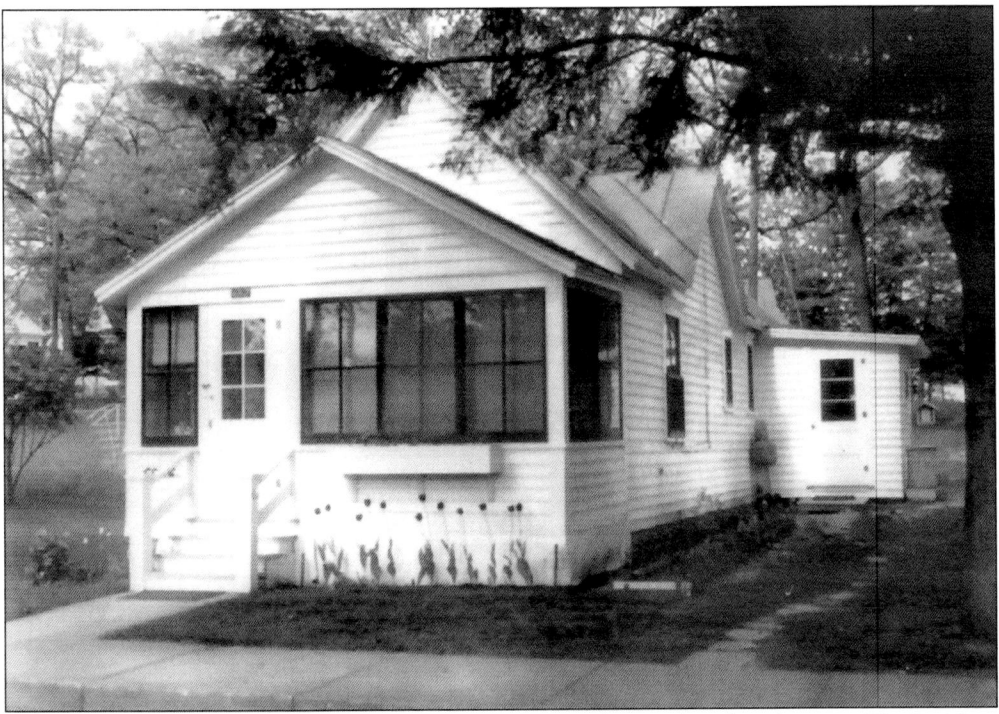

COTTAGE NUMBER 117. Cottage Number 117 was located on Milwaukee Avenue. The building was later removed.

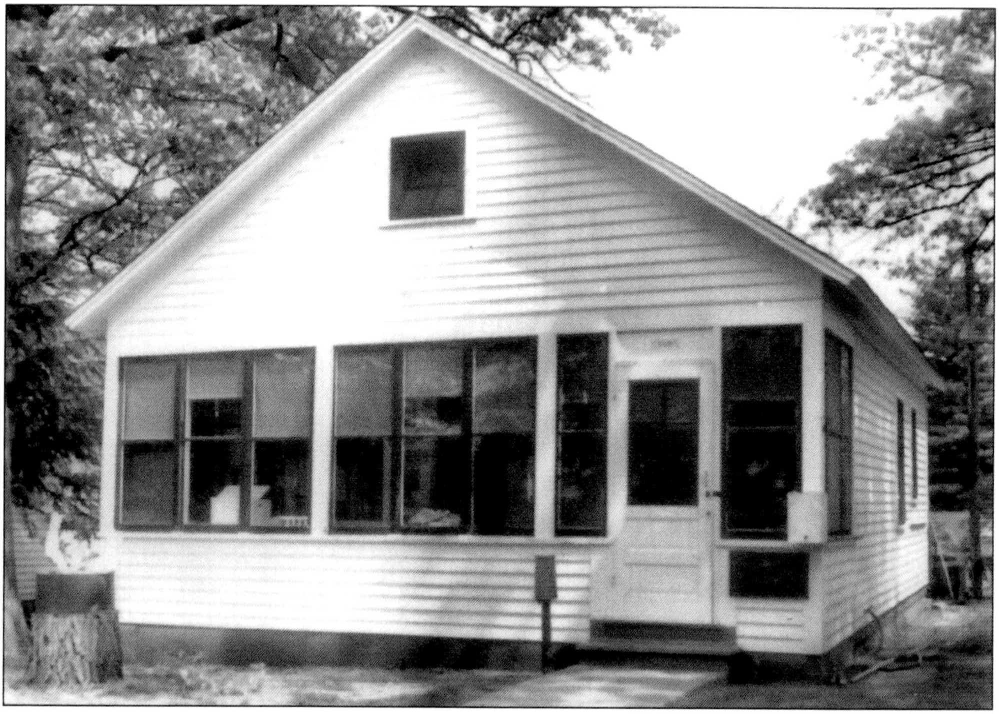

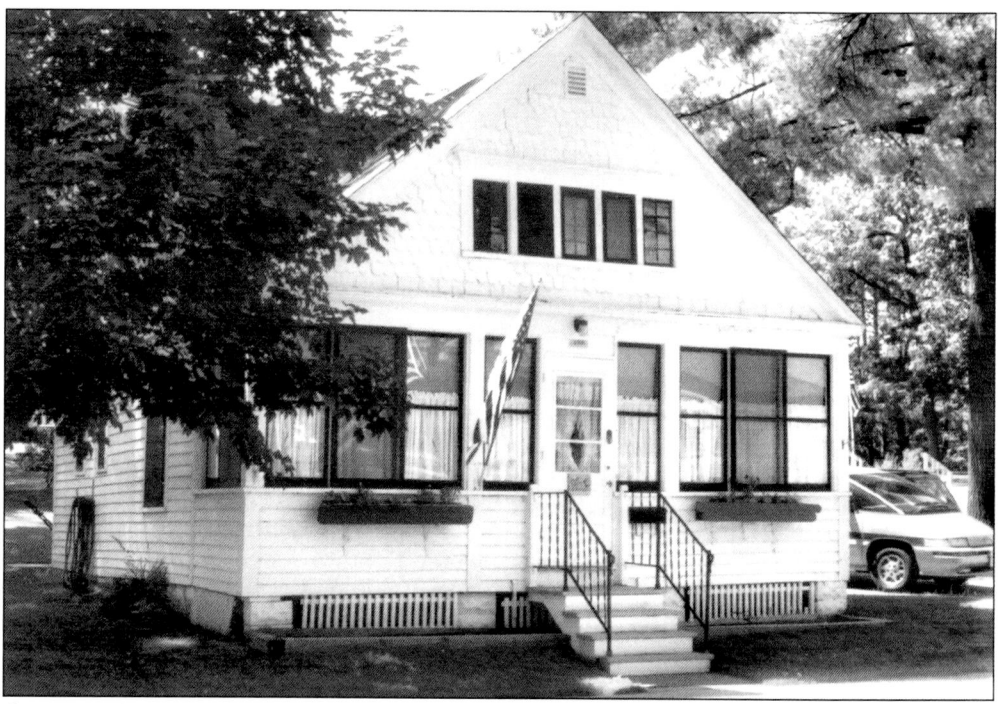

COTTAGE NUMBER 118. Cottage Number 118 was located on the north corner of Milwaukee Avenue and Wright Street. The building was later removed.

COTTAGE NUMBER 120. Cottage Number 120 was located on Milwaukee Avenue. This building still remains today, though the street is now named Bragg Avenue.

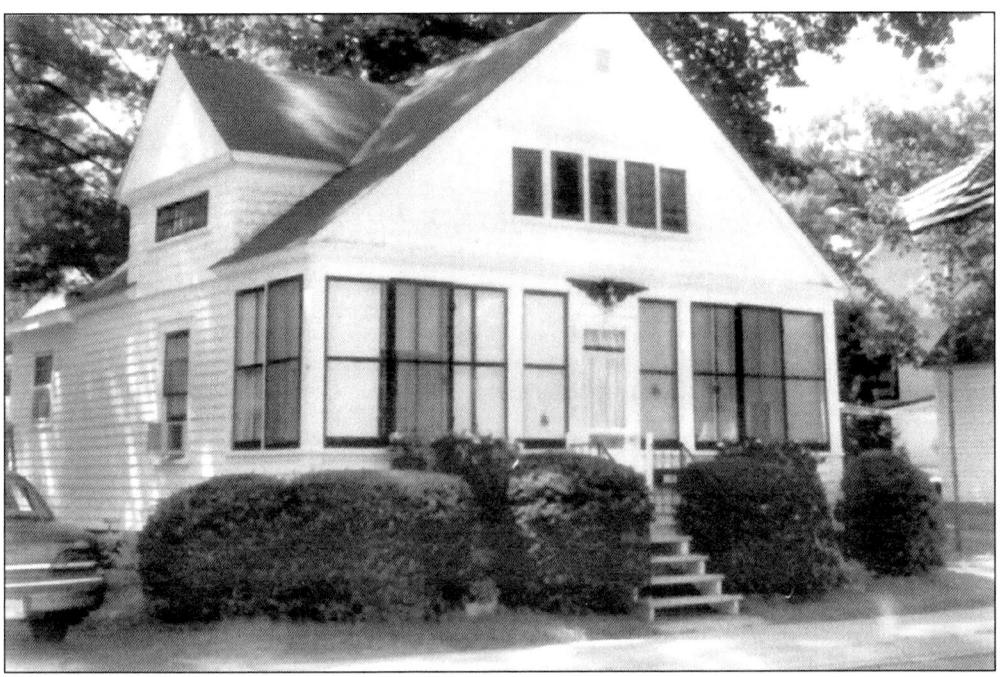

COTTAGE NUMBER 121. Cottage Number 121 was located on Milwaukee Avenue. This building still remains on its original site.

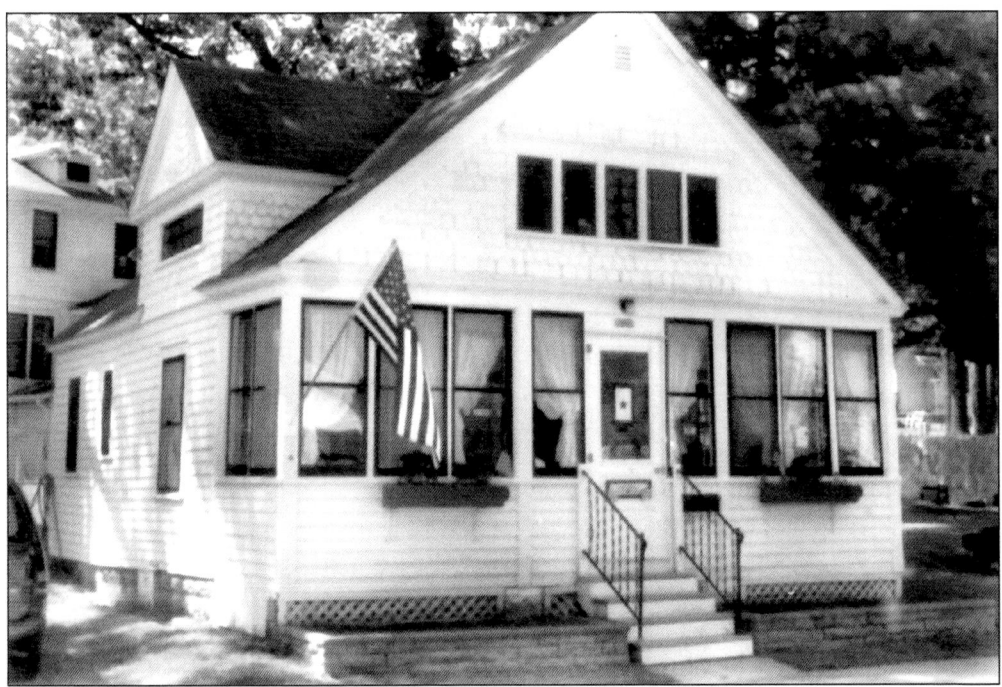

COTTAGE NUMBER 122. Cottage Number 122 was located on Milwaukee Avenue. It remains on its original site.

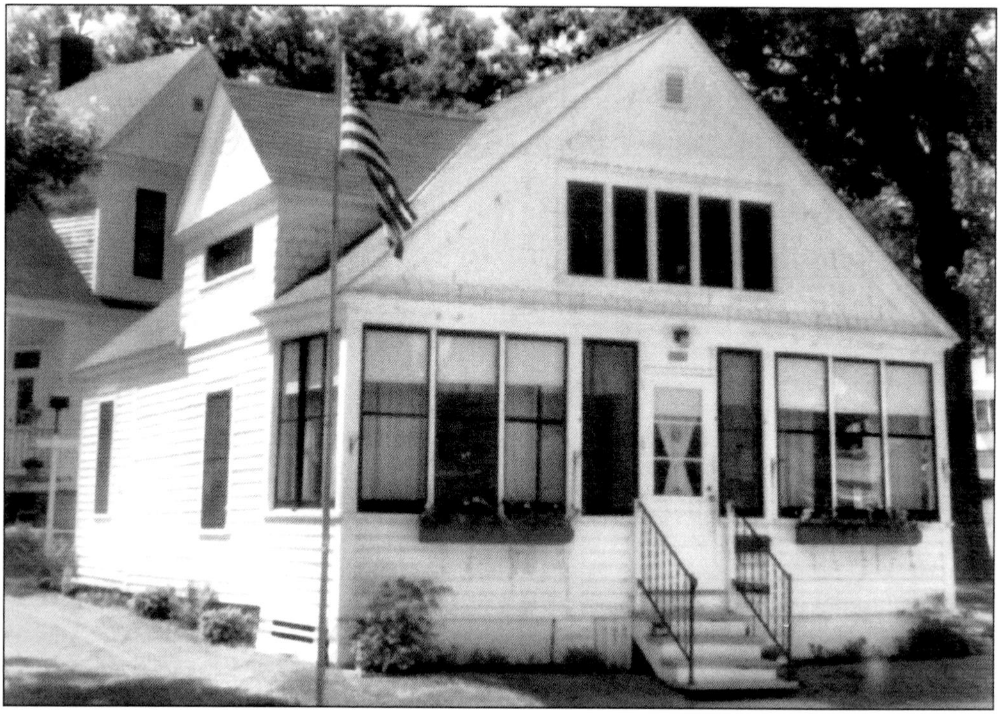

COTTAGE NUMBER 123. Cottage Number 123 was located on Milwaukee Avenue. It is still on its original site.

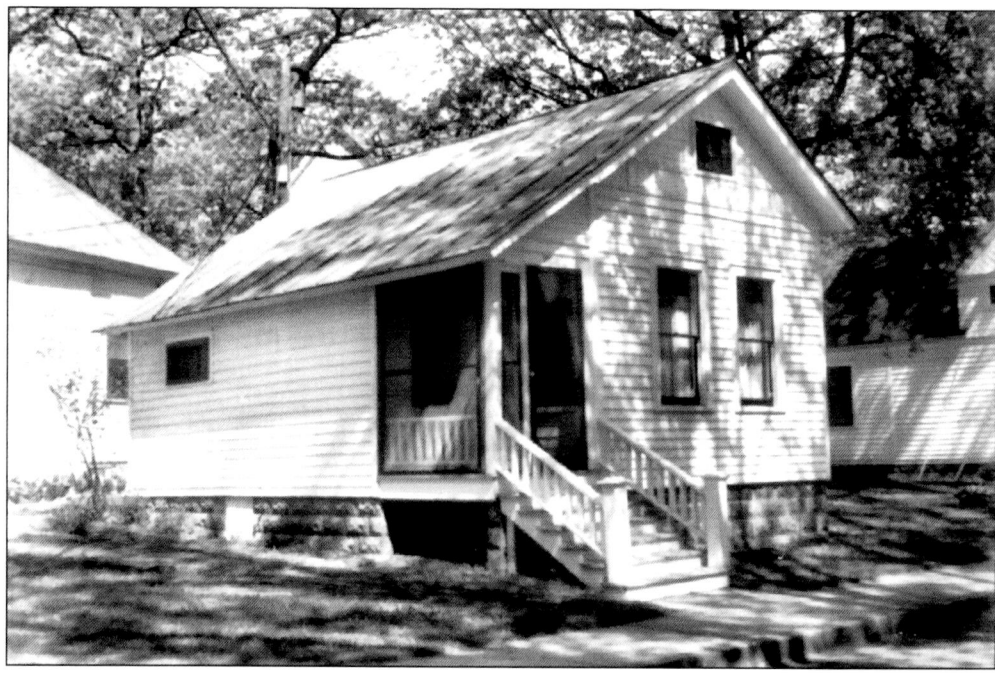

COTTAGE NUMBER 124. Cottage Number 124 was located on Milwaukee Avenue. It still remains there today on its original location. This view shows it as a regular cottage. The next view will show it as a Women's Relief Corp. sponsored building.

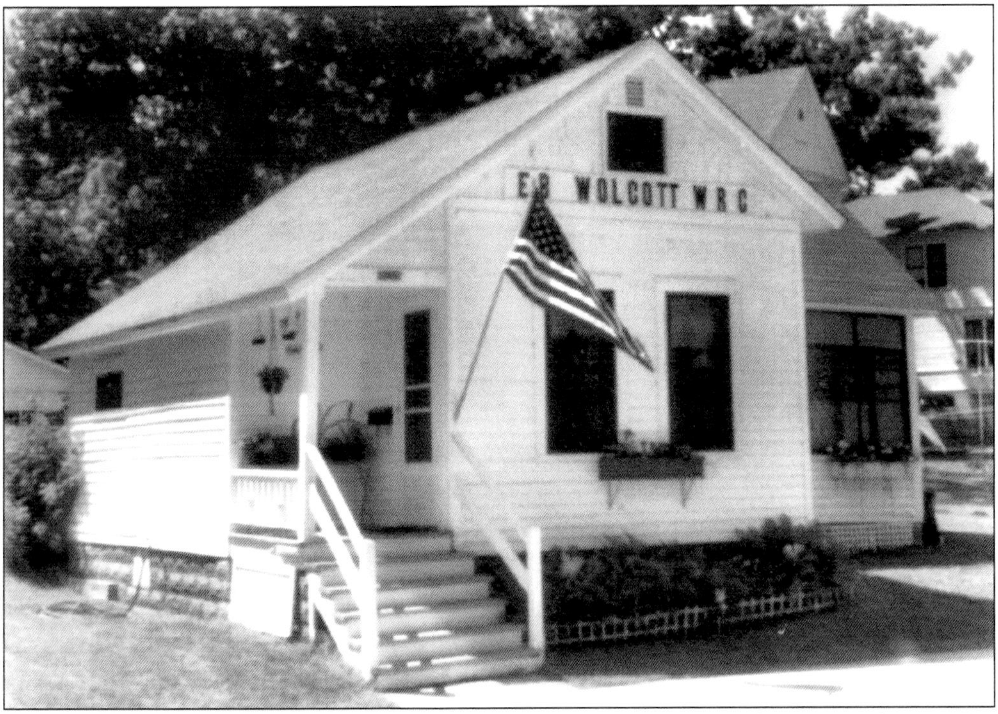

COTTAGE NUMBER 124 AS WRC BUILDING. Cottage Number 124 as the E.B. Wolcott WRC building. The Women's Relief Corp. sponsored 10 of the small cottages.

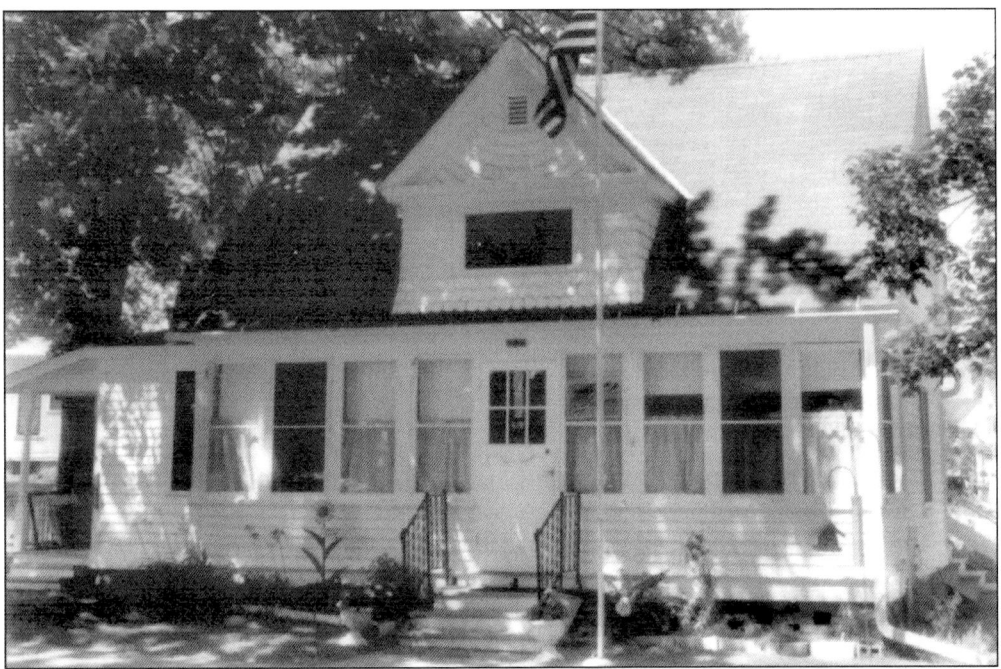

COTTAGE NUMBER 125. Cottage Number 125 was located on Marden Avenue, sandwiched between Milwaukee Avenue and Lake Street. The building still remains on its original site. The front door faces the park.

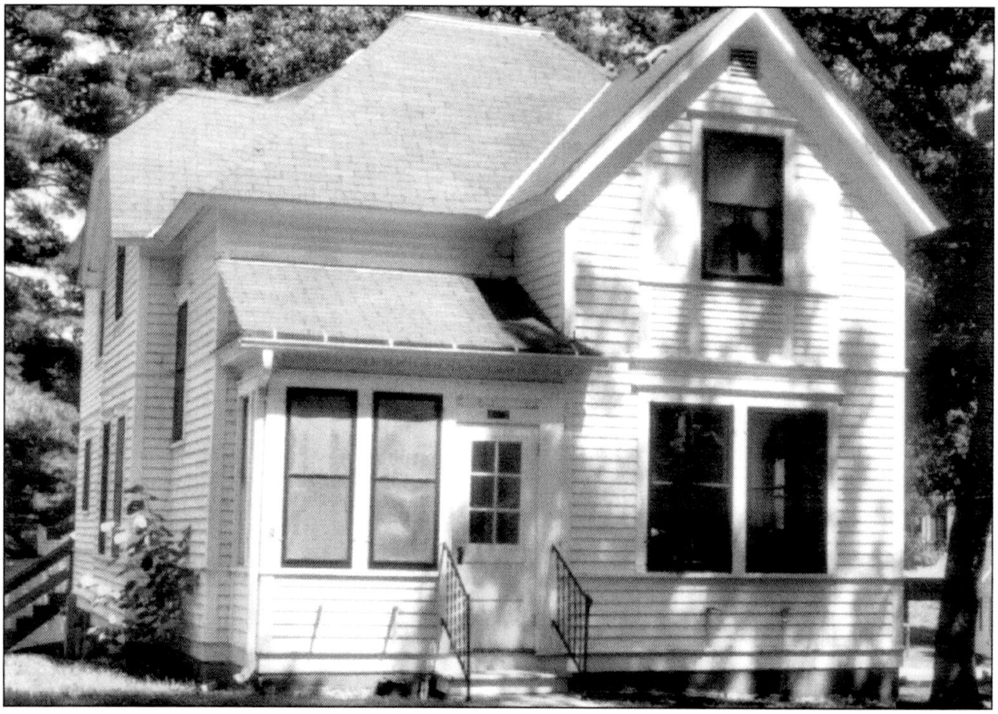

COTTAGE NUMBER 216. Cottage Number 216 was at the north end of Milwaukee Avenue, across from Cottage Number 116. This building was moved next to the adjutant's residence where Cottage Number 105 once stood.

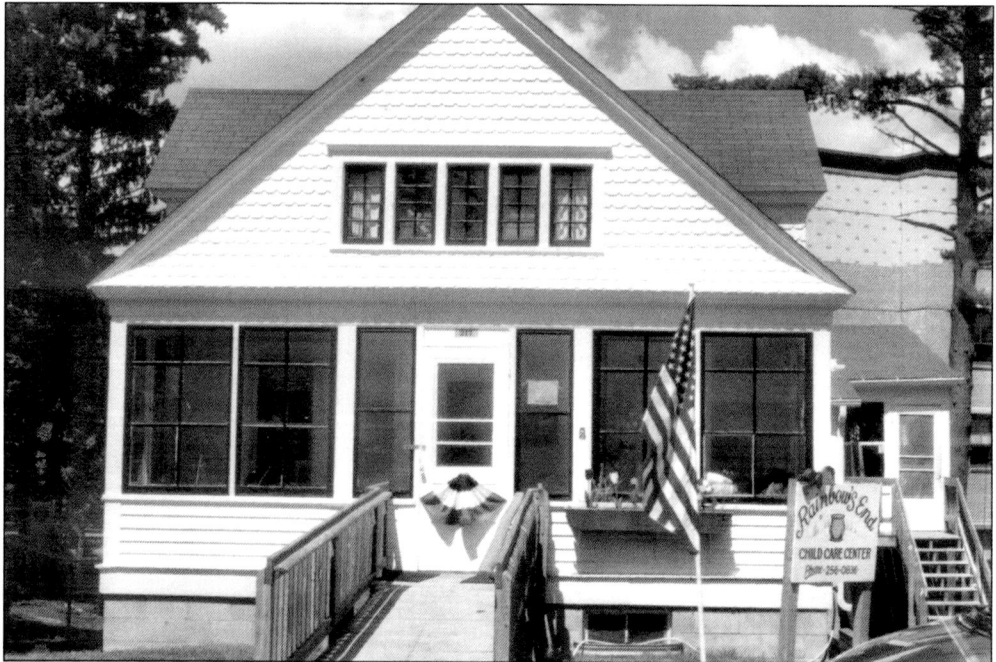

COTTAGE NUMBER 217. Cottage Number 217 was located on Milwaukee Avenue. It was moved to Wright Street and remains there today. It is now a daycare center for the employees' children.

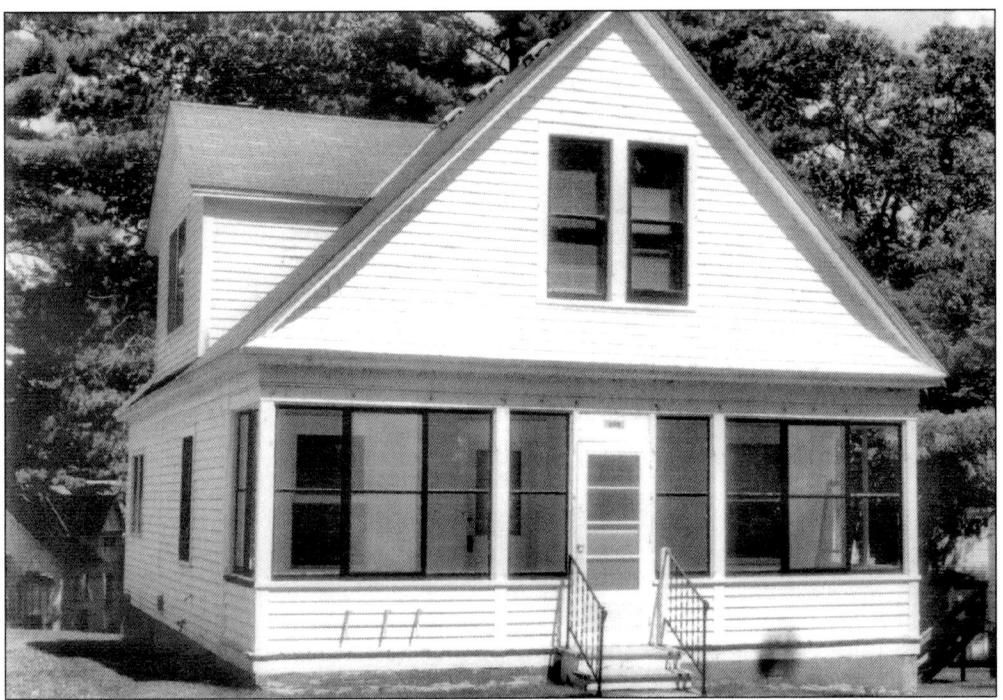

COTTAGE NUMBER 218. Cottage Number 218 was located on Milwaukee Avenue. It was moved later onto Wright Street, about where Cottage Number 106 once stood.

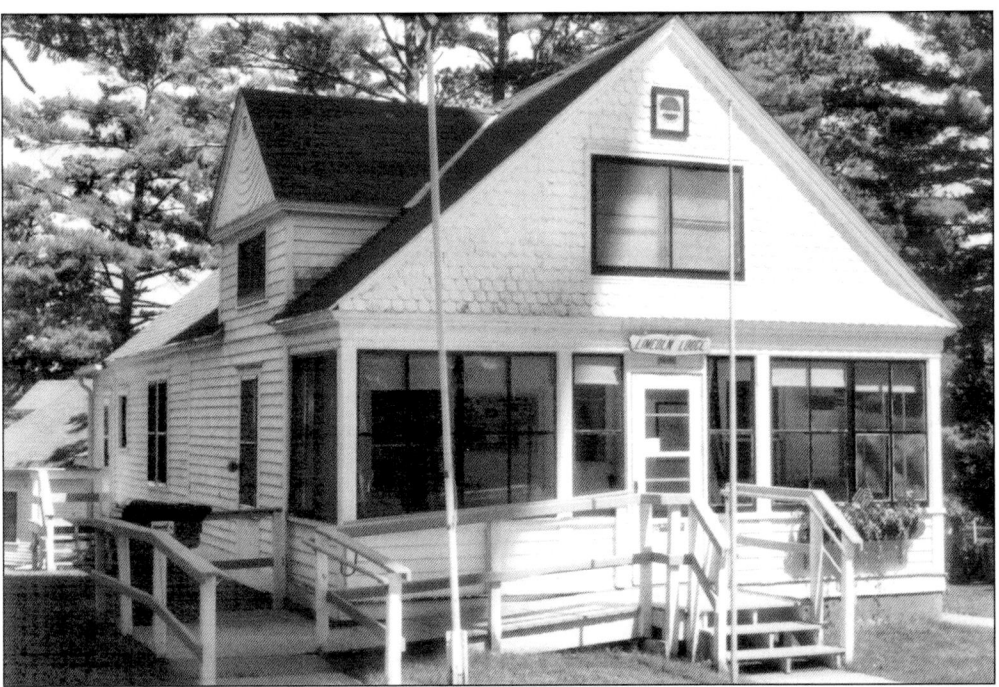

COTTAGE NUMBER 219. Cottage Number 219 was located on Milwaukee Street. It was moved later onto Wright Street where it stands today.

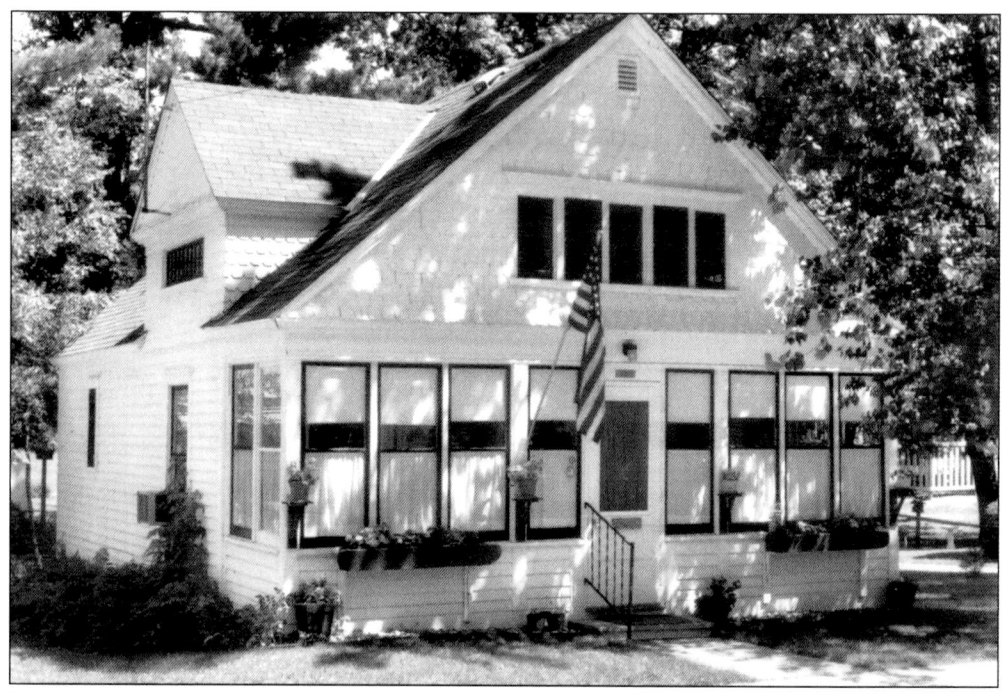

COTTAGE NUMBER 220. Cottage Number 220 was located at approximately the middle of Milwaukee Avenue. This building still remains in its original location.

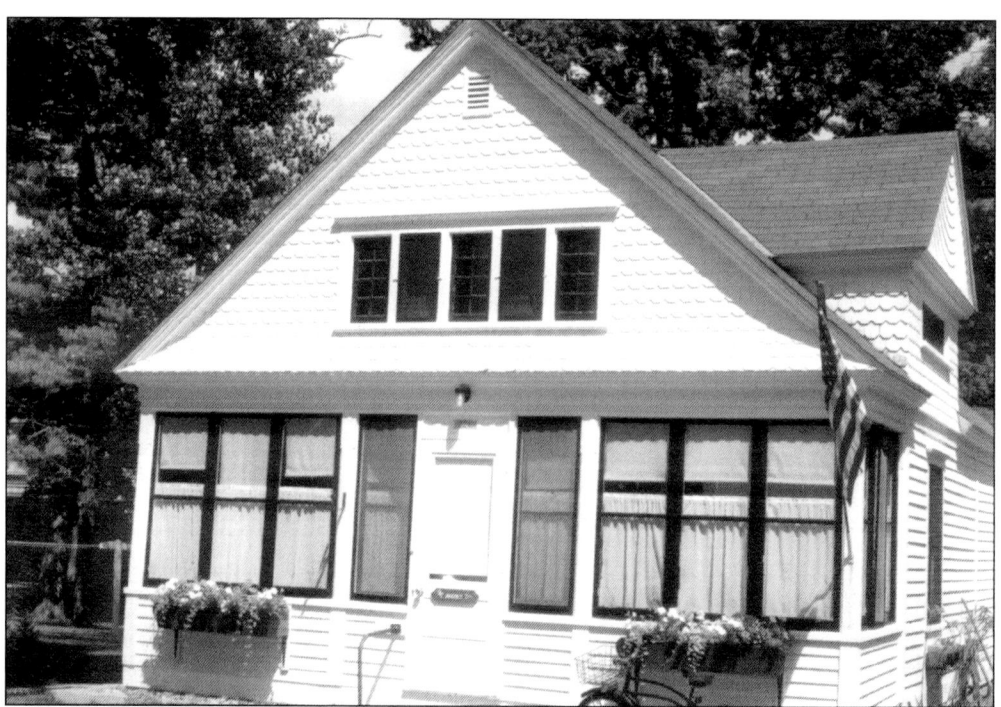

COTTAGE NUMBER 221. Cottage Number 221 was located on Milwaukee Avenue. It remains on its original site.

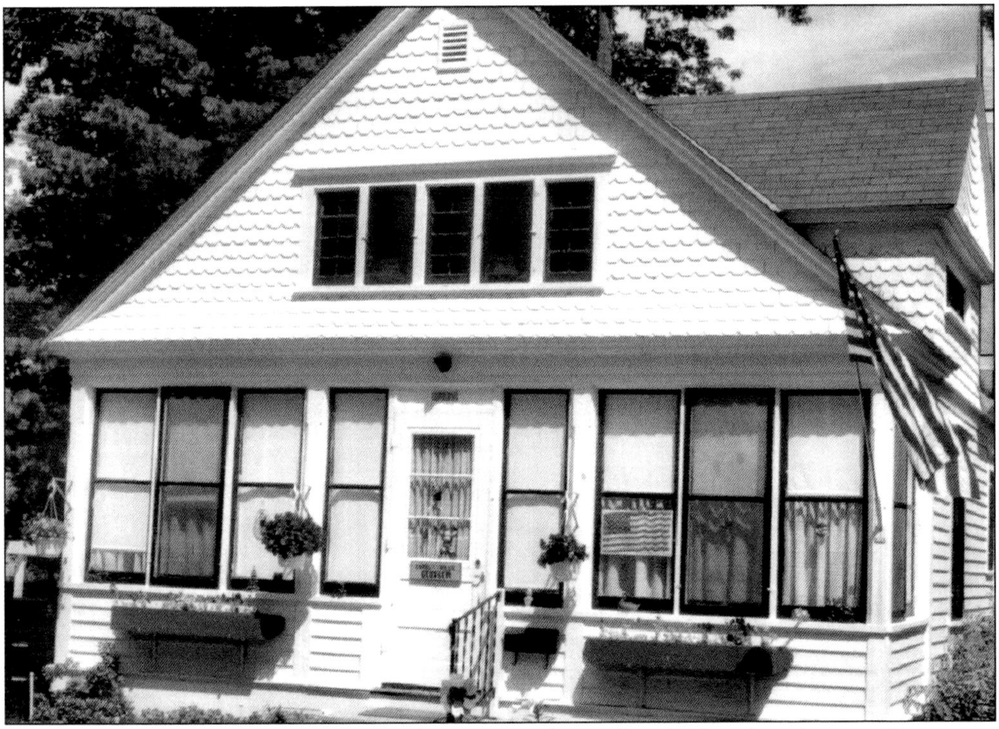

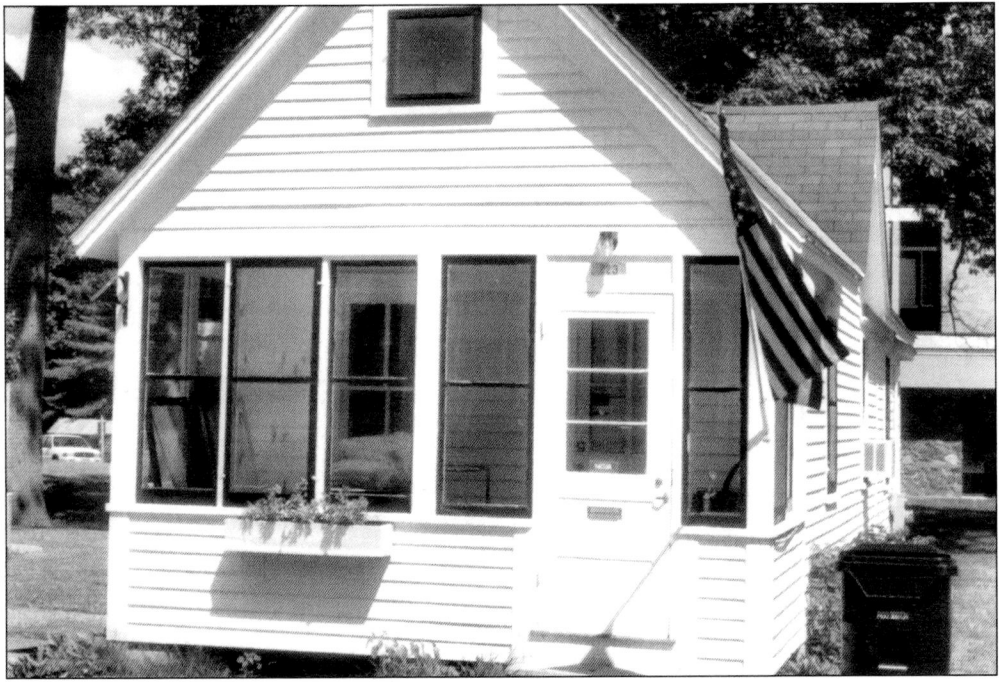

COTTAGE NUMBER 222. Cottage Number 222 was located on Milwaukee Avenue. It remains on its original site.

COTTAGE NUMBER 223. Cottage Number 223 was located on Milwaukee Avenue. It remains on its original site.

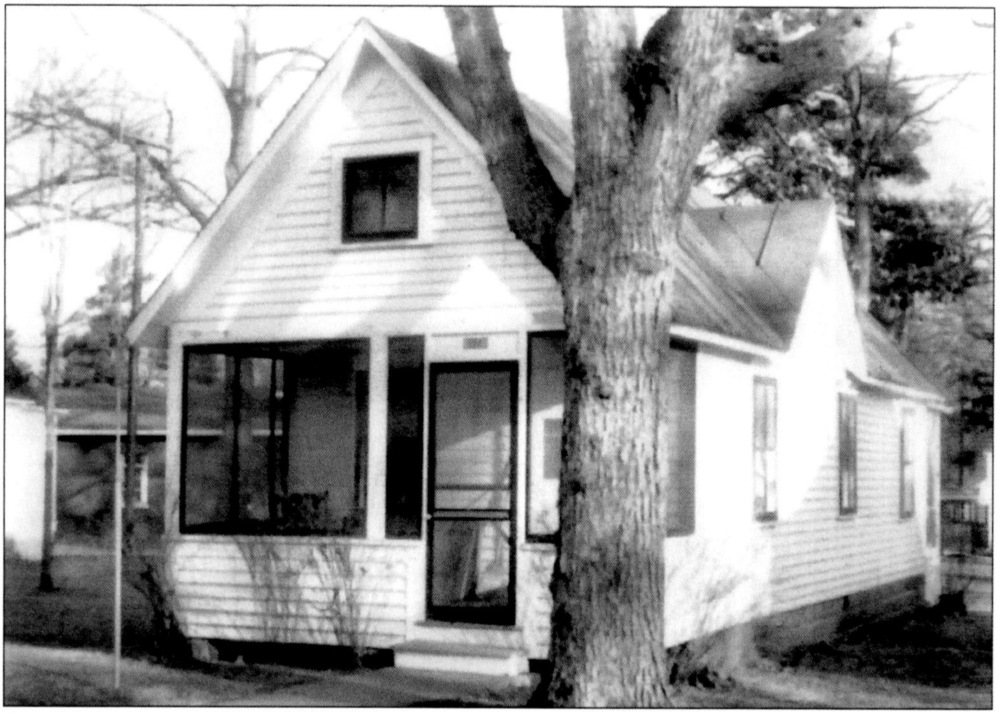

COTTAGE NUMBER 224. Cottage Number 224 was located on Milwaukee Avenue. It was removed.

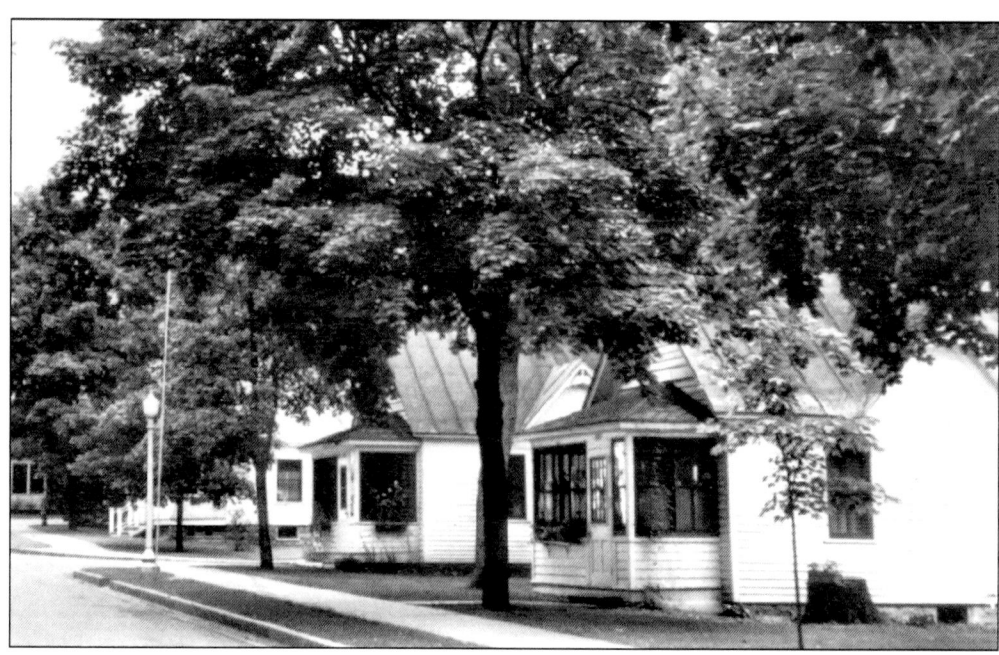

COTTAGE NUMBERS 225, 226, AND 227. This view is of Marden Avenue, looking west toward the commandant's residence. The post card shows, from left to right, the commandant's residence, Cottage Number 225 partially hidden by the trees, Cottage Number 226, and Cottage Number 227.

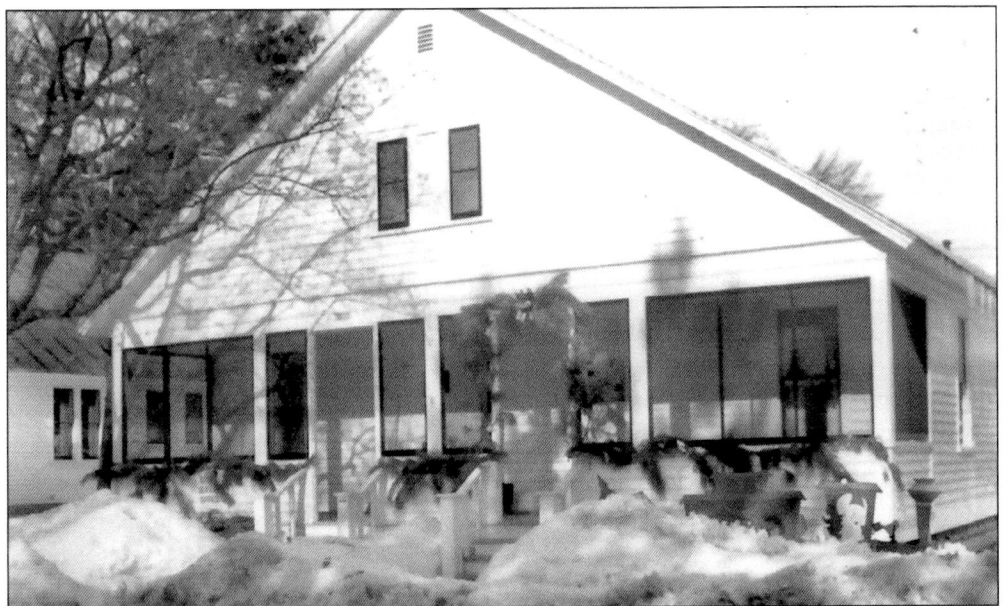

DUPLEX COTTAGE NUMBER 231–232. This cottage is one of the duplex cottages on Marden Avenue. It could be either duplex Cottage Numbers 231–232, or 229–230, since the duplex east of these was the Home Exchange, the only other duplex cottage.

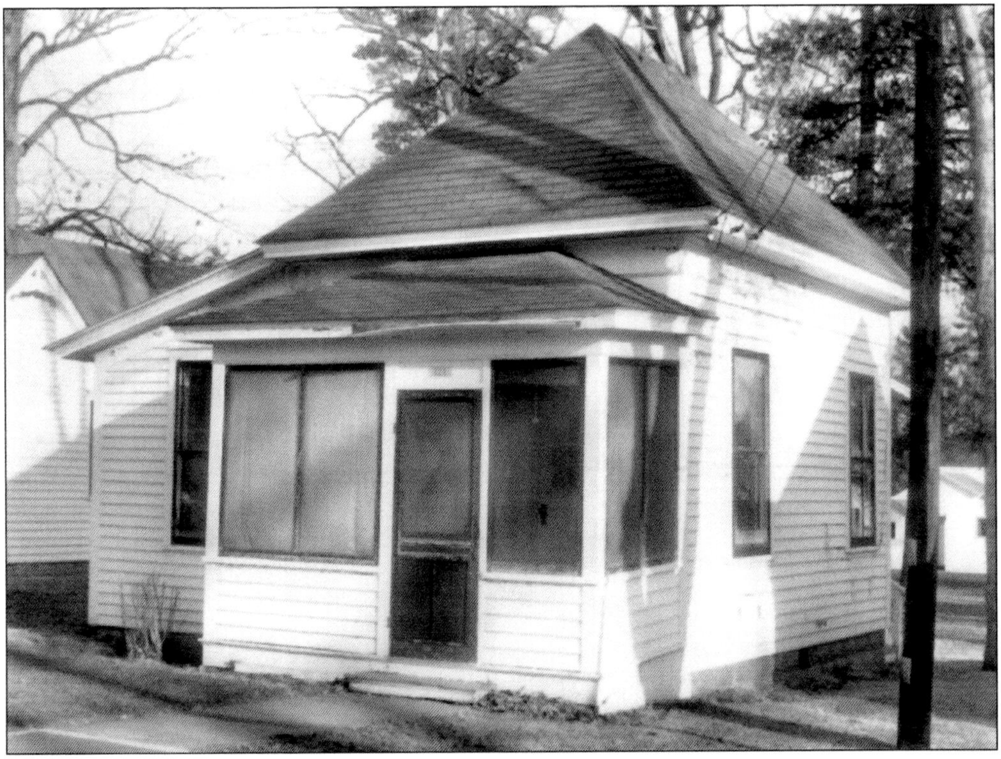

COTTAGE NUMBER 225. This cottage was located on Milwaukee Avenue. It was later removed.

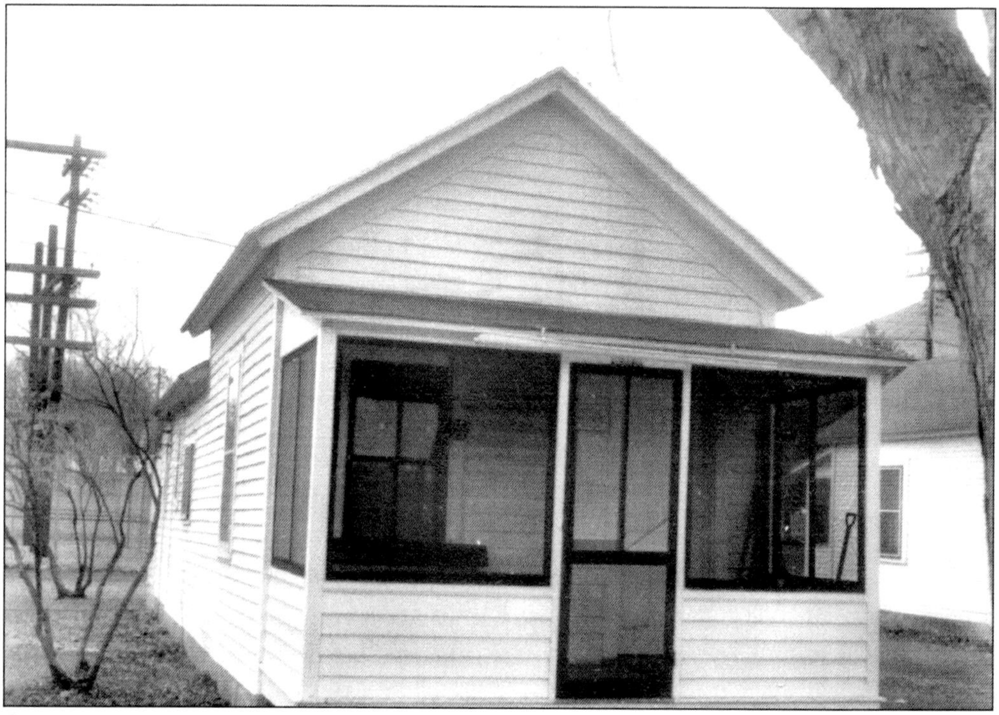

COTTAGE NUMBER 312. Cottage Number 312 was the first cottage encountered on the left from the Bell Avenue entrance. The cottage was located on Bell Avenue and was the weaving shop at one time. It was later removed.

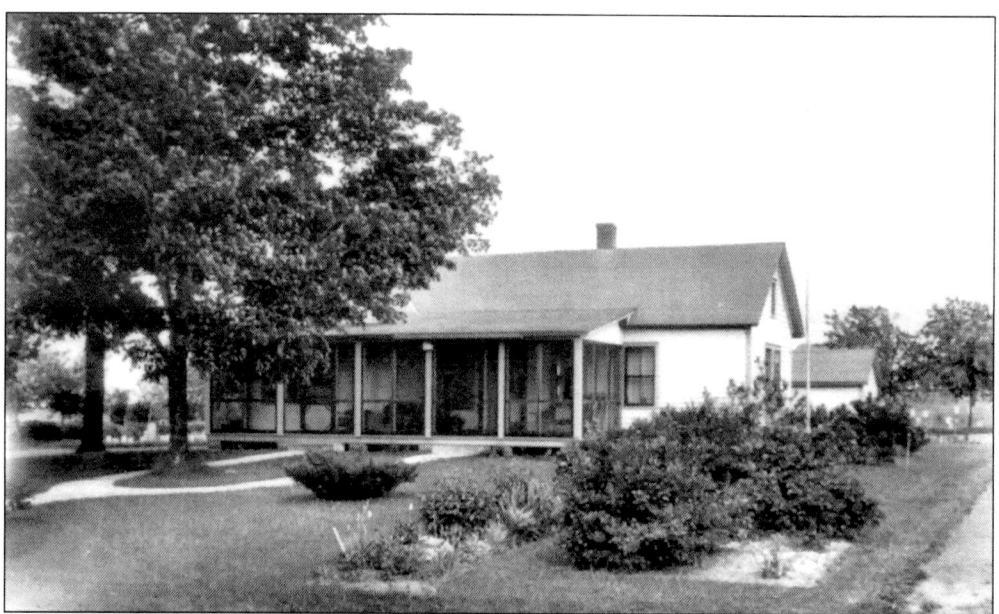

FARM COTTAGE NUMBER 321. This might be the only view of this building. On the right in the background, there are headstones seen from the Home Cemetery. Also in the view is the Farm Shed Number 322. The Farm Cottage was located across the highway next to the cemetery, just south of Marston Hall.

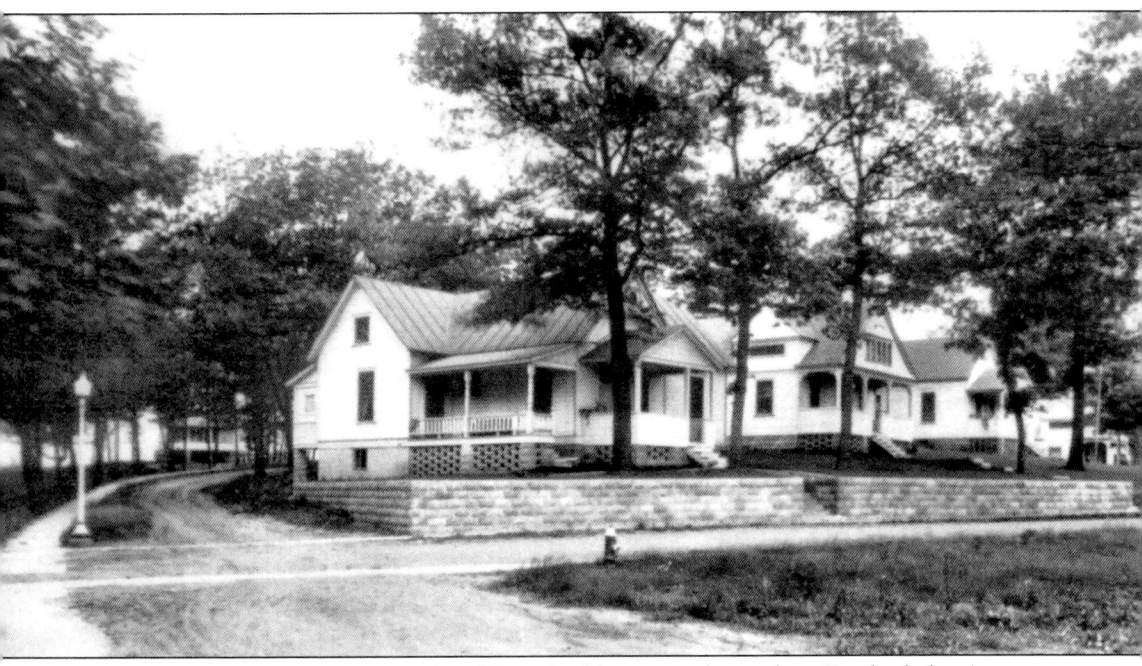

COTTAGE NUMBERS 409, 410, AND 411. These buildings were located on Cumberledge Avenue facing the east. They were later torn down to make room for the new infirmary.

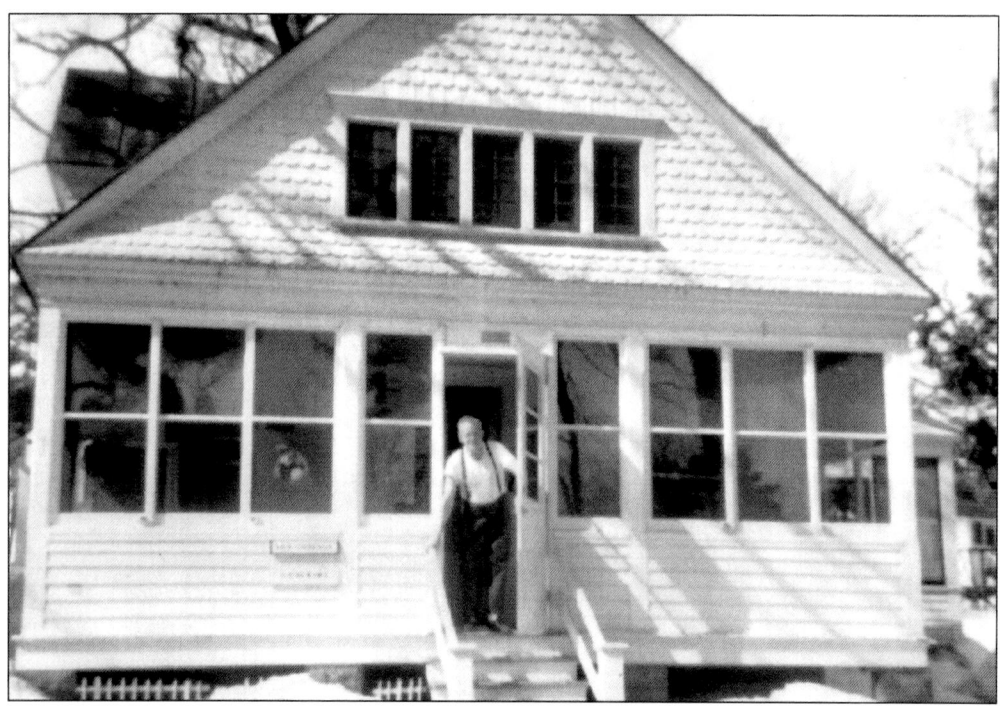

COTTAGE NUMBER 412. Cottage Number 412 was located on Cumberledge Avenue just east of the 21st Regimental Building. The building was in the middle of the cottages on Cumberledge Avenue. It was later moved to Milwaukee Avenue, near Marden Avenue.

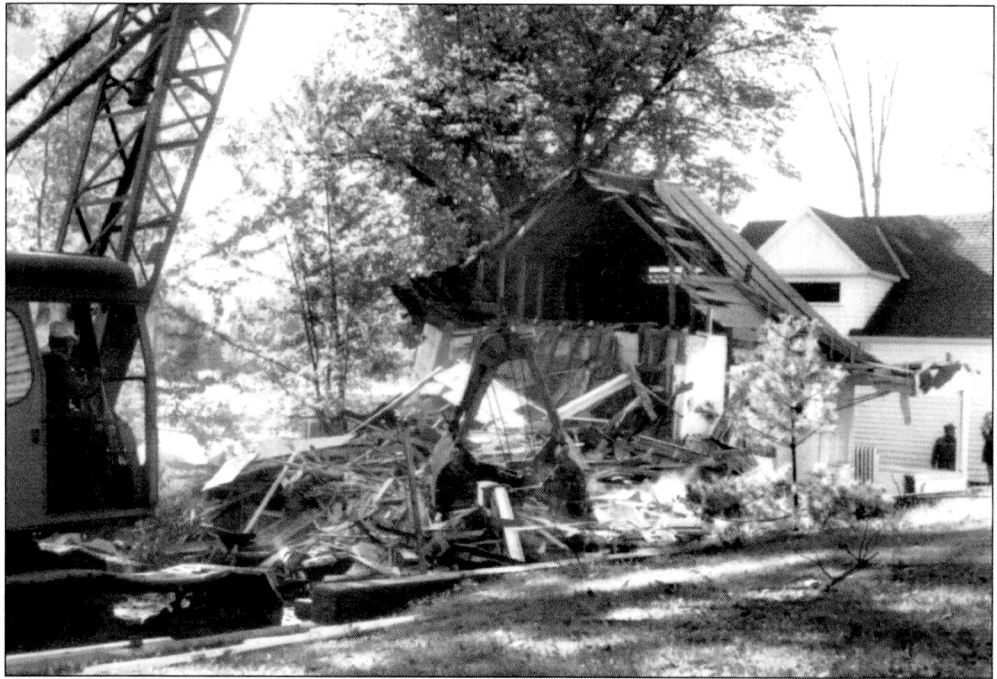

TEARING DOWN COTTAGE NUMBER 413. Cottage Number 413 was on Cumberledge Avenue. This view was taken in 1971.

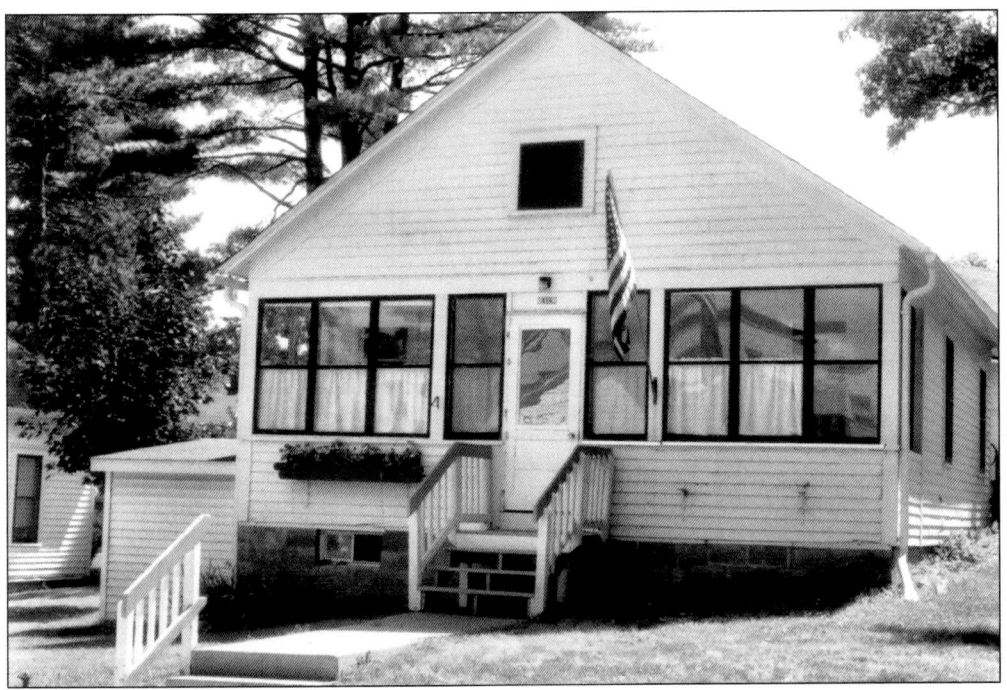

COTTAGE NUMBER 414. Cottage Number 414 was located on Cumberledge Avenue. It was later moved to Wright Street.

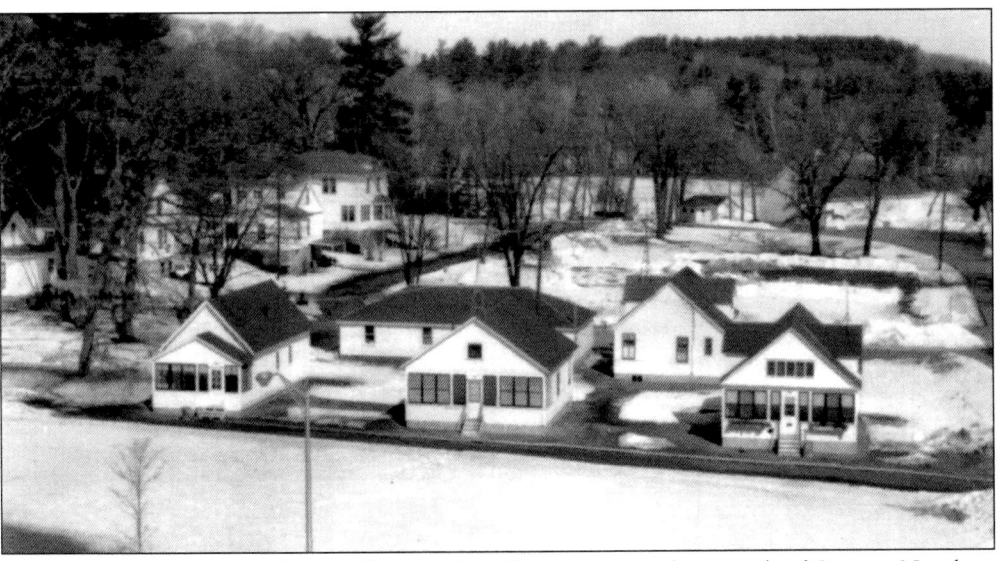

COTTAGE NUMBERS 412, 414, 415, AND 416. This is a group photograph of Cottage Numbers 412, 414, 415, and 416. Also in the photograph is Garage Number 308N. Removed from the area is Garage Number 308S, which was to the right of Cottage Number 412. This area was west of Mitchell Avenue where Ainsworth Hall now stands. Cottage Number 412 was at one time located on Cumberledge Avenue. This cottage was moved again to Bragg Avenue, where it remains today. The Cottages are pictured, left to right, (in front) Numbers 415, 414, and 412; and (in back) Garage Number 308N and Cottage Number 416. The Ice House can be seen in the background and on the left is the backside of Milwaukee Avenue.

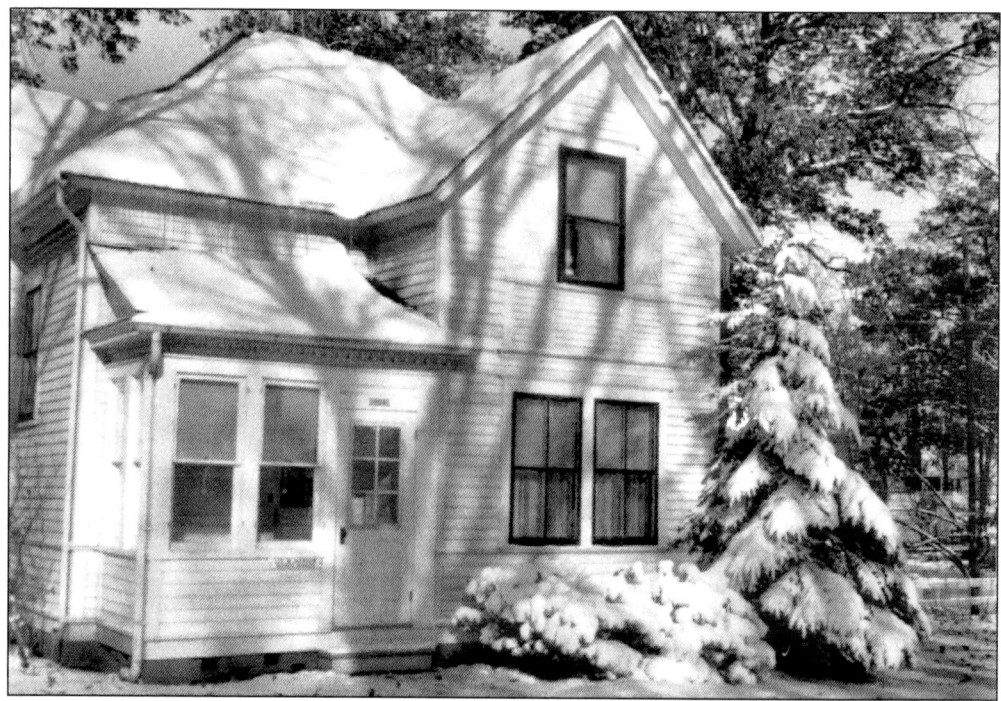

ADJUTANT'S RESIDENCE, BUILDING NUMBER 505. The adjutant's residence was Building Number 505. This building was also the quartermaster's residence at one time. It was located between Manchester Avenue and Cumberledge Avenue, near the hospital's circle drive. This building was later removed.

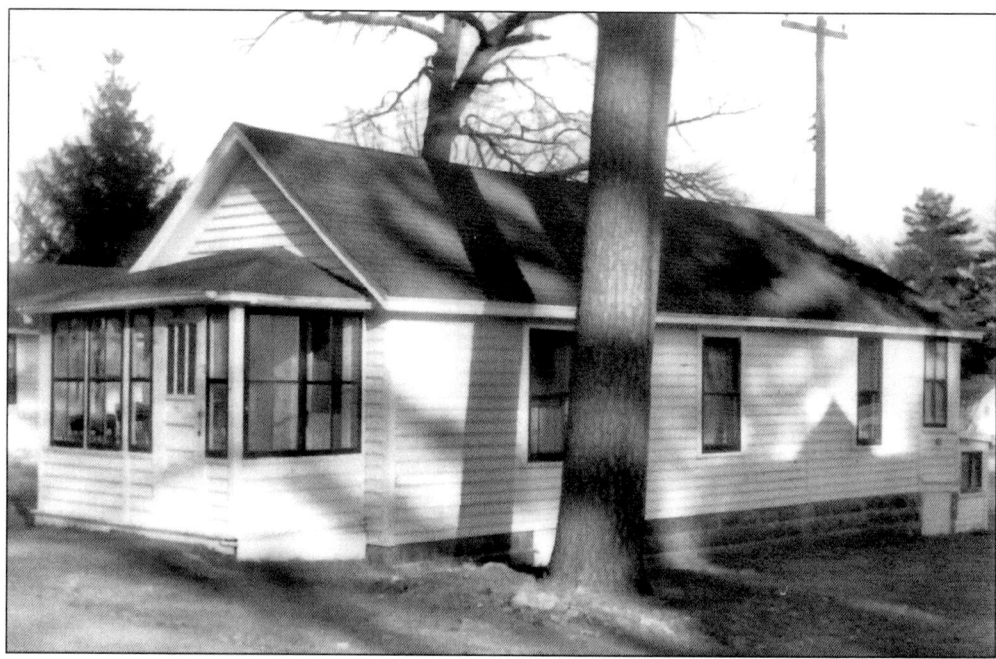

UNKNOWN COTTAGE. The true cottage number is unknown. The original photograph listed it as Number 218, but it might have been changed throughout the years.

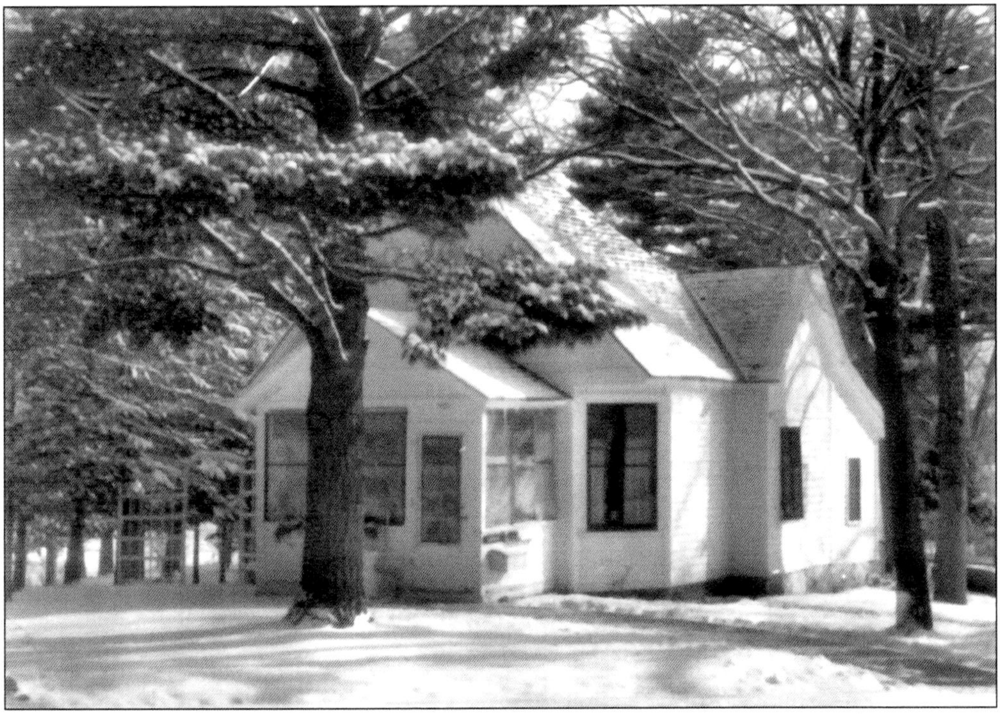

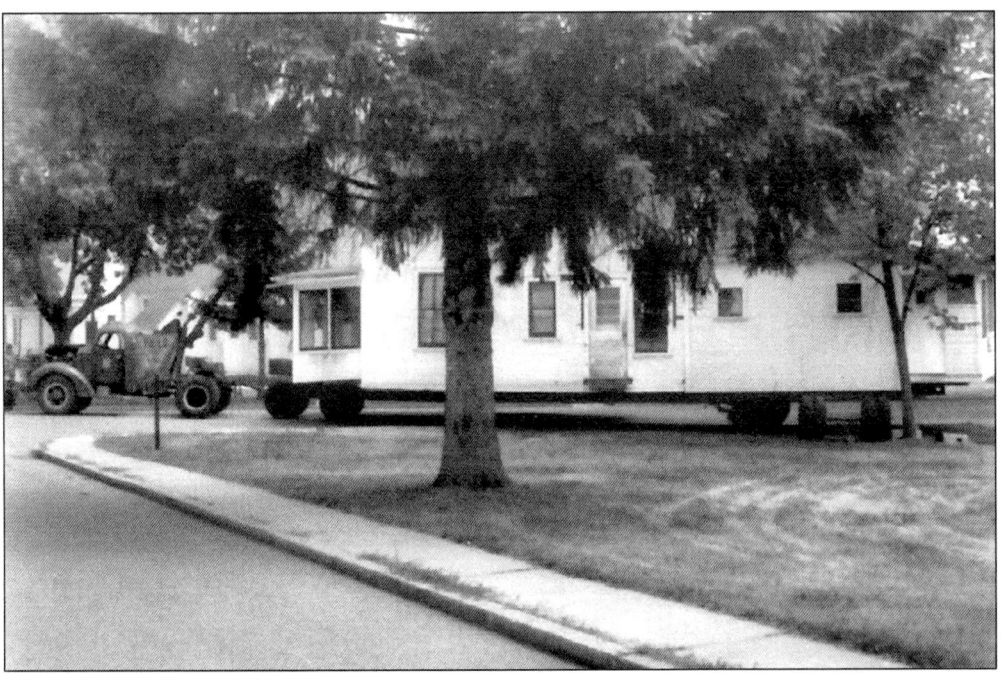

SECOND UNKNOWN COTTAGE. This cottage number is unknown. It appears to be in an area by itself.

REMOVAL DAY. This 1974 view shows one of the cottages being hauled away. It was either moved to another location on the grounds or sold. Some of the cottages were sold for a price of $250. Nolan Movers did some of the removal.

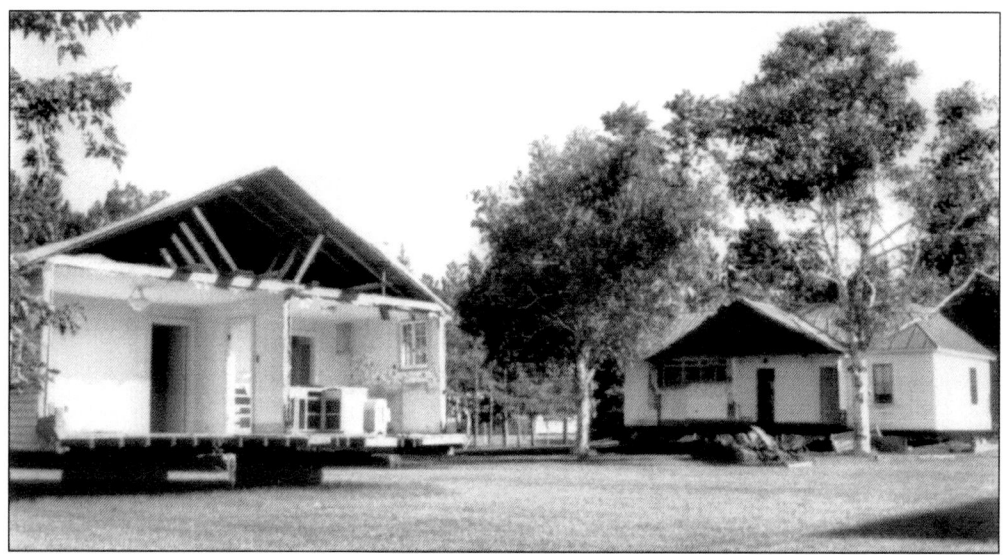

DUPLEX COTTAGE REMOVAL. This duplex is ready to be moved in this 1974 photograph. The duplexes were located on Marden Avenue, close to the post office. They were not moved to another location on the grounds.

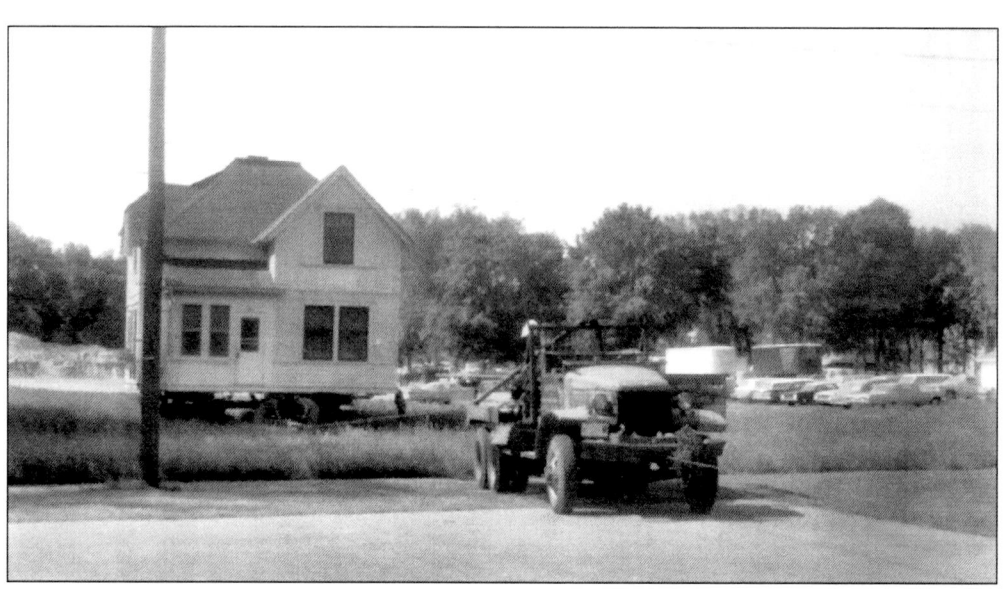

MOVING COTTAGE NUMBER 216. Cottage Number 216 was raised and ready to be moved in this photograph. It was moved from Milwaukee Avenue to Lake Street.

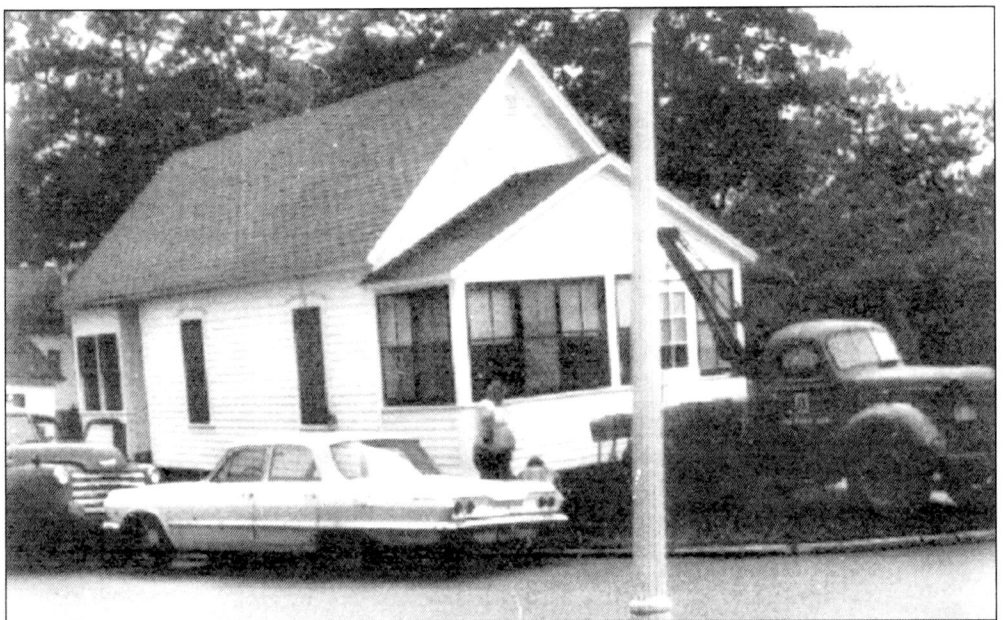

MOVING FIRST COTTAGE 1974. This photograph shows the first cottage to be moved in 1974 to make way for the new Stordock Hall. Notice the peaked trim on top of the windows. This was the only cottage photograph found to have peaked window trim. This cottage bears a strong resemblance to a cottage bought from the Home and is located on Crystal Road southeast of the Home.

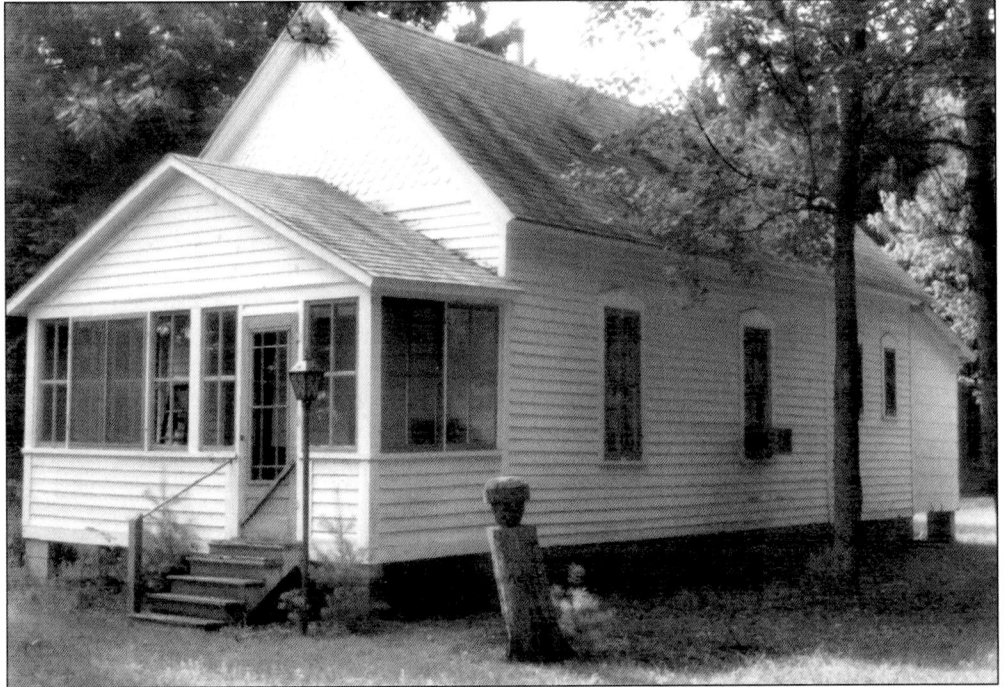

ONE OF THE MOVED COTTAGES. This is one of the cottages bought and moved from the home for $250. It is now a clubhouse for the Rainbow Stag Club on Crystal Road.

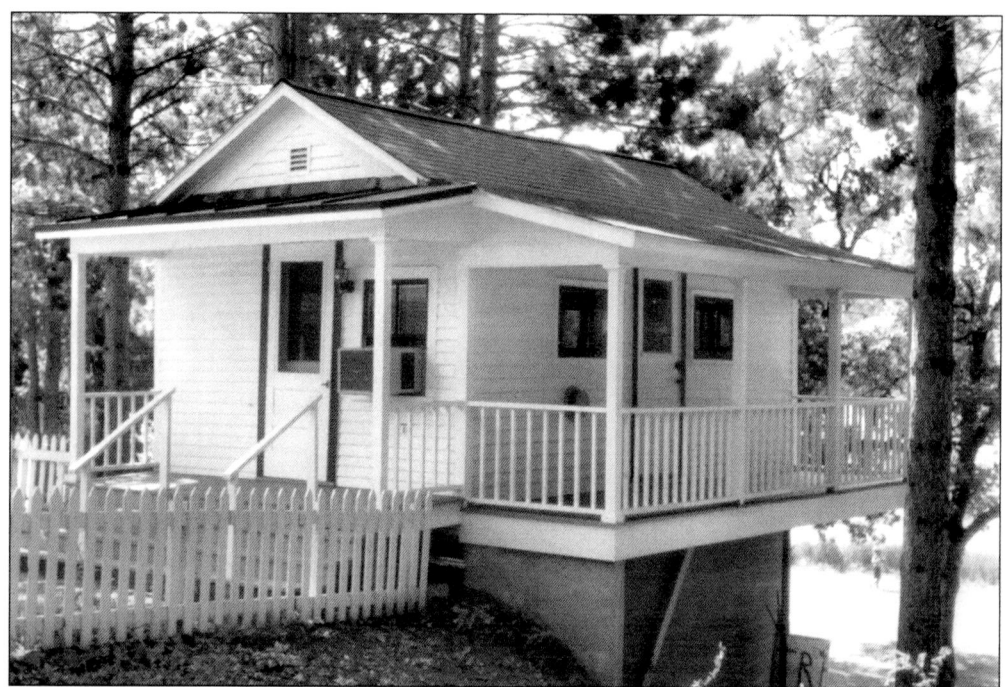

COTTAGE MOVED TO SOUTH PARK. This cottage was moved to South Park in Waupaca. It sits behind the Hutchinson House in the park. It had porches added to it.

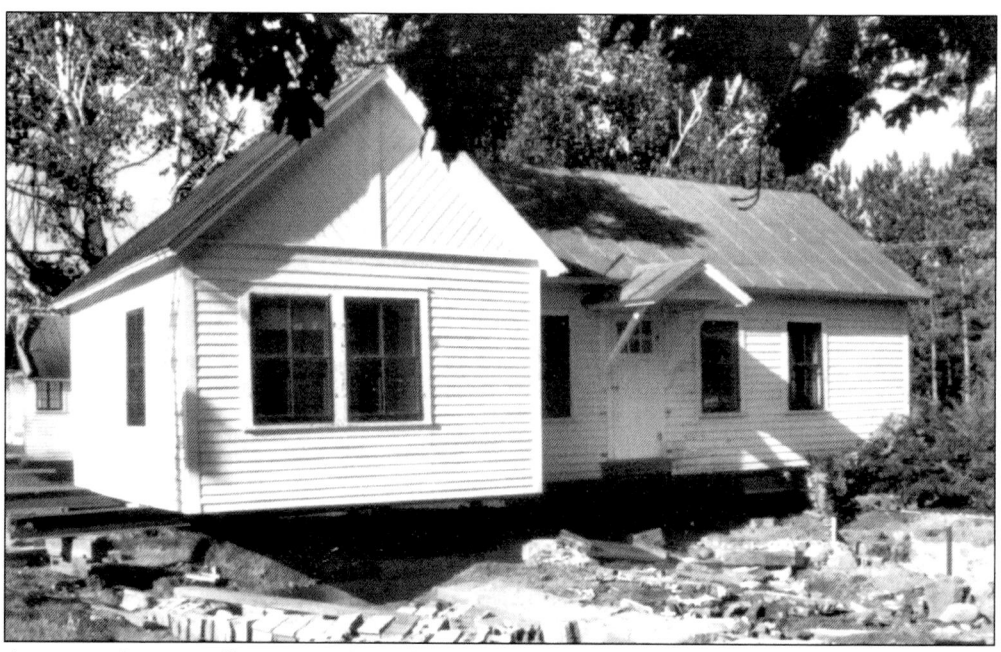

ANOTHER COTTAGE READY TO GO. This view shows another cottage ready to be moved in 1974. The cottage number is unknown.

Seven
PEOPLE, PLACES, AND THINGS

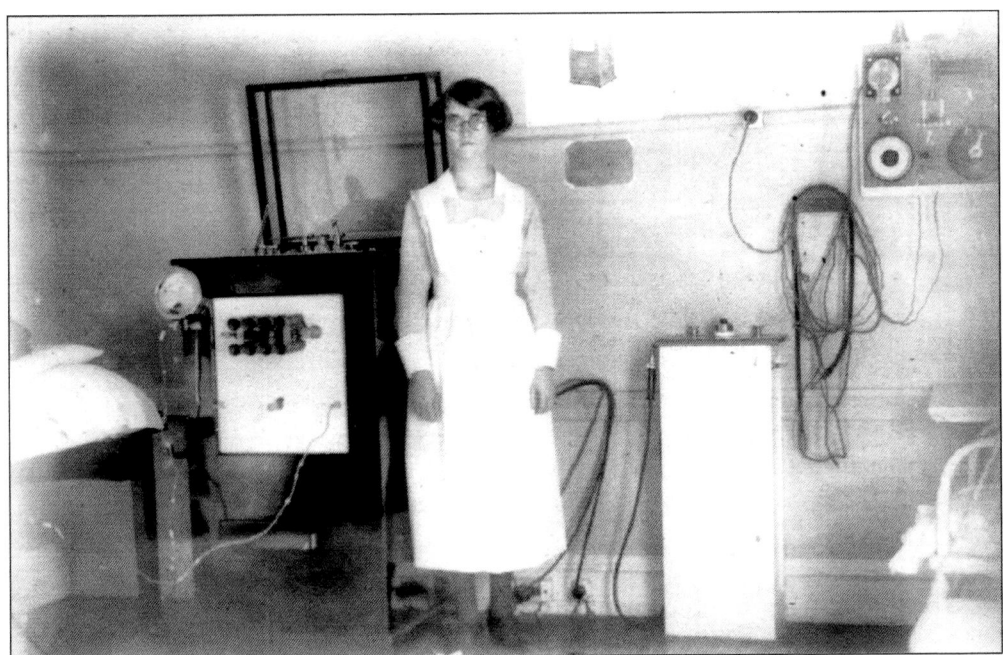

ELECTRICAL LAB. In this very rare view of the Electrical Lab taken in 1923 or 1924, an employee stands to have her photograph taken. With crude equipment by today's standards, treatment awaits the patient whose head is barely seen on the pillow to the left of the photograph.

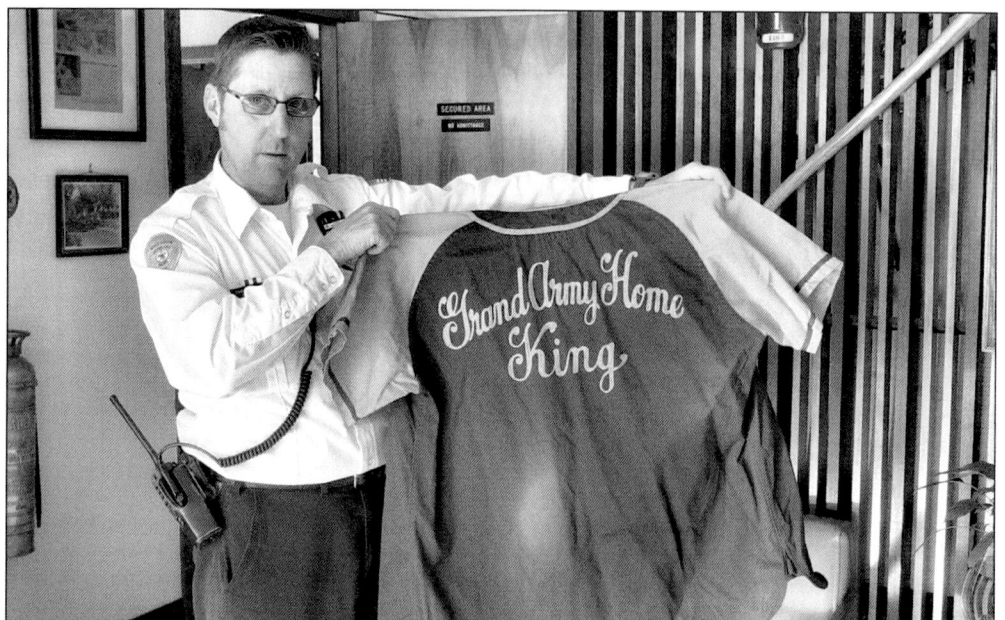

BASEBALL UNIFORM. A security employee, Gary Hartleben, holds the only known remaining baseball jersey from the Grand Army Home baseball team. There was a baseball diamond on the grounds at one time. A photograph of the field is almost non-existent. A glimpse of the field can be seen on a home movie, but it was taken at dusk.

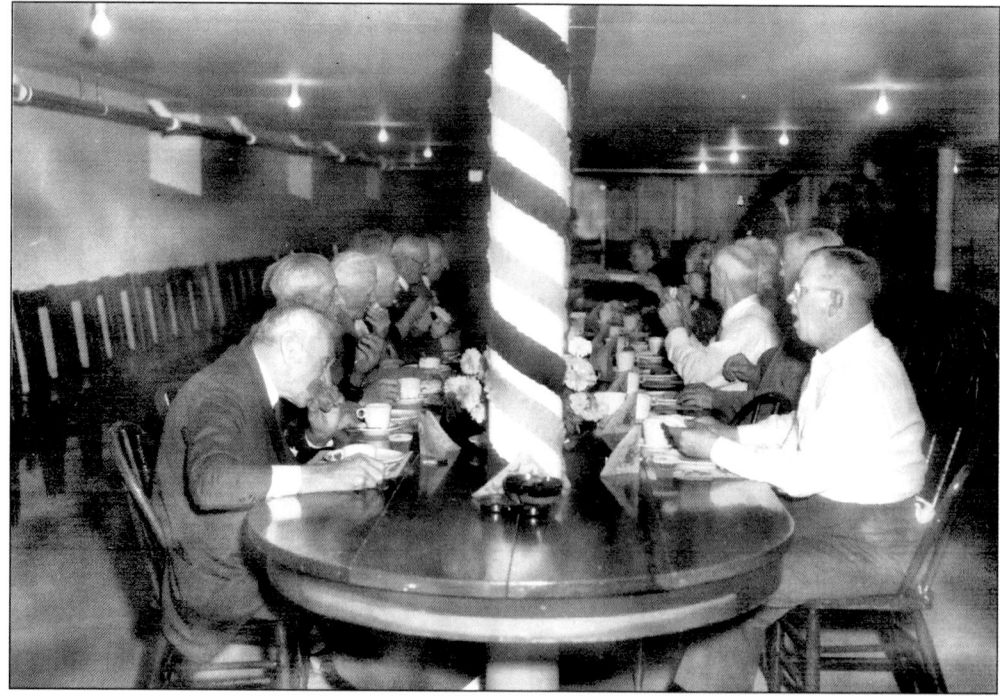

VFW PARTY. Many small parties are held at the Home each year. Each veteran group gathers to celebrate the anniversary of a particular event. Here, members of the Veterans of Foreign Wars celebrate a birthday with a party.

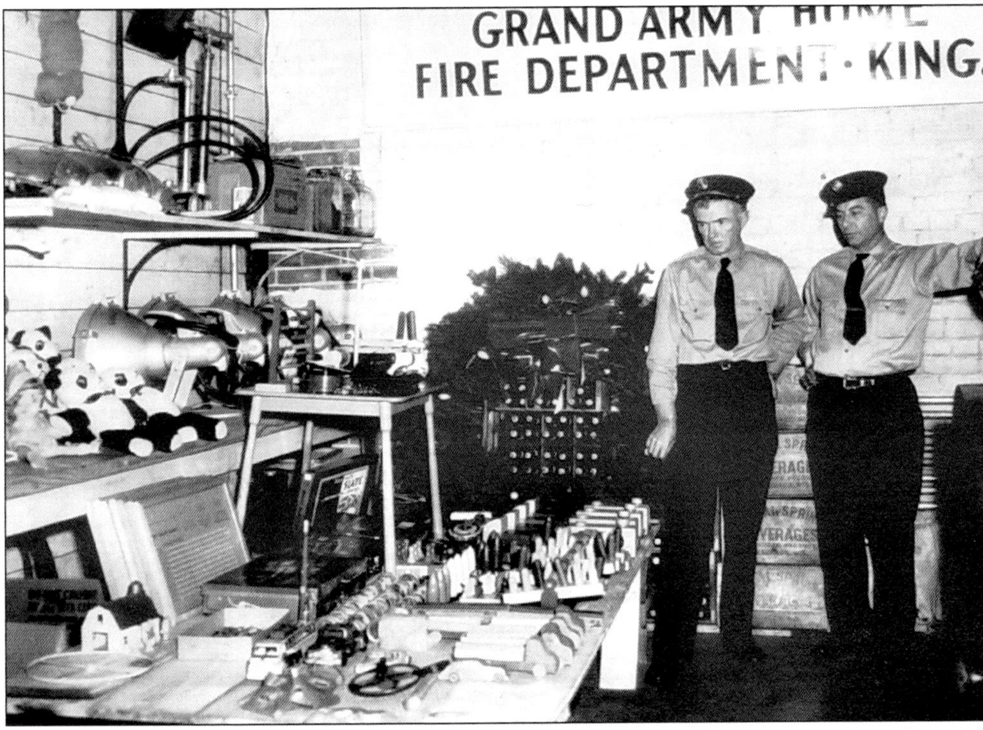

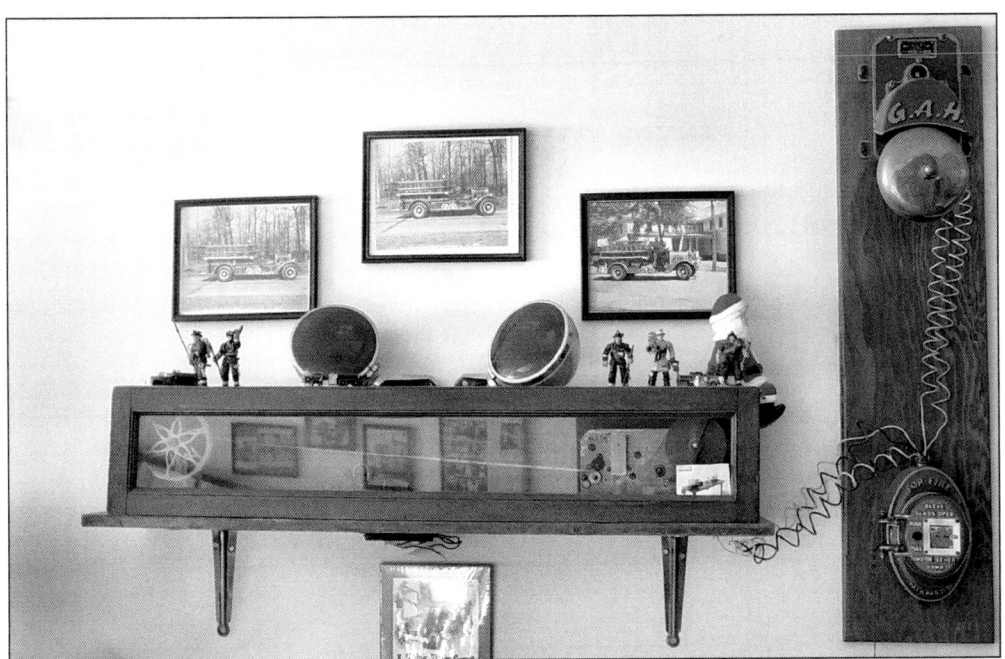

FIRE DEPARTMENT AT CHRISTMAS. Two of the fire department employees are seen with a table of goods that will be gifts for the employees' children at a Christmas party. The fireman on the right is Leonard Tappa, while the fireman on the left is unidentified.

OLD FIRE ALARM. The old fire alarm system from the Home was saved from being scraped and hangs on the wall in the back room of the Security Building.

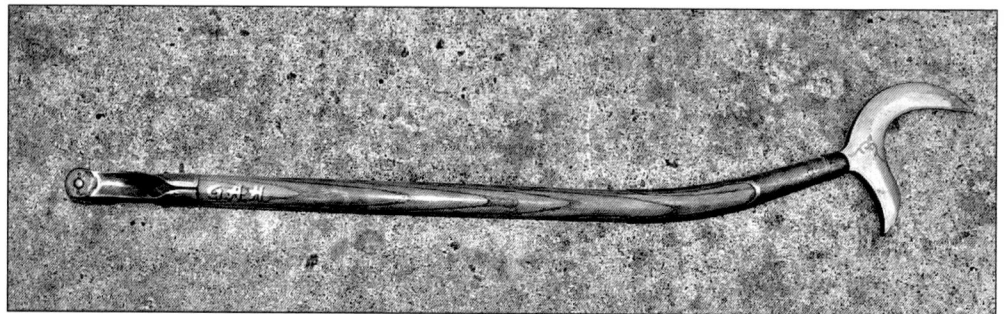

THE CAN OPENER. This device was for the firemen to use on the steel roofing of old wooden buildings. It worked much like a can opener. Without this tool, the firemen would never be able to open the roof to relieve the pressure and heat from a burning building. It is most likely a one of a kind tool. Note that GAH is painted on the tool.

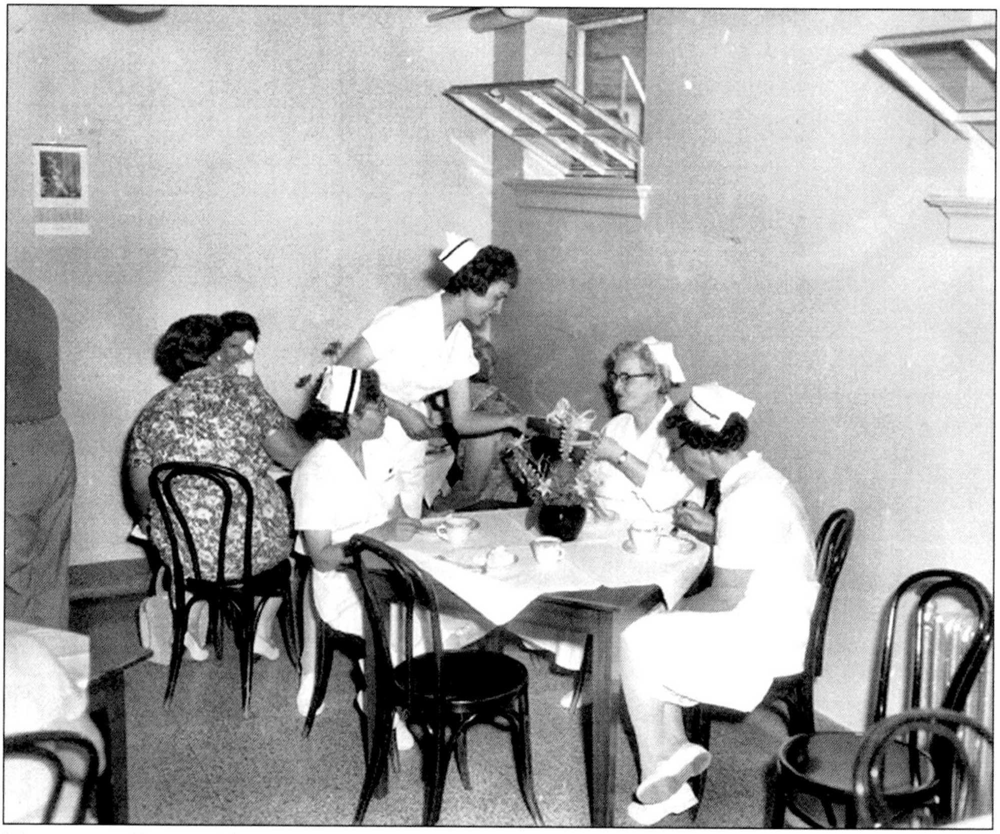

NURSES ON BREAK. These nurses are taking a break in a small break area. Most photographs have nurses mingling with the members. This was a hard photograph to find with just nurses.

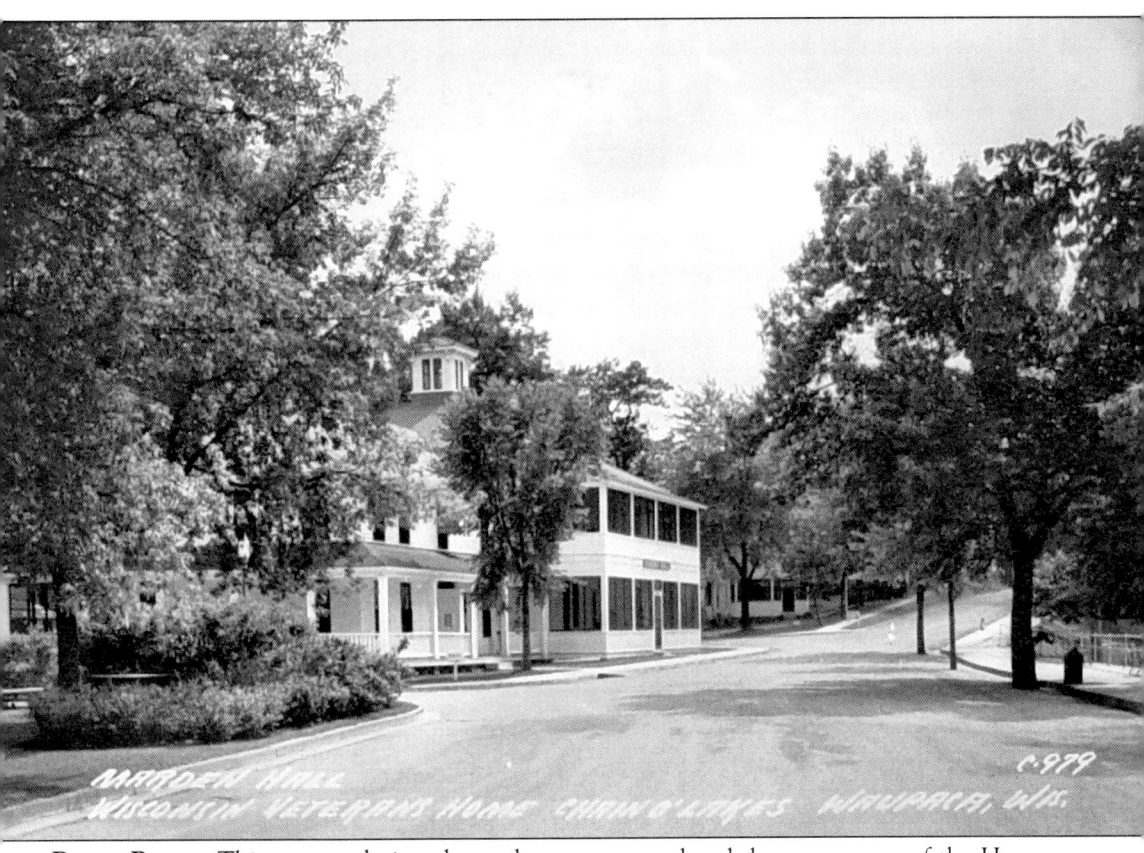

PAVED ROADS. This post card view shows the streets paved and the appearance of the Home modernized. This is another photograph of Woodnorth Avenue in front of Marden Hall.

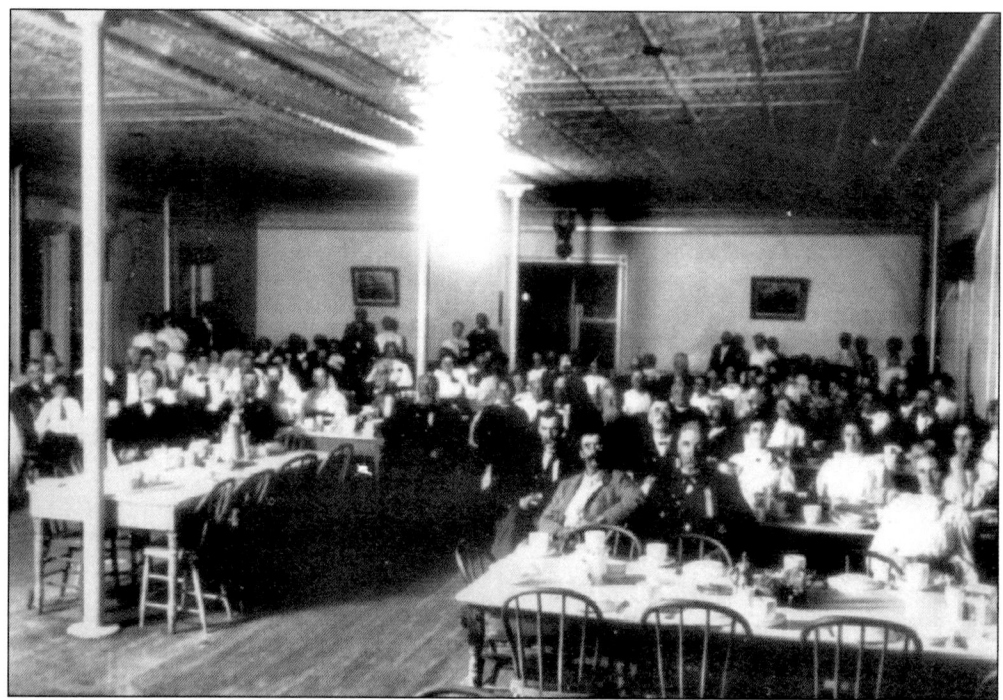

MEAL TIME. This is another view of the Bryant Hall Dining Room. Feeding hundreds of members is a huge job. The Home had an 18-acre garden at one time to feed the Members. It was started in 1911 under the direction of Henry C. Smith, a then new board member. The garden gave Members something to do as volunteers. The meal quality was good and the members enjoyed the social time of meal preparation.

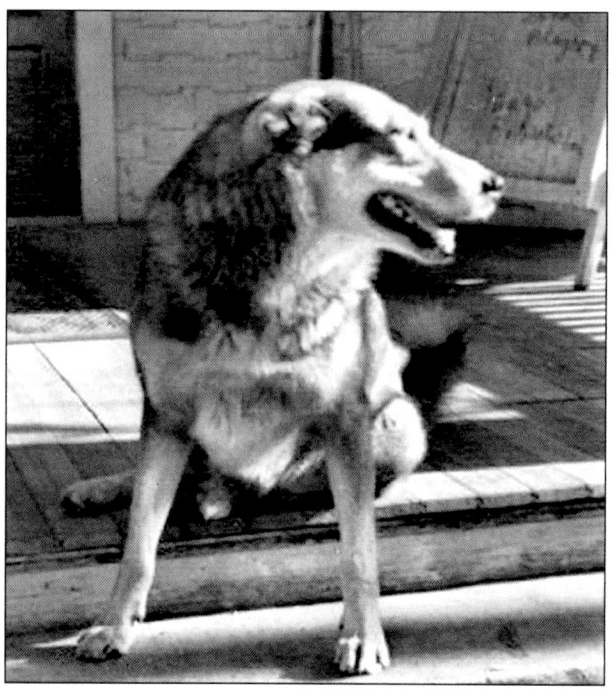

A PHOTOGRAPH OF BROWNIE. The headstone of Brownie was seen earlier. The men must have thought a lot about this dog to have it buried amongst them. He was returned to his owner after the war. Brownie frequently followed his owner's mother to the Home, where she worked as a waitress. He died in 1949 when hit by a car on the highway in front of the Home. He was so well liked that the Home commandant got permission to have him buried in the Veterans Cemetery.

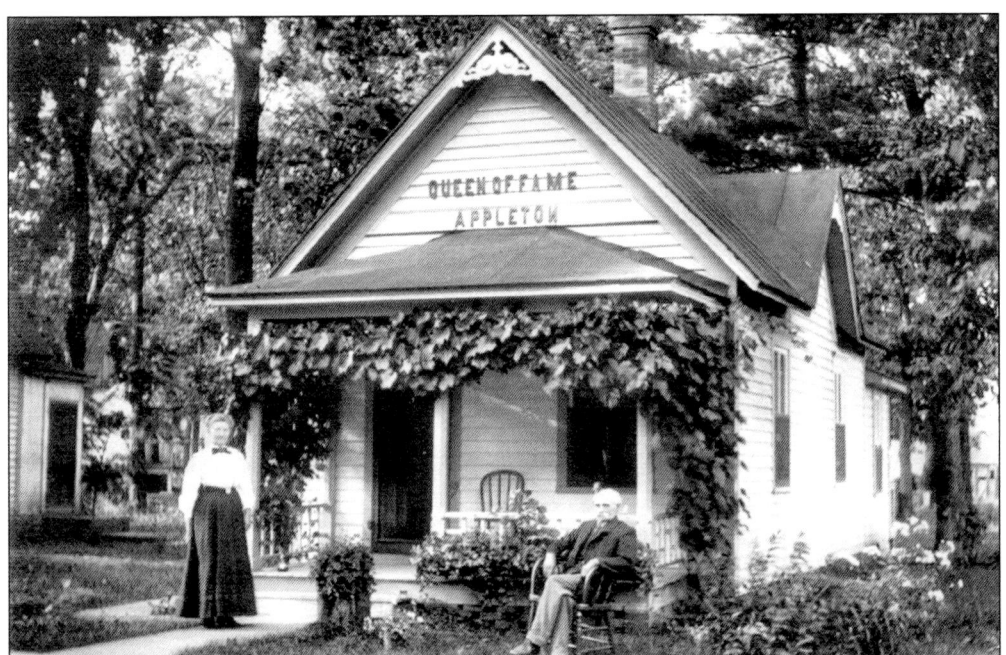

QUEEN OF FAME. A husband and wife relax in front of their cottage. The cottage was sponsored by one of the Appleton, Wisconsin posts. It is a nice photograph to illustrate how the members enjoyed the scent of pine trees and the fresh lake breeze.

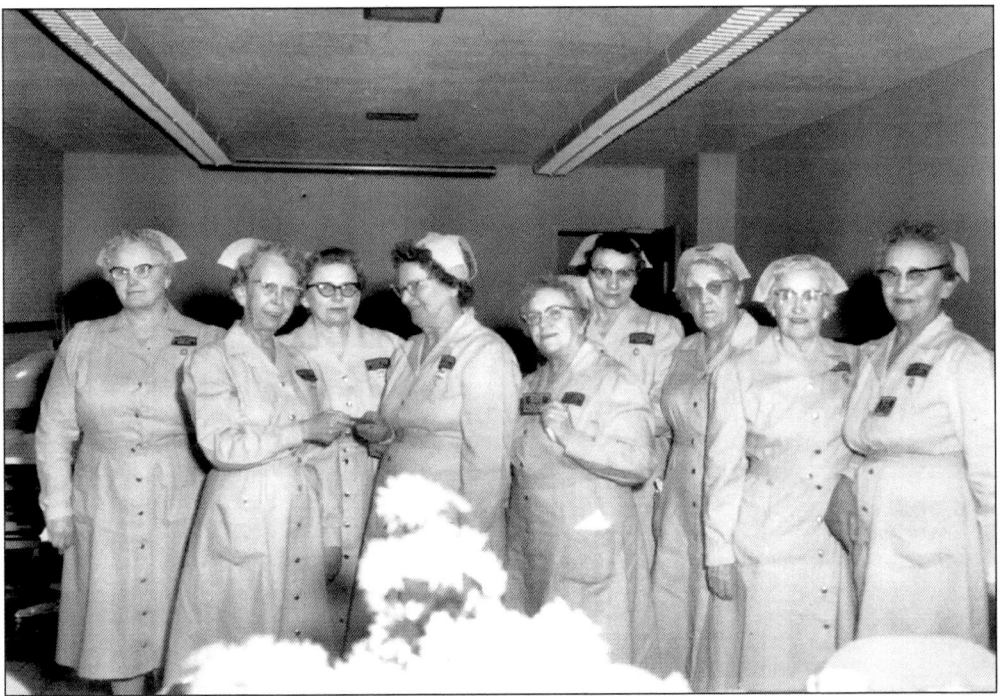

GRAY LADIES. There have been many volunteer groups working at the Home. These women, working on behalf of the Red Cross, formed a nurse's organization called "The Gray Ladies." They were honored for their service to the Home.

Turn of the Century View.

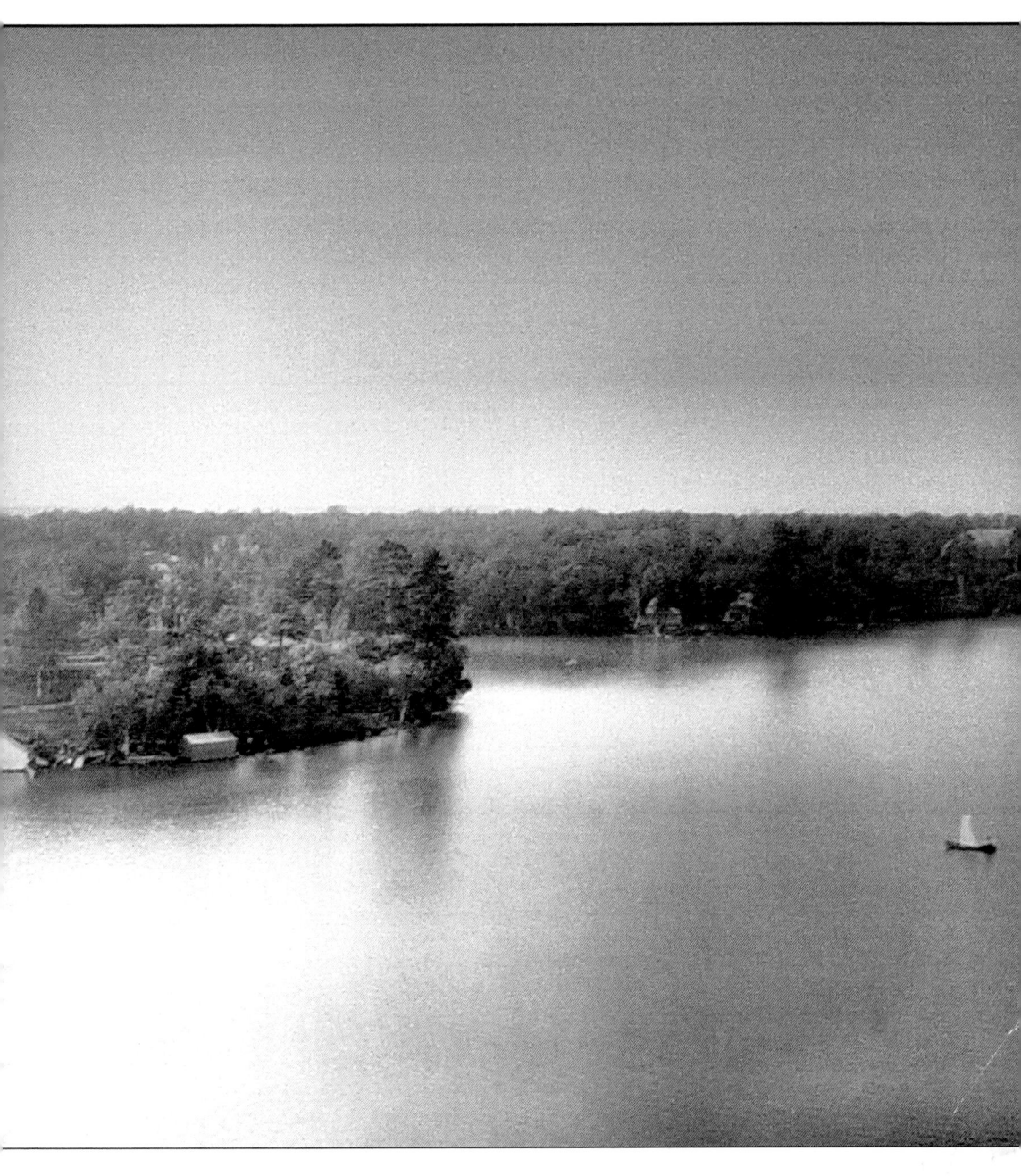

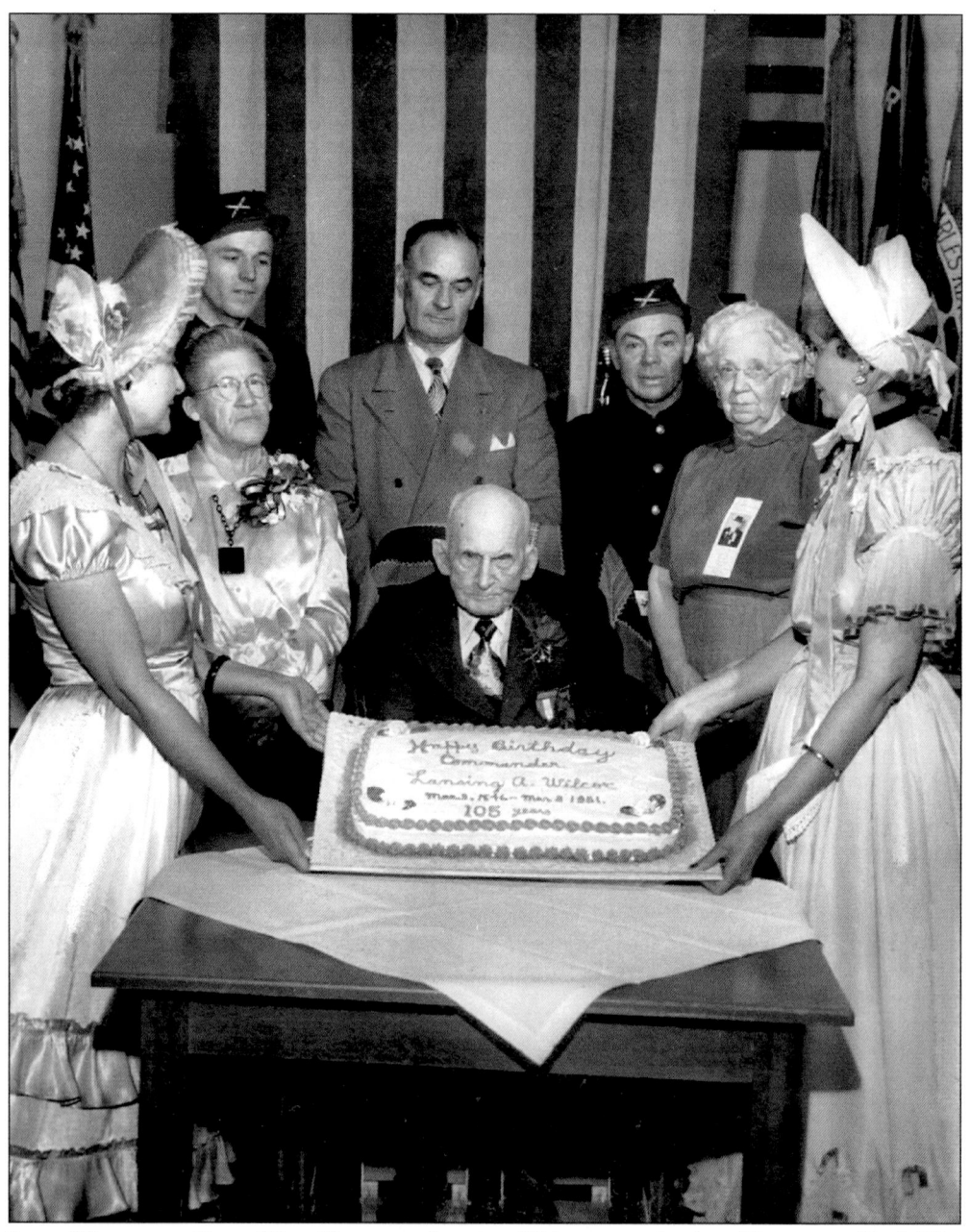

LAST WISCONSIN CIVIL WAR VETERAN. Lansing Wilcox was the last Wisconsin Civil War veteran to live. He was admitted to the Home on July 27, 1950. This photograph shows Commander Wilcox on his 105th birthday, March 4, 1951. His wife, age 74, is on the left side of the commander. He married her when he was 96 years old. He died at the Home six months later in September. This was his fifth time as a Home member. Wilcox fought in the Civil War with the 4th Wisconsin Cavalry.

In memory of all those that served this country.